Where to Stash Your Cash...Legally:
Offshore Havens of the World

Robert E. Bauman, JD

ISBN 1-903590-10-8

Printed by: Victor Graphics, Inc., 1211 Bernard Drive, Baltimore, MD 21223, USA

Notice: This publication is designed to provide accurate and authoritative information in regard to the subject matter covered. It is sold and distributed with the understanding that the authors, publisher and seller are not engaged in rendering legal, accounting or other professional advice or service. If legal or other expert assistance is required, the services of a competent professional advisor should be sought.

The information and recommendations contained in this brochure have been compiled from sources considered reliable. Investment and other recommendations carry inherent risks. As no investment recommendation can be guaranteed, the Society takes no responsibility for any loss or inconvenience if one chooses to accept them.

The Sovereign Society advocates and encourages full compliance with all tax and financial reporting laws applicable in the United States and elsewhere. The Sovereign Society does not receive any fees or commissions for any investment recommendations made in this publication

Acknowledgments

Robert E. Bauman, JD

Mr. Bauman, legal counsel to The Sovereign Society Ltd., served as a member of the U.S. House of Representatives from 1973 to 1981. He is an author and lecturer on many aspects of wealth protection. A member of the District of Columbia Bar, he received his juris doctor degree from the Law Center of Georgetown University in 1964. He received a degree in international relations from the Georgetown University School of Foreign Service in 1959 and was honored with GU's Distinguished Alumni Award in 1975. He is the author of *The Gentleman from Maryland* (Hearst Book Publishing, 1985), *How to Lawyer-Proof Your Life* (Shot Tower Press, 1995), *The Complete Guide to Offshore Residency, Dual Citizenship and Second Passports* (The Sovereign Society, 2002), *The Offshore Money Manual* (The Sovereign Society, 2000), and editor of *Forbidden Knowledge* (The Sovereign Society, 2003). He also is editor of *The Sovereign Society Offshore A-Letter*, an Internet e-letter that is received each week by over 100,000 readers worldwide. His writings also have appeared in *The Wall Street Journal*, *The New York Times*, *National Review* and many other publications.

Special thanks to Erika Nolan, executive director of The Sovereign Society, and Shannon Crouch, Daniel Aponte, Jr. and Claire Greaves of The Sovereign Society staff for their devotion to duty and editorial prowess in the production of this volume. This book could not have been produced without them.

Where to Stash Your Cash...Legally:
Offshore Havens of the World

Robert E. Bauman, JD

The Sovereign Society
5 Catherine Street, Waterford, Ireland
USA Toll Free Tel: 888-358-8125
E-mail: info@thesovereignsociety.com
Web site: http://www.sovereignsociety.com

Table of Contents

Author's Comment ix

Chapter 1 - A Safe Haven Offshore = Peace of Mind 1

Chapter 2 - Creative Offshore Financial Strategies 13

Chapter 3 - What You Need To Know About
Offshore Havens 61

Chapter 4 - The World's Best Offshore Havens..........................77

Chapter 5 - The United Kingdom...123

Chapter 6 - The United Kingdom's Offshore Havens 139

Chapter 7 - Special Havens in Europe 153

Chapter 8 - The Atlantic and Caribbean Havens 189

Chapter 9 - Emigrate to Canada, Leave Taxes Behind 244

Chapter 10 - The United States as an Offshore Tax Haven 268

Appendices

Glossary...289

Recommended Offshore Professionals 299

Recommended Reading 301

Author's Comment

For approaching fifteen years now I have been researching and writing about offshore financial matters – about tax havens, asset havens, offshore banking, asset protection trusts, international business corporations, family foundations – and about the state of the offshore financial world.

Even though I had earned a law degree and served eight years as a member of the U.S. House of Representatives, when I began this work I quickly discovered how little I knew about the "offshore" world.

My limited acquaintance with "offshore" had created the erroneous mental impression that many of us harbor after too many Hollywood movies and TV shows. There, offshore was depicted in the sensational shorthand of numbered bank accounts, sinister con men and fraudsters, money launderers, drug kingpins, and corrupt foreign politicians taking bribes on tropical islands.

The truth about offshore is far different.

But finding the truth for the first time offshore adventurer can be frustrating, discouraging, and, if you get burnt, a very short journey.

The offshore world offers real tax savings, though not as many as slick promoters claim. It offers tax deferral, and most of all, in this lawsuit-happy age, it offers ironclad asset protection and far more financial privacy (and, yes, secrecy) than can now be found in the United States and all other major nations.

That's what this book is all about – legal ways to save on

taxes, protect your wealth, invest and grow your money, and find financial peace of mind.

I tell you the who, what, why, when, and wherefore of the offshore world – based on my own experience, and that of the many experts I work with across the globe, the professionals you'll find listed here for your own use.

Welcome to the offshore world.

Robert E. Bauman, BSFS, JD
Fort Lauderdale, Florida USA
August 2004

Notice for all American Citizens and Residents:

The Sovereign Society advocates full compliance with all applicable tax and financial reporting laws. The U.S. government taxes all worldwide income wherever it is earned and wherever the U.S. person may live or have residence(s). U.S. citizens and resident aliens (known in tax law as "U.S. persons") must, by law, report all of their income annually and pay U.S. taxes accordingly. If a U.S. person has direct or indirect control over an offshore bank account or other financial account, this fact must be reported. If the aggregate amount of financial activity in such accounts amounts to $10,000 or more in a year, additional reporting is required.

You should consult with a qualified U.S tax attorney or accountant to insure that you know, understand and meet these and all other mandatory reporting requirements.

Chapter 1
A Safe Haven Offshore = Peace of Mind

SUMMARY: Here I explain the reasons for using an offshore haven; the ways and means of moving your assets and wealth offshore to a tax-free or low-tax nation – where you can invest with maximum profitability, minimum taxes and greater financial privacy.

Today, vast technological change already has created a new world economic structure.

It's a system that offers huge financial opportunities based on instant communications, interlinked databases, electronic commerce, and digital cash flows. And, in many ways, it has shifted power from the nation state to the individual citizen, greatly increasing personal financial freedom and the chance for profit. In turn, this new freedom has caused a reaction by governments everywhere, trying desperately to keep control over their citizens and eager to know what we are doing, especially with our finances.

And yet many people don't have a clue about the major financial revolution that has taken place. This book goes beyond the clues and reveals the secrets. It tells you how to profit from these changes and what you can do to reap the benefits.

By now most thinking people understand the meaning of the huge advances in computer and software technology and the vast expansion of the Internet. With cell phones and Palm Pilots buzzing, today's economic news travels fast and insider information is no longer confined to Wall Street and the City of London. Nervous waves of news and rumors ripple daily through world time zones and stock markets as 24-hour television covers events live – an example of the irresistible technological advances that have forced a totally new operational reality on financial and banking systems.

All this constitutes the government bureaucrat's worst fear: millions of cell phones and computers linked worldwide, electronic banking and on-line investment accounts, "smart card" money, easily available encryption; free communications, all of it unmediated by governments. As one astute observer says: "You get untraceable banking and investment, a black hole where money can hide and be laundered, not just for conglomerates or drug cartels, but for anyone."

You can see why government bureaucrats are frantic. The freedom potential of this new world money system runs counter to all the Big Brother socialist policies that have bled taxpayers and crippled prosperity for most of the last century.

And believe it; government is doing all it can to stifle these liberating trends. But I believe they will fail.

Why Go Offshore?

Until relatively recently, most of us thought "personal finance" meant checking and savings accounts, home mortgages and auto loans. Even now, with widely available international offshore mutual and hedge funds – many of them successful even in the face of world economic turmoil – relatively few investors take advantage of worldwide diversification. Among the reasons to go offshore are:

1. *Investment diversification.* Many of the world's best investments and money managers will not do business with U.S. citizens directly. They have made the choice that it is easier to do business with the rest of the world than to comply with the

draconian U.S. rules. By going offshore you can gain access to these U.S.-restricted investments. Only about 1,600 foreign securities are traded on U.S. markets, representing a tiny percentage of the securities traded on foreign markets. The only practical way to buy these offshore shares is through a foreign bank or broker.

2. *Higher returns.* There are opportunities in the traditional financial markets, such as offshore mutual funds and London-traded investment trusts with much higher returns than are generally available in U.S. markets. For example, the BFS Income and Growth Fund returned 75% the year 2002-2003; and the Jupiter Financial Fund has a one-year return of 57.1%! These "split capital" trusts aren't normally available to U.S. investors.

3. *Currency diversification.* Investors wishing to stabilize portfolios can protect their wealth against the falling U.S. dollar by simply holding other currencies (such as the Japanese yen or Swiss franc). Foreign currency opportunities are plentiful, such as earning nearly 20% during 2003 on the declining dollar versus the euro. For decades, the U.S. dollar has been losing value in relation to stronger currencies. In 1970, a U.S. dollar would purchase 4.5 Swiss francs. Since 1971, the franc has appreciated nearly 300% against the U.S. dollar. In September 2003, the dollar purchased only 1.4 Swiss francs. While U.S. investors can purchase foreign currencies through a few U.S. banks, offshore banks generally offer higher yields, lower fees, and lower minimums.

4. *Safety and security.* Fifteen years ago, the United States experienced a wave of bank and savings and loans failures at a rate unmatched since the Great Depression. In contrast, the off shore banks I recommend in these pages aren't exposed to risky investments such as third-world debt and highly lever aged derivative investments. Further, these banks are located in politically neutral countries that do not conduct offensive interventionist foreign policy. Thus, they are a much less like-

ly target for the kind of terrorist attacks that forced the closure of U.S. financial markets on September 12-15, 2001 after the 9/11 terror attacks.

5. ***"Insurance" against closure of U.S. securities markets.*** We all learned the need to have part of our assets outside of the United States when our markets were shut down for five full trading days following the terrorist attacks of September 11, 2001. But, although U.S. markets were closed, individuals with foreign accounts were able to trade securities on foreign exchanges.

6. ***Asset protection.*** Lawsuits have reached epidemic proportions in the U.S. If a creditor gets a judgment against you in the state where you live, the judgment is easily enforced. In contrast, if you invest in a suitable jurisdiction – Switzerland, for instance – you can be configured to be essentially judgment-proof. The prudent use of offshore havens provides U.S. persons with an enhanced ability to protect assets from the threat of lawsuit, civil forfeiture, business failure, divorce, foreign exchange controls, regressive legislation, or political instability. It largely avoids the vast U.S. asset-tracking net work, which permits investigators to easily identify the unencumbered assets of a potential defendant.

7. ***Financial privacy.*** Many people want protection from the prying eyes of business partners, estranged family members and identity thieves surfing the Internet. Financial privacy can be the best protection against frivolous lawsuits that end with big judgments – if you do not appear to have enough assets to justify the time and expense of an attack in an attorney's mind, he will not view you as a target. Simply put, assets you place "offshore" are off the domestic asset tracking "radar screen." The United States is one of the few nations lacking a federal statute that protects bank or securities accounts from disclosure except under defined circumstances. Many disclosures that would be illegal in other countries, either under international agreements such as the European Privacy

Directive, or under national laws guaranteeing financial secrecy, as in Switzerland, are commonplace in the United States.

These advantages have especially strong application when it comes to placing assets offshore.

More and more people are becoming comfortable with offshore bank accounts that also can be used as investment vehicles. But the use of more complicated offshore techniques, such as the international business corporation (IBC) and the foreign-based asset protection trust (APT), has been ignored for the most part. While these methods take a bit more time and effort, they can greatly enhance your financial strategy. In these pages, I will explain them and how you can use them.

In addition, you may wish to consider relocating your personal residence offshore in a tax haven nation that welcomes foreigners with tax exemptions and special privileges that make life easier and less complicated. I will explain which nations offer such inducements and how you can take advantage of them.

Important Privacy

The world now lives in an era when terrorism has become a major concern of every nation. Part of that concern is manifested in a whole host of recent national laws that severely curtail financial and personal privacy. These laws were originally premised on fighting drugs and combating money laundering and other crimes. By now, these laws have all but abolished any privacy – at least for those accused or suspected of crimes of any nature.

But for the average offshore investor or person otherwise financially active offshore, there is little to fear from anti-crime laws that compromise privacy. So long as you learn and obey the financial reporting laws and tax obligations imposed on you by your home nation, you will remain in the clear. Professional advice will help you in this essential education.

As I will note repeatedly in these pages, the financial privacy and bank secrecy laws of many nations are still very much stronger than those in the United States. This can be a definite advantage for you – and an added shield for your financial activities.

More Investment Profits Offshore

For more than a decade, the trend has been towards foreign investment. In 1980, less than 1% of U.S. pension fund assets were invested abroad. By 2000, that figure had risen to 20%. More than pension funds, mutual funds and stock purchasers, banks have bought into emerging markets in a very big way, especially European and Japanese banks.

"When history books are written 200 years from now about the last two decades of the 20th century," former U.S. Treasury Secretary Lawrence Summers told *The New York Times*, "I am convinced that the end of the Cold War will be the second story. The first story will be about the appearance of emerging markets – about the fact that developing countries where more than three billion people live have moved toward the market and seen rapid growth in incomes."

In 1980, less than 1% of U.S. pension fund assets were invested abroad. By 2000, that figure had risen to 20%.

Cross-border investments have proven profitable, despite temporary setbacks. What used to be tagged "Third World" investment funds have become the more appealing "emerging market funds."

The global economy of today is very different from that of past times. Finance and technology now dominate the economic scene. On a typical business day, the total amount of money moving in just the world's foreign exchange markets is US$2 trillion. That's ten times more than in 1986. It's also a sum equivalent to the total current world trade for a full four-month period!

Investment capital has exploded. By 2000, mutual funds, pension funds, and other institutional investors controlled US$25 trillion, 12 times the comparable 1980 figure. Where once autos, steel and grain dominated world trade, now trade in stocks, bonds and currencies reign supreme.

Wealth has become stateless, cash without a country, circulating wherever the owner finds the highest return and the greatest freedom. From 1970 to 2000, spending by investors in industrialized nations on offshore stocks increased 197 times over, and national capital markets have merged into one fast-moving, global capital market. As stock markets close in London, they open in New York, and as U.S. exchanges end the day, markets in Hong Kong and Tokyo come to life.

But far too few Americans realize that information about most of these profitable offshore investments are denied to U.S. persons. Cumbersome rules and regulations imposed by the U.S. government on foreign investment funds drive them away. Unwilling to waste time and money on bureaucratic registrations, most will not even do business with anyone with a U.S. address.

Avoiding Roadblocks to Prosperity

This global economic integration continues despite outdated U.S. laws that hinder offshore activity and hobble American investors. One of the main obstacles remains restrictive securities legislation. Any "investment contract" for purchase of a security sold in the United States must be registered with the Securities & Exchange Commission, and often with similar state agencies. This is an expensive process. The U.S. also requires far more stock disclosure by sales entities than most foreign countries, burdening the process further with U.S. accounting practices that differ from those used abroad.

International fund managers are practical people who keep their eyes on the bottom line. Many correctly calculate that operating costs in the U.S. would wipe out any possible profit margin. Ironically, several mutual funds and hedge funds with top performance records are run from the U.S. by U.S. residents, but do not accept investments from Americans. To avoid SEC red tape and registration costs, investment in these funds is available only to foreigners.

Ironically, several mutual funds and hedge funds with top performance records are run from the U.S. by U.S. residents, but do not accept investments from Americans.

Fortunately, there are ways for U.S. citizens to get around these government obstacles. In these pages I explain how you can access such offshore investments, legally and safely, using offshore entities such as a trust or international business corporation, or even a family foundation, located in a haven nation.

The Exodus Offshore Grows

Much of the revolution in world economics occurs as an escape from leech-like national tax systems that financially prop up dying welfare states. People in ever greater numbers are seeking havens where hard work is rewarded, not punished by wealth confiscation. Places where business is free to make its own decisions, without regulatory predators hovering over every attempt at free enterprise.

The United States offers a good example of this growing emigration trend. Every year, about 250,000 U.S. citizens and resident aliens leave America to make new homes in other nations. Admittedly, this quarter of a million people leaving must be compared with the millions clamoring to get in.

But there's a huge difference in the economic status of these two groups. Those seeking admission are, by and large, poverty stricken persons desperately trying to better their lot with new lives in the Promised Land. They'll settle for low paying jobs, welfare, free education for their kids, and U.S. government subsidized housing and health care.

Those seeking to escape the growing tyranny aimed right at

them by the United States government are typically wealthy people. It is this gusher of fleeing rich people who take with them the lion's share of the U.S. tax base. These are the very people who pay for all of those programs the new immigrants covet.

John Gaver, an astute observer of the American scene, writes: "The problem is that, increasingly, the wealthy perceive, whether correctly or incorrectly, that they are under attack by their own government and they are taking the only rational option left open to them. They're taking their wealth and leaving."

In a startling, extraordinary review of the government attack on wealth during the last decade, Gaver outlines U.S. congressional legislation that has all but abolished domestic financial privacy, reversed the burden of proof forcing an accused to prove his own innocence, allowed property confiscation by police fiat – all this wrapped in the U.S. flag held high in the phony wars against drugs, money laundering, and the latest ruse to gain government power, anti-terrorism.

But, as they say about us humans, "Old habits die hard." Despite the occasional financial excursion abroad, human nature dictates that most prefer to make and save money at home. We tend to be comfortable with the familiar and less threatening domestic economy of our home nation.

Taxes Drain Wealth

People who move some or all of their assets offshore simply recognize the present reality – that the government is engaged in the systematic destruction of hard-earned wealth. It's been called the "Nazification" of the economy. That's certainly true in the United States, the United Kingdom and most European Union (EU) nations. Sadly, in ever greater numbers, Americans must look to a select list of foreign lands for the kind of economic freedom once guaranteed by the U.S. Constitution.

The tax collectors know the most talented citizens of the U.S., U.K., EU and other welfare states are deserting, setting up financial shop where they and their capital are treated best. What has been called the "permeability of financial frontiers" now empowers investors instantly to shift vast sums of money from one nation to another and from one currency to another.

Lovers of freedom see in these developments the potential for liberation of "the sovereign individual," the courageous person who declares independence from "decrepit and debilitating welfare states," as The Wall Street Journal described them. (For more about this, see *The Sovereign Individual*, by James Dale Davidson and Lord William Rees-Mogg, [Simon & Shuster, 416 pp., US$25, 1997] an excellent book that explains the mass exodus of wealthy people from high-tax nations).

No wonder the U.K. Inland Revenue, the U.S. Internal Revenue Service and other tax hounds are worried. In Europe "undeclared" (and untaxed) work now exceeds 15% of Europe's combined gross domestic product (GDP), up from 5% in the 1970s. In the somewhat freer U.S., the underground "black market" economy accounts for over 10% of GDP. That means billions of dollars slipping through the eager hands of the taxman.

Why the growing black market? Confiscatory taxes, exorbitant labor costs, over-regulation – all failures of big government. All things bureaucrats love.

Diminished Privacy In The Digital Age

In many ways, life in modern America and the U.K. parallels the chilling description of life in the ultimate totalitarian state foretold in George Orwell's famous book, *1984*. In part, we have ourselves to blame. Although we claim to value freedom and privacy, too many of us willingly surrender personal information piecemeal, until we stand exposed to the world.

Those who conduct their financial affairs with reckless openness make the work of government snoops easy. As you read this, corporate and government computers hum with detailed binary facts about you and your family. Nothing is sacred: health, wealth, tax and marital status, credit history, employment, phone calls, faxes and e-mail, travel, eating and reading habits, even individual preferences when cruising the Internet are recorded.

In an age of digital cash, interconnected databases, electronic commerce, and instant worldwide communication, no area of financial activity offers more pitfalls than personal and commercial banking. Once considered discreet and honorable, banks and other financial institutions have been forced to become a brownshirt brigade, a U.S. version of Big Brother's thought police.

Case in Point

There was immense criticism of a U.S Department of Defense proposal called "Total Information Awareness" (TIA). In 2003, the U.S. Congress tried to halt most TIA funding, but other similar projects remained in the works. The Pentagon wants to create a government database with a huge data quantity, gathered from many different sources, to expose "potential terrorism." This would be accomplished with several technologies like speech recognition, "collaborative reasoning," and "data mining." TIA envisioned combining data about millions of Americans and foreigners to create profiles of potential terrorists. But in the process, everyone would be stripped of privacy and exposed to the stupidity of error-prone bureaucratic analysis.

Taking Back Your Sovereignty

Sadly, in today's world, you need to conduct your financial affairs with the utmost privacy, caution and discretion. In this book, we'll discuss concrete legal and practical steps you can take to guard against being victimized by government run amok.

To protect your privacy and wealth, you should consider taking the following steps:

1. Establish an offshore bank account in a tax-free, privacy-oriented, financial friendly nation. When done correctly, your cash will be secure from almost all U.S.-based claims. But first carefully investigate any foreign bank you consider using.

2. As part of your overall estate plan, create your own offshore

corporation and/or asset protection trust to hold title to specific assets.

3. Precisely document all financial transactions so you always have ready proof that your activities are legal.

4. Educate yourself about and comply with all laws, rules and regulations concerning reporting of your financial activities to government agencies.

5. Before you act, consult an experienced professional attorney and/or accountant and find out the U.S. or other tax implications of your plans.

6. Get a firm and reliable estimate of the cost of what you are planning, both immediately upon implementation and for the first few years of operation.

For a complete list of trusted professionals and financial institutions, see the Appendix, p. 299.

Chapter 2
Creative Offshore Financial Strategies

SUMMARY: In this chapter, you will learn about specific strategies for offshore living, residency, second citizenship, investing, bank accounts and conducting your business for maximum profit and the greatest tax savings. And I'll tell you about U.S. reporting requirements for offshore financial activity.

Later in these pages, I will explain which tax and asset havens are best for fulfilling your own personal wealth and estate management goals. After you read this chapter, keep in mind these strategies as I explain which offshore tax and asset havens offer them.

But before I get to geography and specific places, let's consider several proven personal, financial, and business strategies you can employ offshore, once you choose your own tax or asset haven. These varied strategies can be used individually or in combination, as your situation requires. But each one of them is fully legal and each has been used by many thousands of people worldwide – with highly satisfactory results.

Later in this book, when I discuss and describe individual tax havens and asset havens, I'll tell you where these strategies are best employed.

One or all of these strategies may be just what you are looking for.

Part 1. Personal Living Strategies

Strategy 1: Expatriation: the Ultimate Estate Plan

Expatriation: It's been called "the ultimate estate plan" and it's a legal, step-by-step process that can lead to the legal right for you to stop paying U.S. or other national income taxes – forever.

In sum, it requires professional consultations, careful planning, movement of assets offshore and acquisition of a second nationality. When all that's done (and done exactly right), you must leave behind your home country and become a "tax exile" with an established domicile in a low or no-tax jurisdiction. And, for U.S. citizens, this unusual plan requires, as a final step toward tax freedom, the formal relinquishment of citizenship.

A drastic plan? You bet. And in truth, there are many other perfectly suitable offshore strategies that I recommend that can result in significant tax savings. These include international life insurance policies and offshore investments made through retirement plans. But for U.S. citizens and long-term residents who seek a permanent and completely legal way to stop paying all U.S. taxes, expatriation is the only option.

The Blueprint to Ultimate Tax Avoidance

Individuals have been leaving their own land to seek opportunities elsewhere since the dawn of mankind. But it has only been since the development of the modern nation-state, and its taxation of the worldwide income of its citizen-residents, that expatriation has taken on significant tax consequences.

One of the first tax advisors to appreciate the potential tax savings of expatriation was my friend and colleague, Marshall Langer, JD, a valued member of The Sovereign Society's Council of Experts.

Langer is an international tax attorney and the respected author of several major international tax treaties, but also the daring creator of a now out-of-print book, *The Tax Exile Report*. This title gained international notoriety when the late U.S. Senator Daniel Patrick Moynihan (D-NY), red-faced and angry, waved a copy of the book at a televised Senate hearing, denouncing it as "a legal income tax avoidance plan."

In explaining why "expatriation" is so attractive to wealthy Americans (and others), a few years ago a *Forbes* magazine article gave the compelling arithmetic: "A very rich Bahamian citizen pays zero estate taxes; rich Americans – anyone with an estate worth US$3 million or more – pay 55%. A fairly stiff 37% marginal rate kicks in for Americans leaving as little as US$600,000 to their children." Even though U.S. estate taxes have been reduced since then, an even more impressive part of the Langer plan is the ability to escape American income, capital gains and other taxes.

When it comes to expatriation, however, Americans face a nearly unique burden. Unlike almost every other nation, with one or two minor exceptions, U.S. citizens and long-term residents cannot escape home country taxes by moving their residence to another nation. The only way to leave U.S. taxes behind is to give up their citizenship.

Toothless Penalties

Becoming a tax exile is not without problems, but, so far, they are more political than legal.

The source of the current controversy over expatriation was a sensational article in the November 24, 1994 issue of *Forbes* magazine, entitled "The New Refugees." Filled with juicy details (famous names, luxury addresses, big dollar tax savings), the story described how clever ex-Americans who became citizens of certain foreign nations, paid little or no U.S. federal and state income, estate and capital gains taxes.

Ever since, expatriation has been a favorite "hot button" issue kicked around by the American news media and "soak-the-rich" politicians. While current anti-expat provisions in the U.S. Tax

Code are relatively toothless, this status may soon change. On July 25, 2003, legislation (HR 2896) was introduced in the U.S. House of Representatives by Rep. William M. Thomas (R-CA), powerful chairman of the tax-writing Committee on Ways and Means. This bill includes an ominous Sec. 2005, entitled "Revision of Tax Rules on Expatriation of Individuals."

To the average uninformed U.S. taxpayer, expatriation seems like just another rich man's tax loophole.

This section, in effect, would impose an immediate tax on unrealized capital gains on anyone who ends their U.S. citizenship. It uses an arbitrary test of net worth and/or income tax paid over a period of years to assume an ex-citizen is trying to escape income taxes. Similar net worth/income tax provisions have been the law since 1996, which I'll explain in a moment.

It's understandable why politicians keep this political football in play. To the average uninformed U.S. taxpayer, expatriation seems like just another rich man's tax loophole. Before *Forbes* raised the issue, few people had even heard of the concept of formal surrender or loss of U.S. citizenship.

Taken together with the controversy over U.S. companies re-incorporating offshore to avoid U.S. corporate taxes (which is completely legal), candidates for federal office have in expatriation a convenient straw man that they can beat unmercifully. Former U.S. Treasury Secretary Lawrence Summers (now president of Harvard University) went so far as to call tax expatriates "traitors" to America. He later was forced to apologize.

Your Right to Give Up U.S. Citizenship

As a national political issue, expatriation is hardly new.

In the bitter aftermath of the U.S. Civil War (1860-65), Congress hotly debated the status of people in the southern states that formed the Confederacy. Ultimately, Congress decided "rebels" who swore allegiance could again become U.S. citizens. The "Expatriation Act of 1868" formally recognized that all Americans do have a right to give up their citizenship, if they so choose.

A century later, in the Foreign Investors Tax Act of 1966, Congress again decided to make an issue of expatriation. In that Act, lawmakers tried to impose onerous taxes on exiting wealthy Americans who relinquished their U.S. citizenship "with the principal purpose of avoiding" U.S. taxes, a highly subjective intention that was virtually impossible to prove. The IRS couldn't prove such "intent" and very rarely even tried.

A 1996 anti-expatriation law inspired by the *Forbes* article asserts limited U.S. tax jurisdiction for a period of 10 years over persons who renounce their U.S. citizenship "with the principal purpose of avoiding U.S. taxes." Also covered by this law are permanent resident aliens ("green card" holders) or anyone else who has resided in the United States for any eight of the preceding 15 years.

For the purposes of this law, tax avoidance is presumed to be the true purpose if, at the time of expatriation, an expatriate's net worth exceeds US$552,000 or he or she pays an annual tax bill exceeding US$110,000, figures that are indexed for inflation annually. However, with proper planning, it is relatively easy to avoid U.S. taxes during this 10-year period.

The lengths to which politicians will go to penalize expatriates is demonstrated by a never-enforced provision of U.S. law, also enacted in 1996, which permits the Attorney General to bar from returning to the United States anyone who renounces their U.S. citizenship to avoid U.S. taxes. In this manner, Congress lumped individuals exercising their legal right to avoid taxes with narcotics traffickers and terrorists.

Amidst the furor, thoughtful experts criticize what they see as a much broader and dangerous U.S. anti-expatriation precedent. They point out that these laws involve not only retaliatory government acts against resistance to high taxes, but pose possible human rights violations guaranteed by others laws and even the Human Rights Charter of the United Nations. It is worth noting that the U.S. Supreme Court has repeatedly affirmed the right of U.S. citizens to end their citizenship as well as the right to enjoy dual citizenship.

In reality, this political frenzy probably reflects collective envy more than any sense of patriotism by Americans or their congressional representatives. Expatriation is not as serious a problem as some pretend: fewer than 800 Americans, rich or poor, have formally given up their citizenship in recent years. Most expatriates give up their U.S. citizenship because they are return-ing to their native land or marrying a non-U.S. citizen.

Save Millions of Dollars, Legally

Amidst the controversy, there remain very substantial tax sav-ings for wealthy U.S. citizens who are prepared to give up their citizenship. While only a handful of very rich Americans have legally expatriated, these individuals include some prominent names:

In 1962, John Templeton, respected international investor, businessman and philanthropist, surrendered his U.S. citizenship to become a citizen of The Bahamas. This move saved him more than US$100 million when he sold the well-known international investment fund that still bears his name. Other wealthy ex-Americans who have taken their formal leave include billionaire Campbell Soup heir John ("Ippy") Dorrance, III (Ireland); Michael Dingman, chairman of Abex and a Ford Motor director (The Bahamas); J. Mark Mobius, one of the leading emerging market investment fund managers (Germany); Kenneth Dart, heir to the billion dollar Dart container fortune (Belize); Ted Arison, head of Carnival Cruise Lines (Israel); and Fred Kreible, million-aire head of Locktite Corporation (Turks and Caicos Islands).

How It Should Be Done

Long before you formally give up your U.S. citizenship, you should reorder your financial affairs in such a way as to remove from possible government control and taxation most, if not all, of your assets.

Here are the steps you must take:

* Move abroad and make your new home in a no-tax foreign nation so you are no longer a "resident" for U.S. income taxes;

* Obtain alternative citizenship and passport;

* Give up U.S. citizenship and change your legal "domicile" to avoid U.S. estate taxes;

* Arrange your affairs so that most or all of your income is derived from non-U.S. sources; and

* Title your property ownership so that any assets that remain in the United States are exempt from U.S. estate and gift taxes.

> Here's the process and time table you might follow: decision to expatriate leading to consultation with expert advisors (1-2 years); leading to liquidation of U.S. assets (1-2 years); leading to selection of appropriate jurisdictions for alternative citizenship and residency (1-2 years); leading to move to selected residency haven leading to alternative citizenship (0-10 years); leading to giving up U.S. citizenship.

One of the most important decisions is the choice of a second nationality. Millions of Americans already hold a second nationality; millions more qualify almost instantly for one by reason of birth, ancestry, or marriage. For instance, in many countries (Ireland is one), having a parent or grandparent born in that country will qualify children or grandchildren for immediate citizenship and passport after presenting the appropriate documentation.

Otherwise, you will need to qualify for alternative citizenship through prolonged residency (2-10 years) in a country in which you qualify for residency based on your economic status or investments you make there. For instance, both Panama and

Belize have formal tax advantaged residency plans for foreign nationals who wish to make their home there. After five years, sometimes less, you can apply for citizenship.

Alternatively, you may choose to purchase economic citizenship, which can be obtained in a matter of months, but only at significant cost (US$75,000 or more). The only two legitimate economic citizenship programs still in existence are from the Commonwealth of Dominica and St. Kitts & Nevis. For more on these programs, see the Henley & Partners Web site at www.henleyglobal.com.

Before making any move, it's absolutely essential to consult qualified professionals. See Appendix, page 299 for a list of qualified professionals who can assist you.

Strategy 2: Foreign Residence in a Tax Haven

For foreigners, tax havens can also be places for better living.

Even though U.S. persons are taxed on their worldwide income, there are many attractive places to live where taxes can be reduced on business and related activities conducted away from America in a tax haven. These hospitable places exempt foreigners from local income and business taxes and from many other local taxes.

Personal income tax rates in many major welfare states are now 50% or higher. This tax burden, combined with Social Security taxes, capital gains taxes, net worth taxes and inheritance taxes has led many to seek out low or zero tax havens where they may be able live tax-free or nearly tax-free.

Dozens of countries provide at least limited tax incentives to qualified new residents. It's easiest to qualify if you're healthy and have sufficient income and assets so that you won't need a job in the local market. However, it isn't easy to find a haven offering both low taxes and high quality of life including a wide range of amenities, excellent medical facilities, easy residence requirements, and a warm climate, all within easy reach of major cities. But a few countries come fairly close to this ideal.

For instance, in Italy, if you receive a fixed income from foreign bonds, you pay a flat 12.5% tax, and inheritance taxes have been abolished altogether. Unfortunately, for most other types of income, taxes in Italy are quite high.

For people of great wealth, both Austria and Switzerland have special immigration and tax arrangements for foreigners who wish to make their home or retire there.

Malta is one of the most attractive locations for foreigners looking for a warm climate as well as low taxes. Permanent residents enjoy a privileged tax status, as only 15% tax is charged on income remitted to Malta, subject to a minimum tax liability of about US$5,000 per year. To obtain permanent residence, you must show proof of an annual income of about US$25,000 or capital of about US$375,000. Although a residence permit entitles you to live in Malta, you don't actually have to spend a minimum length of time there. This is particularly useful if you are often away for lengthy periods.

Panama offers one of the most attractive locations for tax advantaged residence in the Americas. It offers a special *pensionado* program for foreign retirees that provides tax-free living with discounts on many goods and services. Residents pay no tax on income earned outside Panama not brought into the country. You may acquire residence as a financially independent person/retiree or as an investor. Belize offers a similar special program for foreign retirees with zero taxes and other incentives.

For people of great wealth, both Austria and Switzerland have special immigration and tax arrangements for foreigners who wish to make their home or retire there. Indeed, it's fair to say that there are havens for tax advantaged residence in almost every corner of the world.

For more information about offshore residency, contact Christian H. Kalin, member of The Sovereign Society's Council of Experts, and partner in Henley & Partners, Zurich, specialists in relocation and residence for private clients worldwide. Contact: Henley & Partners AG Kirchgasse 22, 8001 Zurich, Switzerland; Tel.: +41-44-266-22-22; Fax: +41-44-266-22-23; Web site: http://www.henleyglobal.com.

Strategy 3: Dual Citizenship

Dual Citizenship

If you have decided to take up a new residence in an offshore tax haven, you may want to consider the acquisition of a second passport or dual citizenship. Under U.S. law, this is fully legal, as it is under the law of many nations.

A second passport, quite literally, could save your life. Your existing passport may not permit you to travel internationally if it becomes necessary for you to leave "home." That's because your passport is the property of your government. In most countries, the government can seize it anytime.

At the very least, a second nationality is a hedge against unknown events. Because it gives you the option to reside in another country, it may also offer tax advantages, although this is of limited benefit to U.S. citizens.

You may be able to acquire a second nationality and passport based on ancestry, marriage or religious affiliation. If you don't qualify on these grounds, your options are limited to obtaining citizenship through residency for some time (anywhere from 2 to 12 years) or obtaining citizenship by investment.

Citizenship by investment is the granting of citizenship by a sovereign country in exchange for a financial contribution to that country, or an investment in a business, real estate, etc. in that country.

In recent years, such programs have been heavily criticized.

There have been allegations that passports are being sold to international organized crime figures and terrorists. These allegations are totally false, but have led to the termination of the citizenship by investment program in Belize and the indefinite suspension of the Grenada program.

St. Kitts & Nevis and Dominica are now the only countries that offer legal citizenship by investment programs, although in Austria it is also possible under certain conditions to obtain citizenship without prior residence based on a substantial investment. All of these programs require that applicants pass a rigorous screening process.

The best value for the money is the St. Kitts & Nevis program. Citizens enjoy a passport with an excellent reputation and do not need a visa to travel to most countries. You are required to make a real estate investment of at least US$250,000 and pay application fees that total US$35,000 for a single applicant plus US$15,000 for each dependent, plus a "due diligence" fee of US$2,000 per adult applicant.

In Dominica, there are two options for obtaining citizenship by investment: a Family Option (requiring a US$100,000 payment) and a Single Option (requiring a US$75,000 payment). Application, agent and registration fees total approximately US$17,000. You must also travel to Dominica for an interview.

In Austria, you may qualify for citizenship if you make a substantial investment that creates jobs in Austria. There is no "program" as such and few cases are approved each year. An equity investment of approximately US$1 million is normally required, along with application and legal fees of approximately US$250,000. However, the Austrian passport is the only possibility to obtain a first world passport through an investment.

Since citizenship by investment remains controversial, these programs, particularly in Dominica, may be terminated at any time. If you are interested in this potentially life saving option, now is the time to act.

For more information about second citizenship, contact Christian H. Kalin, member of The Sovereign Society's Council of Experts, and partner in Henley & Partners, Zurich, specialists in relocation and residence for private clients worldwide. Contact: Henley & Partners AG, Kirchgasse 22, CH-8001 Zurich, Switzerland; Tel.: +41-44-266-22-22; Fax: +41-44-266-22-23; Web site: http:// www.henleyglobal.com.

Part 2. Personal Financial Strategies

Strategy 1: An Offshore Bank Account

Until relatively recently, only the wealthiest investors could benefit from having an offshore bank account. Only the richest of the rich could afford the fees and legal advice associated with going offshore. Now, after dramatic changes in international banking and communications, even a modest offshore account can be your quick, inexpensive entry into the world of foreign investment opportunities.

Put aside the erroneous popular notion that foreign bank accounts are designed for shady international drug kingpins and unscrupulous wheeler dealers unwilling to pay taxes. For some people, offshore accounts will always evoke images of cloak and dagger spies from the U.S. Central Intelligence Agency or the U.K.'s MI-5, of shadowy clandestine operations and crooked officials in third world nations.

A foreign bank account can be employed as an integral tool in an aggressive, two-pronged offshore wealth strategy.

Although these sinister images are entertaining, they hardly relate to our present practical purposes: to build offshore financial structures to increase your wealth legally and protect your assets. Forget the intrigue and embrace the fact that an offshore bank account is a highly effective and economic way to achieve your legitimate financial goals. There is nothing underhanded or sinister about protecting the wealth you have worked so hard to earn.

A foreign bank account can be employed as an integral tool in an aggressive, two-pronged offshore wealth strategy. One goal is to increase your asset value by cutting taxes and maximizing profits. The other is to build a strong defensive asset protection structure. As I will show you in these pages, the possible variations on these important themes are nearly endless.

Offshore banking is big business worldwide. Recent estimates calculate that US$2 trillion to US$5 trillion is stashed in nearly 40 offshore banking havens that impose no taxes, have less onerous regulations, guarantee privacy, and cater to nonresidents. One-third of the entire world's private wealth is stashed in Switzerland alone!

The Benefits of Offshore Banking

Your offshore bank account is not just a place for safekeeping cash. One of the great advantages of an offshore bank account is the ability to trade freely and invest in foreign-issued stocks, bonds, mutual funds and national currencies that are not available in your home country.

An offshore account is an excellent platform from which to diversify investments and take advantage of global tax savings. You can have instant access to the world's best investment opportunities, without concern about your home nation's legal restrictions. Offshore foreign stock, bond and mutual fund trading are not covered by laws such as the U.S. Securities and Exchange Act or its administrative arm, the SEC. You can purchase attractive insurance and annuity products not available in the U.S. and some other nations. Tax savings may result from deferred investment earnings, capital gains, or appreciation, rather than receiving ordinary income that is not only taxed currently, but at a much higher rate.

An offshore bank account can mean opportunities to profit from currency fluctuations, easy ability to purchase foreign real estate, and earnings from high interest rates available only in foreign countries. You also can trade precious metals and other tangible personal assets through most foreign accounts.

Another important benefit is the relatively strong asset protection foreign bank accounts can provide.

Another important benefit is the relatively strong asset protection foreign bank accounts can provide. The existence of your offshore account is not readily known to a possible claimant seeking to collect a judgment against your assets. The existence of the account must be revealed on your U.S. income tax return (Form 1040), but that's not part of the public record. At times in a judicial proceeding, you may have a legal obligation to reveal an offshore account in a statement of your assets and liabilities. But there are times when it makes good financial sense to discourage a potential litigant by letting him know just how difficult it will be to reach your assets.

Because of defendant-friendly local laws in asset protection haven nations, foreign judgment holders often have a very difficult time enforcing a judgment obtained in their own country. To reach your assets, a successful creditor must start all over using the foreign judicial process to press a claim against your offshore assets. To do that, they must bear the expense of hiring foreign lawyers, travel and witness transportation.

Besides promoting compromise, the delay in such a strung-out process allows ample time for a defendant to fight the action, or simply move cash or assets to an account in another country. Because of such offshore local laws, courts in these countries only rarely issue orders prohibiting such transfers, especially in civil cases.

Many of these nations have one- or two-year statutes of limitations accruing from the date an initial claim arises. Since a U.S. lawsuit takes years to get through the courts, this means any American court judgment would be void under the foreign nation's one-year cutoff date. In fact, the U.S. process often takes so long that time runs out in nations with five-year statutes of limitations.

Choosing and Opening Your Offshore Bank

Before you choose a bank, you must pick the right haven nation where you believe your needs will be met. I'll help you make that decision in these pages.

But, first ask yourself your real purpose for having an offshore account. To expand investment opportunities? Increase privacy? Protect yourself from potential claims and creditors? These can all be accomplished offshore. Different strategies offer unique benefits, and this book will show what can work best to meet your specific needs.

Your next step is to learn all about your offshore bank of choice and the services it provides. Check its reputation, financial condition and all associated costs. Later in the book, I will give you reputable banking contacts to get you started.

In many countries, banking fees are rather expensive, far more than Americans are used to paying. Often, the net benefits of an offshore account are diminished by high fees. Run a mathematical model and find out what your net profit (or loss) might be. Few countries tax nonresident bank accounts per se, but some do collect withholding taxes on interest earnings.

If you want maximum privacy and strong protection from intrusive government officials, litigation, and lawyers, avoid any offshore bank with established branches or subsidiaries located within your home country, especially if you live in the United States, its territories, possessions, or dependencies. American courts have been known to threaten instant shutdown or confiscation of U.S. branches or subsidiaries when their offshore parent bank fails to comply with a court's orders.

You should also avoid transactions that send personal offshore bank checks (with your name on them) through units of the U.S. or Canadian banking system. Carelessness like that leaves an audit trail a mile wide. Restrict yourself to personal cash withdrawals from your offshore account – no checks please. Never use your offshore account as a checking account for payment of home country bills. Bank fees for international check payments are extremely costly and far worse, this creates recorded links that undermine privacy.

But, under no circumstances, should you attempt to hide reportable home nation income in your offshore bank account.

On the other hand, if you're unconcerned about creditors or personal claims, and you want ease and speed in setting up and managing an offshore account, head for the U.S. branch office of a foreign bank. You might also pick a major international bank like **Citibank** or **HSBC** with many offices and subsidiaries overseas. This latter course allows you to go offshore without ever leaving home. Just realize that this option offers little asset protection or privacy.

A more convenient and very private course of action is to obtain a **Barclays**, **Visa**, **MasterCard**, or other international credit card from your offshore bank. While offshore cards are more expensive than their U.S. equivalents, the offshore bank can deduct your monthly charges from your account balance. This means you earn money offshore, incur bills offshore, make deposits into and pay with your offshore account, all beyond the scrutiny of your home country. As with offshore checks, never use that offshore credit card in your home country. Do that and your financial privacy is shattered.

But, under no circumstances, should you attempt to hide reportable home nation income in your offshore bank account. Nor should you use an offshore bank credit card as an unreportable piggy bank to conceal income or personal expenses.

Source for Offshore Bank Information

U.S. laws force banks and financial institutions licensed to do business in the U.S. to disclose information about transactions in other branches, even if the branches are in another country. Many nations have similar laws. Failure to disclose can mean the bank and its officers may be held in contempt of court, fined, and/or its managers imprisoned. Indeed, U.S. courts have imposed sanctions on the American branch of a foreign bank, even when refusal is based upon a foreign court order or law that forbids production of the requested data.

To find an offshore bank **without** domestic branches in your country, visit your local library and ask for the *Thomson/Polk World Bank Directory* (International Edition). This standard reference has a complete listing of banks in over 212 countries, including the U.S., with updated sections issued twice a year. It also analyzes a bank's financial size and strength, tells you how and whom to contact. One of its four volumes is a 300-page reference that includes industry ranking tables for banks with worldwide and U.S. holding companies, credit ratings, international banking holidays, Central Banks, currency exchanges, attorneys experienced in banking law, regulatory agency contact information, and trade association contact information.

It also lists funds processing information including ABA routing numbers and Fed telegraph names for U.S. banks, Canadian transit numbers for Canadian banks, and country routing or sort codes for international banks. The "Worldwide Correspondents Guide" section contains correspondent information for over 12,500 banks worldwide and includes city locations, phone numbers and routing numbers. If you want to know more about this series, visit: http://www.tfp.com/reference.html.

Opening Your Account

Except for the geography involved, opening an offshore bank account differs little from starting a domestic, home country account. Just like your local banker, offshore bankers want to see you face to face before your relationship begins. In reputable offshore banks, a new account applicant must produce positive identification, a passport and/or birth certificate, a certified balance sheet, and business and personal references that are checked carefully. Personal first-time contact is the preferred method. Most nations now have anti-money laundering statutes similar to the U.S. or U.K., so new customers must appear in person to open accounts.

The "know-your-customer" rules are now normal policy in international banking. Bank officials always want more business, but they don't want it from drug merchants, terrorists, or crooked politicians. Only if your financial activity is likely to involve relatively small amounts of money will you be able to open the account by mail. Many offshore banks decline to provide even this small exception.

Except for the geography involved, opening an offshore bank account differs little from starting a domestic, home country account.

This one-on-one contact should be reciprocal. When you establish your account, immediately get to know your contact in the bank personally. That person should speak your language, understand your business, and be totally reliable. Always have a "back-up" contact at the bank who knows who you are, in case your usual representative becomes unavailable for any reason.

Increasingly, offshore banks are demanding that depositors sign a letter giving the bank permission to release account details to foreign investigators, thereby waiving the depositor's rights under bank secrecy laws. The waiver letters previously applied only to U.S. depositors, but now may be requested from Canadians as well. If an offshore bank you are considering makes such a request, take your business elsewhere.

Out in the Open

Here's a tip that may help you to avoid unwanted scrutiny while accomplishing your offshore financial goals in relative peace.

Let's be honest: many offshore jurisdictions known for no-tax, privacy, and anti-creditor banking laws are also prime suspects for certain unsavory financial activities. When your name appears on a bank account in places like The Bahamas or the Cayman Islands, it immediately raises red flags for suspicious U.S. government agents.

If you create your own "privacy haven" out in the open, instead of rushing to a small bank in some exotic, far-flung locale, your money usually will be much more secure.

If privacy is the goal, you should never use your own name on an offshore account. Instead, use the name of a corporate substitute under your direct or indirect control. If need be, set up your own international business corporation (IBC) or trust in the nation where you chose to locate your offshore banking.

Still another way to obtain banking privacy is to "get lost in a crowd." Why not establish your offshore account in a major banking nation where privacy is better protected than in the U.S.? A good choice might be the **United Kingdom** or **Switzerland**. Such nations have highly respected private banks that do a high volume of business. IRS officials are less suspicious of accounts held in these established institutions. But even in these nations, caution is required.

You might choose a country where you have family ties, or one with an active international financial role, such as **Hong Kong**, **Singapore**, **Ireland** or **Austria**. In London, Vienna or Dublin, your bank dealings will not be deemed especially noteworthy, since thousands of Americans hold accounts in these places. If you create your own "privacy haven" out in the open, instead of rushing to a small bank in some exotic, far-flung locale, your money usually will be much more secure.

Let us make clear that true banking secrecy does exist in many reputable haven jurisdictions. Tax havens such as **Panama**, **Nevis**, **Belize**, and **Gibraltar** officially impose banking privacy by law, waiving this protection only in criminal situations, and usually only under court order. Unlike the U.S., where bank employees have been turned into surrogate government spies, many offshore nations impose fines and prison sentences on bank employees who violate the privacy of account holders.

But you should put one notion to rest right now – there is no such thing as a totally "secret" bank account anywhere in the world. Even in nations with the strongest bank privacy laws, like Austria, a bank account holder's true name is on record some-where in that institution's files. Even if the account is in a corpo-rate name, or the name of a trust or other legal entity, there's always a "paper" (or computer) trail to be traced, especially if government agents want to know about alleged criminals and their finances.

Check page 311 for information about the special Sovereign Society Convenient Offshore Bank accounts available to *Sovereign Society* members.

Strategy 2: The Offshore Asset Protection Trust (APT)

One of the very best methods for asset protection is an asset protection trust (APT) located in an offshore haven jurisdiction.

A trust is a formal legal arrangement voluntarily created and funded by a person (the grantor) that directs another person (the *trustee*) to take legal title and control of the grantor's donated property, to be used and managed for the benefit of one or more other persons the grantor designates (the *beneficiaries*). The bene-ficiary of a trust receives income or distributions of assets from the trust and has an enforceable equitable title to the benefits, but does not control trust assets or manage trust operation. An offshore asset protection trust may also include another party to trust operation, the *protector*, a person vested with certain powers to monitor the performance of the trustee.

The creation of a trust arrangement is usually a planned, calculated, intentional act. It can serve a specific purpose or as part of a general estate plan. The trust grantor signs a written declaration describing his or her intentions, stating specific details of trust operation, income distribution, and the extent and limits of trustee powers.

The trust process may seem complex and difficult, but, in fact, a trust is one of the most flexible yet efficient legal mechanisms recognized by law.

A well-drafted trust document will reflect the grantor's precise intentions. Drafting a trust *declaration* as part of an overall estate plan requires expert advice based on a thorough examination of all existing arrangements that affect the grantor's estate. To create a proper estate plan, the status of all other legal documents or devices, such as a will, or jointly owned assets, must be reviewed and coordinated with the trust. Conflicts must be resolved consistent with all applicable trust and tax laws. However, a targeted trust is drafted only to accomplish limited or even a single goal, such as asset protection.

Most offshore asset protection trusts are drafted as *discretionary trusts*, a form which allows greater planning flexibility. This means the trustee is given the power to decide how much will be distributed to beneficiaries and, in some case, who qualifies as a beneficiary. The trust declaration may vest a trustee with the right to make payments for purposes, at times, and in amounts, the trustee decides. A trustee often is given the authority to recognize beneficiaries within named classes of persons ("my children and their heirs"), or the trust may contain a right known

as a power of appointment allowing the trustee to choose beneficiaries from a class of eligible persons.

What a Trust Can Do

A trust may be created for any purpose that is not illegal or
void as against public policy.

A trust can hold title to and invest in real estate, cash, stocks,
bonds, negotiable instruments, and personal property. Trusts can
provide care for minor children or the elderly; or pay medical,
educational, or other expenses. A trust can provide financial support in an emergency, for retirement, during marriage or divorce,
or even carry out premarital agreements.

To the uninformed, the trust process may seem complex
and difficult, but, in fact, a trust is one of the most flexible yet
efficient legal mechanisms recognized by law. Compared to the
alternatives, it can provide superior asset protection and can
assure that your bounty will be distributed exactly as you see fit.

The APT

In recent decades, asset protection using the trust format as a
vehicle has gained wide popularity amongst people of wealth "in
the know."

The foreign asset protection trust (or APT) is a targeted form
of trust created by a grantor resident in one nation under the
statutes of another nation where the trust operations are based.
Because the trust is governed by the laws of the nation in which it
is registered or administered, it serves as a shield for the grantor's
business and personal assets, deflecting would-be creditors, litigation and potential financial liabilities, perhaps even an ex-spouse
bent on revenge.

Here are a few reasons why an offshore APT can be so
effective:

* Start Over: The courts of foreign asset haven nations will not recognize the validity of U.S. or other nations' domestic court orders in many cases. A foreign judgment creditor seeking collection must re-litigate the original claim in the local court after hiring local lawyers. He may be required to post a bond and to pay legal expenses for all parties if he loses. The sheer legal complexity and cost of such an international collection effort is likely to stop all but the most determined adversaries.

* **Minimal Needs:** An offshore APT need not be complex. Creation can be little more than the signing of formal documents and opening a trust account managed by your local trustee in a bank in the foreign country you choose. Respected offshore multi-national and local banks routinely provide experienced trust officers and staff to handle trust matters. Most international banks have U.S. dollar-denominated accounts, often with better interest rates than U.S. financial institutions offer.

* **Greater Protection:** Under the laws of asset haven nations, assets placed in an offshore asset protection trust have far more protection than permitted under domestic U.S. trust law. The law in such countries is especially drafted to provide an asset protection "safe harbor" that is unavailable in the U.S. and many other nations. With an offshore APT, foreign-held trust assets are not subject to the jurisdiction of your local or home country judicial system.

* **Fast Acting:** The statute of limitations imposed on initiating a foreign creditor's suit varies. In many jurisdictions, the statute begins to run from the date the APT was established. Some haven nations, such as the Cook Islands, have a limit of one year for initiation of claims. Others, such as St. Vincent and the Grenadines impose a claims filing limit for certain creditors of within two years after APT formation. As a practical matter, it may take a creditor longer than that just to discover the existence of a foreign APT to which most of your assets have long since been transferred.

* **Better Investments:** An offshore APT is an excellent platform from which to diversify investments and benefit from the global

tax savings I described in these pages. The APT permits taking advantage of the world's best investment opportunities, without concern about your home nation's legal restrictions. As I explained previously, offshore foreign stock, bond, and mutual fund trading are not covered by laws such as the U.S. Securities and Exchange Act or its administrative arm, the SEC. An offshore APT can also purchase attractive insurance and annuity products not available in the U.S. and some other nations. Tax savings may result from deferred investment earnings or capital gains, rather than ordinary income that will not only be taxed currently but at a higher rate.

* **Confidentiality:** The APT can provide far greater privacy and confidentiality, minimization of domestic, home country inheritance taxes and the avoidance of the probate process in case of death. It provides increased flexibility in conducting affairs in case of personal disability, allows easy transfer of asset titles and avoids domestic currency controls in your home nation. An APT is also a good substitute for, or supplement to, costly professional liability insurance or even a prenuptial agreement, offering strong protection for your heirs' inheritance.

* **Estate Planning:** An offshore APT can serve the same traditional estate planning goals achieved by domestic strategies. These include using bypass trust provisions to minimize estate taxes for a husband and wife, trusts that allow maximum use of gift tax exemptions through planned giving, and trusts that provide for maintenance and tax-free income for a surviving spouse.

Asset Transfer

As a practical matter, regardless of the time of APT creation, any assets physically remaining within your home country and its courts' jurisdiction generally are not protected from domestic judgment creditors. Simply placing title to property in the name of a foreign trustee is at best, paper thin protection unless the property actually is moved offshore. If tangible assets actually are transferred to the foreign jurisdiction, as when funds or stock shares are moved to an offshore trust account or the trustee's safe deposit box, a home country creditor will have great difficulty in reaching them, provided he even discovers the existence of the trust.

As a mandatory precaution, the APT and its trustee should always employ an offshore bank that is not a branch or affiliate of any bank within your home country. This helps insulate the offshore bank officials (and APT accounts) from foreign pressure. It gives greater legitimate protection from home country pressures or just informational snooping, whether government or otherwise.

While high cost once may have been the rule, the APT costs have changed for the better.

Even with this enhanced financial privacy, in a given situation there can be great tactical advantage in letting a harassing party know your assets are securely placed well beyond their reach. The cost and difficulty of pursuit may well discourage any action on their part.

Up-Front Costs

Traditionally, the cost of creating a highly complex asset protection in a foreign nation has exceeded US$15,000, plus several thousand dollars in annual maintenance fees. Unless the total assets to be shielded justify such costs, a foreign APT may not be practical. A few years ago, *Business Week* estimated that "as a rule of thumb you should have a net worth of around US$500,000" or more in order to justify a foreign asset protection trust. The magazine cited expert's fees for establishing and administering such trusts running as high as US$50,000, with some demanding a percentage of the total value of assets to be transferred.

While high cost once may have been the rule, the APT costs have changed for the better. These days, offshore trusts are not just for the very rich. The Sovereign Society has investigated and recommends several offshore asset protection trusts with much lower costs. If you would like information about these trusts, see our Web site: www.sovereignsociety.com, or send an E-mail to: info@thesovereignsociety.com. Ask about our *Offshore Trust Report*. For a list of attorneys who can assist you with trust formation, see page 299.

Strategy 3: US$80,000 a Year – U.S. Tax-Free

If you decide personally to follow your cash, assets and investments offshore, there's a very useful provision of U.S. tax law about which you should know.

The so-called "foreign-earned-income exclusion" allows a U.S. citizen who lives and works outside the U.S. to exclude up to US$80,000 of foreign-earned income from taxable gross income. With a working spouse, you both can get US$160,000 annually, plus exclusion of housing allowances if an employer pays those.

It is important to note this is not a tax deduction, credit, or deferral. It is an outright exclusion of the earnings from taxable gross income. There are no taxes due at all on this offshore earned amount. To qualify for these benefits you must:

* establish a "tax home" in a foreign country;
* pass either the "foreign-residence test," or the "physical-presence test";
* actually have earned income;
* live in the U.S. for no more than one month per year; and
* file a U.S. income tax return for each year you live abroad.

Your "tax home" is the location of your regular or principal place of business, not where you live. But the definition of "tax home" is broader when determining eligibility for the foreign-earned-income exclusion. Confusion over this point snags many Americans overseas who think they are earning tax-free income. If you work overseas *and maintain a U.S. residence*, your tax home is not outside the U.S. In other words, to qualify for the foreign-earned-income exclusion, *you must establish both your principal place of business and your residence outside the United States.*

There is a complicated test that can also determine if you get this tax exclusion. It involves counting the maximum number of days you are in or out of the country. The more subjective test, known as the "foreign-residence test," is probably easier for most taxpayers to pass. You must establish yourself as a bona fide resident of a foreign country or countries for an uninterrupted period that includes an entire taxable year, and you must intend to stay there indefinitely. If you do not pass this test, you are considered a transient, or sojourner, and will not qualify as a foreign resident.

According to the tax law, your residence is a state of mind. It is where you intend to be domiciled indefinitely. To determine your state of mind, the IRS looks at the degree of your attachment to the country in question. A number of factors, none of them decisive or significantly more important than the others, are examined. The bottom line is that you must establish yourself as a bona fide member of a foreign community.

Strategy 4: Offshore Variable Annuities

Even though the U.S., the U.K., and the European Union continue to tighten the tax and financial reporting screws on wealth, there still remain private and profitable, yet strictly legal ways to protect and invest assets. One of these is the offshore variable annuity.

"Offshore annuities are becoming an investment vehicle of choice for those who have oodles of money they want to shelter from taxes."

This is one of the easiest, least expensive methods to invest in offshore funds. Moreover, you obtain deferral of taxes until funds are actually withdrawn. Another plus: your annuity investments can be transferred from one fund manager to another with no immediate tax consequences. Plus, you achieve significant asset protection. According to *The Wall Street Journal*, "Offshore annuities arc becoming an investment vehicle of choice for those who have oodles of money they want to shelter from taxes."

Offshore variable annuity investments typically start at least US$250,000, commonly exceeding US$1 million or more. In contrast, the average domestic U.S. annuity buyer's initial investment is only US$25,000 or less. The primary objectives in purchasing insurance offshore are asset protection, greater wealth accumulation, and access to international investment opportunities.

Because they are offshore, away from restrictive U.S. laws, foreign insurance companies can be flexible in negotiating fees. But keep in mind that, unless eliminated by a tax treaty, a one-time 1% federal U.S. excise tax is levied on all life insurance and annuity contracts issued to U.S. persons by foreign insurers.

Deferred Taxes

Foreign or domestic, a variable annuity is a contract, usually denominated in U.S. dollars, between you and an insurance company that provides tax deferred savings. It can serve as a savings or retirement vehicle using investment structures much like mutual funds, sometimes called "sub-accounts."

Here's how it works: you buy a variable annuity contract (policy) for an agreed upon sum, often referred to as a "single premium." These monies are invested by the insurance company in one or more investments that you approve, such as an offshore hedge fund.

The annuity contract requires periodic payments by the insurance company to you representing the increased value of investments on which the annuity is based. The money compounds, tax deferred, until you withdraw part or all of it, at which time it is taxed as regular income. This tax deferred accumulation can continue until the contract maturity date, usually when you are 85 or older – usually a time when total income is lower. An annuity is not "life insurance," so you need not take a medical examination to determine "insurability."

In most cases when the annuity matures, it either must be surrendered or converted to a life annuity that pays out a specified sum, at least annually, for the rest of your life, or for some other agreed period of time. Because most investors buy variable annuities for their tax deferred savings features, withdrawing funds as needed, most variable annuities never convert to a life annuity.

Strong Asset Protection

Variable insurance annuities offer significant asset protection, shielding the cash invested and the annuity income from creditors and other claimants. Practical asset protection exists since: 1) The policies are issued by offshore insurance companies with no affiliates in the United States; and 2) The policy's underlying assets are held entirely outside your home jurisdiction. Any domestic investments are made in the name of the insurance company, not your name.

Statutory asset protection exists in many jurisdictions for annuity contracts as well. In the Isle of Man (a jurisdiction that is home to 192 insurance companies), claims by creditors only can be made through the local courts.

...jurisdictions with a well-developed insurance sector provide statutory protection against creditor claims for insurance policies.

When a variable annuity is issued, the investment assets must be placed in this account and used only to satisfy the variable annuity obligation. If the company has financial problems, these segregated assets cannot be reached by insurance company creditors or creditors of other policyholders. The Cayman Islands, home to many leading offshore insurance companies, has a similar "segregated accounts" law.

In Switzerland, according to Swiss attorney Urs Schenkero, "A life insurance policy...is protected from the policy owner's creditors if the policy owner has irrevocably designated a third party as beneficiary or if the policy owner has irrevocably or revocably designated his spouse and/or his descendants beneficiaries."

The Swiss Insurance Act prevents a properly structured insurance contract from being included in a Swiss bankruptcy procedure. The law also protects the contract from foreign seizure orders or orders including them as part of foreign estate proceedings. Under Swiss law, if you are unable to pay your debts or file bankruptcy, all rights under the contract are assigned to the beneficiaries. Other offshore jurisdictions with a well-developed insurance sector provide statutory protection against creditor claims for insurance policies.

Offshore Variable Annuities and Taxes

Section 72 of the U.S. Internal Revenue Code treats both foreign and domestic variable annuities the same. But the IRS rules must be followed by an insurance company in order for accumulations to qualify for tax deferral. Always obtain a copy of legal opinions an insurance company has concerning U.S. tax treatment of annuities issued by that company. Check with your tax advisors if in doubt.

Tax deferral is no longer available to U.S. investors who purchase foreign fixed annuities..

To the extent that the funds you withdraw from a variable annuity represent deferred income, they are taxed at ordinary U.S. income tax rates. A loan against a variable annuity from the issuing insurance company to the owner, or a third party loan secured by a pledge of the annuity, is a taxable distribution. Certain unsecured loans, however, may be tax-free. Also, borrowing against an annuity when it is purchased is not taxable since no deferred income has accumulated.

Thus, you can acquire a US$2 million annuity contract and borrow up to US$1 million of the purchase price, pledging the annuity to secure the loan, with no adverse tax consequences.

Tax deferral is no longer available to U.S. investors who purchase foreign fixed annuities. A "fixed annuity" is an annuity contract guaranteeing a fixed income for a specified period of years or for life. A variable annuity's income varies depending on the performance of the underlying investments. Foreign fixed annuity contracts issued before April 7, 1995 retain tax deferral, as do domestic fixed annuities.

Information on Offshore Variable Annuities

Colin Bowen, Isle of Man Assurance, Ltd., IOMA House, Hope Street, Douglas, Isle of Man IM1 1AP, Channel Islands; Tel.: +44-1624-681-200; Fax: +44-1624-681-397; E-mail: colinb.ioma@ ioma.co.im; Web site: http://www.ioma.co.uk.

Marc Sola, NMG International Financial Services, Goethestrasse 22, Zurich, Switzerland; Tel.: +41-1-266-2141; Fax: +41-1-266-2149; E-mail: marcsola@nmg-ifs.com

Vernon K. Jacobs, CPA, CLU, Research Press, Inc., 4500 W. 72nd Terrace, Prairie Village, Kansas 66208; Tel.: 913-362-9667 / -7843; E-mail: rpi@sky.net; Web site: http://www.offshorepress.com.

Strategy 5: Offshore Life Insurance

Despite all the talk of "tax reform" in the United States, upon death, the combination of income tax and estate tax can consume 50% or more of a U.S. person's estate.

You can avoid these ruinous consequences with several planning techniques, but only life insurance provides these four key benefits: 1) Tax-free build-up of cash value, including dividends, interest, capital gains; 2) Tax-free borrowing against cash value; 3) Tax-free receipt of the death benefit; and 4) Freedom from estate and generation skipping taxes.

These benefits are available in any life insurance policy designed to comply with U.S. tax laws. However, for larger estates, a U.S. tax compliant life insurance policy issued by a carrier outside the U.S. offers five additional benefits:

1) Increased asset protection. No protection for life insurance proceeds exists under federal laws. While many states have enacted laws that provide limited protection for life insurance policies, coverage varies from significant to non-existent. In contrast, many offshore jurisdictions provide statutory asset protection for the death benefit and investments held by an insurance policy. As a practical matter, it is much more expensive for a creditor to bring a claim before a foreign court than a domestic court.

Life insurance remains one of few remaining opportunities for offshore estate tax planning combined with asset protection and tax deferral.

---

2) Access to global investments. Offshore insurance policies provide tax advantaged access to international asset managers and to offshore funds that are generally not accessible to U.S. investors.

3) Increased privacy. Domestic assets, including life insurance policies, can easily be discovered by private investigators with access to any of the hundreds of "asset tracking" services now existing in the U.S. In contrast, assets held offshore are off the domestic "radar screen" and cannot easily be identified in a routine asset search. The confidentiality statutes of some offshore jurisdictions are an additional barrier against frivolous claims and investigations.

4) Not reportable as a "foreign bank account." A life insurance policy purchased from a non-U.S. carrier is not considered a "foreign bank, securities or other financial account." This means that there is no requirement to report the existence of or the income derived from an offshore insurance policy to any U.S. government authority. However, depending on what country you purchase an offshore insurance policy from, it may be necessary to make a one-time excise tax payment to the IRS amounting to 1% of the policy premium.

5) Currency diversification. Life insurance policies are free to make investments in non-U.S. dollar assets that may gain in the event of future declines in the value of the U.S. dollar.

Needless to say, the IRS is not pleased with a planning technique that simultaneously eliminates federal estate taxes, creates a situation where no U.S. person is subject to tax upon transfer of the assets to the beneficiaries and permits the policyholder to invest in highly lucrative offshore mutual funds without paying tax.

To this end, the IRS in 2003 announced rules that would limit the tax benefits for investors in hedge funds that are setting up insurance companies in offshore jurisdictions, but that are not operating as life insurance carriers. It also is concerned with foreign insurance carriers that are investing in hedge funds and has promised to more aggressively enforce existing provisions in the U.S. Tax Code that prohibit life insurance investors from managing their own securities portfolio and that require adequate diversification within the policy.

However, these policy changes have been "in the making" for several years. A properly planned and executed offshore insurance policy should not be affected. But, it is essential that you obtain expert tax advice when considering the purchase of an offshore insurance policy.

Life insurance remains one of few remaining opportunities for offshore estate tax planning combined with asset protection and tax deferral. Without major changes in U.S. federal laws, these advantages will remain for the foreseeable future.

Information contact

Mr. Colin Bowen, Isle of Man Assurance, Ltd., IOMA House, Hope Street, Douglas, Isle of Man IM1 1AP, Channel Islands; Tel.: +44-1624-681-200; Fax: +44-1624-681-397; E-mail: colinb.ioma@ioma.co.im; Web site: http://ioma.co.uk.

Strategy 6: Offshore Investing

Some of the most profitable investments to be made can be found offshore. And throughout these pages I will give you contact information for investment managers and firms that can assist you in your quest for profits.

At this writing, there are approximately 1,500 emerging-market investment funds managing over US$200 billion in equities. Add to that figure the billions denominated in other financial instruments and the total is overwhelming.

By 2000, foreign stocks represented over 65% of the total world stock market capitalization of US$15 trillion plus.

International and "emerging nation" mutual funds offer a simple way for American investors to profit from the growth of foreign companies. Such funds eliminate the inconvenience associated with direct ownership of foreign shares. American investors can also profit from American Depository Receipts, or ADRs. These are listed securities traded on U.S. stock exchanges. ADRs represent shares of a foreign stock and are issued by U.S. banks that take possession of the securities. The banks convert dividend payments into dollars and deduct any foreign withholding taxes. ADRs give investors a greater guarantee of safety, as participating foreign companies have to meet certain U.S. Securities and Exchange Commission (SEC) accounting and disclosure standards.

Over the past 20 years, capital markets outside the U.S. have grown rapidly in size and importance. In 1970, non-U.S. stocks accounted for 32% of the world's US$935 billion total market capitalization. By 2000, foreign stocks represented over 65% of the total world stock market capitalization of US$15 trillion plus.

While top U.S. stocks have performed exceptionally well over the years, international stock markets historically have outperformed Wall Street as a whole. The rapid growth of capital markets around the world has also created abundant opportunities for fixed income investors. Worldwide bond market capitalization now exceeds worldwide equity capitalization. Non-U.S. bonds account for more than half of the world's bond market value. Non-American investors have realized the enormous profit potential of cross-border investment.

Avoiding Roadblocks to Prosperity

This international economic integration continues despite U.S. laws designed to hinder such activity. One of the main obstacles remains restrictive securities legislation. Any "investment contract" for a security sold in the United States must be registered with the SEC and similar agencies in each of the states. This is a prohibitively expensive process. The U.S. also requires far more disclosure than most foreign countries, and burdens the process with different accounting practices.

International fund managers are practical people who look at the bottom line. Many correctly calculate that operating costs in the U.S. would wipe out any profit margin they could achieve. Ironically, several mutual funds and hedge funds with top performance records are run from the U.S. by U.S. residents, but do not accept investments from Americans. To avoid SEC red tape and registration costs, investment in these funds is available only to foreigners.

Fortunately, there are ways for U.S. citizens to get around these obstacles. Although you're a U.S. citizen, you can qualify under the law as an *accredited investor*. As such, you will have a freer hand to buy non-SEC registered foreign stocks and mutual funds directly. An accredited investor is defined by SEC rules as an individual who has a net worth of US$1 million or more, or an annual income of at least US$250,000. In other words, you must have a lot of money.

You can also buy foreign securities through corporations or trusts you have created offshore. Properly structured foreign trusts and corporations – and I do mean properly structured – are not considered "U.S. residents, persons, or citizens." These entities therefore have the unrestricted right to buy non-SEC registered securities.

SEC "Regulation S" has actually made it easier to make such investments. It clearly defines the exemptions allowed by U.S. securities laws. These exemptions permit investment in non-SEC registered securities through a foreign trust and/or corporation. The most important restriction: the grantor who creates such entities must include income from these sources as personal income on annual tax returns.

Typically, the IRS has a web of rules and regulations that aim to wring maximum revenue from Americans who go offshore. These tax laws are extremely complex, so move cautiously and only with expert professional advice. At every step of the way, find out exactly what the U.S. tax consequences will be before you proceed. For professional tax advisors, see page 299.

Part 3. Offshore Business Strategies

Strategy 1: An International Business Corporation (IBC)

One excellent vehicle for offshore tax savings is an international business corporation (IBC). An IBC is simply a corporation registered in an offshore tax haven under its laws. Since the IBC does business offshore but not in the nation where it is registered, it is exempt from most local corporate and other taxes. Usually, there is an initial incorporation fee and then an annual maintenance fee.

An IBC can be used outside of the nation of incorporation for a variety of activities including consulting, investing, trading, finance, holding assets, or real estate ownership. In some cases, an IBC may confer a trade advantage or it may also be used as an integral part of a trust structure.

One excellent vehicle for offshore tax savings is an international business corporation (IBC).

One of the main advantages of an IBC is that it can be used to pay legitimate business expenses, and it can also be used to plough back profits to be used for business. So long as these profits are not paid out as salary or dividends to the IBC owners, this avoids immediate income tax liabilities.

Certain tax havens, such as Panama, make it attractive to incorporate. When selecting a place to incorporate, here's what you need to consider:

* legal and political attitudes of the jurisdiction toward commercial activities;

* corporate laws that facilitate incorporation and continuing management;

* the level and speed of service obtainable; and

* the cost.

All IBC friendly jurisdictions have at least two requirements: 1) maintaining an agent for the service of process; and 2) payment of an annual franchise fee or tax.

One of the best tax haven nations for IBC incorporation that I recommend is Panama.

The following can provide IBC incorporation services in Panama:

Derek Sambrook, Trust Services, Ltd., Suite 522, Balboa Plaza, Avenida Balboa, Panama City, Panama. Mailing Address: Apartado 0832-1630, World Trade Centre, Panama City, Panama; Tel.: +507-269-2438; Fax: +507-269-4922; E-mail: sambrook@trustserv.com; Web site: http://ww.trustserv.com.

Strategy 2: Using Tax Treaties for Profit

There is at least one thing worse than paying taxes in your home country: paying taxes in two or more countries on the same income. In this case, "look before you leap" is very good advice. Careless offshore financial arrangements can result in redundant taxes that eat up most or all of the profits involved.

Bilateral (two-country) tax treaties were developed to avoid these problems. Formally known as "double tax conventions," these agreements usually allow the source country to tax most of the income earned within its borders, while the other country agrees not to tax that income, usually by giving credit for foreign taxes paid against domestic taxes owed. Those are the basic principles, but the variations within each treaty are endless.

Current U.S. tax treaties were negotiated individually over the last half-century and usually remain in effect for set time periods (20 years or more), so re-negotiation is ongoing constantly. Most U.S. treaties are with industrialized countries or nations with major commercial and banking activities. Some European countries, especially the United Kingdom and the Netherlands, have their own network of tax treaties with an extensive list of nations, many their former colonial possessions.

There's little point in discussing the terms of each U.S. tax treaty in detail here, since they change periodically based on re-negotiation or official reinterpretation. The information presented here is as current as I can make it. To be certain you are up to date, obtain professional advice on the status and impact of any tax treaty before investing offshore. Recent U.S. treaties are on the Internet at http://www.irs.gov/businesses/corporations/article/0,,id.

Tax treaty strategies are less important to someone who simply wants to use an offshore bank and investment account as a personal financial tool. But they can be of tremendous value when doing commercial business overseas in one or more nations. Depending on your business and the way a given tax treaty is structured, taxes can be significantly lowered or avoided completely.

The Tax Treaty Loophole

In theory, bilateral tax treaties are supposed to remove or reduce the burden of double taxation. That's the theory, but not always the practical result.

After World War II, with the British Empire crumbling, the

United States routinely agreed to extend the terms of the existing U.S.-U.K. tax treaty to newly independent nations in the British Commonwealth. As the interdependent global economy began to grow, especially in the 1970s, these new countries and creative international tax planners found tremendous profits to be made under the terms of older, existing treaties. Former British colonies became low- or no-tax havens for certain types of exempted income earned by foreign-resident persons, trusts and corporations. Liberal local tax laws combined with the tax treaties created a bonanza in tax-free transactions. Pick the right country, the right business, and you could be "home free" with tax-free profits.

Anyone planning an offshore business should seek guidance from an attorney who knows international tax planning and tax treaties.

The good news for U.S. taxpayers considering going offshore is that no-tax or low-tax countries have a significant financial interest in keeping these liberal provisions available. They have been resisting U.S. Treasury Department efforts to change the rules. In addition, many U.S.-based multinational corporations want these favorable offshore tax provisions continued in order to keep their capital costs in line with those of foreign competitors.

Anyone planning an offshore business should seek guidance from an attorney who knows international tax planning and tax treaties. Choosing the right country in which to incorporate your business could mean a dramatically reduced tax bill. It's well worth checking out.

Strategy 3: Profitable "Stepping Stones"

Creative offshore tax planning often calls for business operations in more than one country. That way, you can use the most advantageous combination of available tax treaties. International tax practitioners like to call this the "stepping stone" principal. The IRS derisively calls it "treaty shopping." Stepping stone transactions are most useful when passive interest or royalty income is involved, though some other commercial and service business structures can also be profitable.

The stones work like this: a German investor naturally wants to earn the highest interest rates available. His tax advisor suggests investing through a Dutch company, because that nation has an extensive, ready-made tax treaty network with all other developed countries. The German could form his own Dutch corporation, but tax authorities prefer that he use an independent, pre-existing business. In effect, the German will invest money in an existing Dutch company that will invest it elsewhere. The Dutch company will charge fees for its middleman role, payments known as "the spread."

The tax treaty network allows a Dutch company to invest money virtually anywhere it wants. Under treaty terms, the interest it receives is not subject to withholding taxes in the countries where the money is invested. For example, the U.S.-Netherlands treaty provides for no withholding of tax by the U.S. on interest paid from the United States to a Dutch company. The Netherlands company is not required to withhold taxes when that interest in turn is paid to the German investor. No taxes all around.

The existing U.S. tax treaty network, and the multiple "stepping stone" possibilities it offers to foreign investors, means the United States is a tax haven for the world, but not for its own citizens. Many foreign businesses and investors using U.S. tax treaties as part of careful structuring make money by basing their operations in America and legally paying little or no U.S. taxes.

There are ways to save taxes offshore, but do it right and be sure you know what you can and cannot do.

Not surprisingly, the IRS disapproves of this wholesale treaty shopping. In tax treaty renegotiations, the U.S. insists, not always successfully, on "anti-treaty shopping" provisions. The actual terms vary, but basically the IRS wants to re-write treaties to limit tax benefits to those who are bona fide residents of the other bilateral treaty nation. In our example, that would have ruled out the German investor.

The IRS hates such arrangements. To them it's tax evasion using phony affiliates of businesses operating within the U.S. Fortunately for astute taxpayers, if it's done right this system is legal and it works. The one key requirement is strict adherence to proper form and no corner-cutting.

The moral: There are ways to save taxes offshore, but do it right and be sure you know what you can and cannot do.

I repeat, tax treaties change constantly, and with those changes come the end of some formerly available tax saving strategies. Internal domestic tax laws change, too. What's here today is gone tomorrow. But serious international business people must pay as much attention to tax treaty developments as they do to daily weather forecast or stock market reports. It can be that essential.

One Last Word About Reporting

So you have gotten your assets offshore. Now what? Do you have to tell the U.S. government that you have opened an offshore account?

The law says: "Each United States person who has a financial interest in, or signature authority over bank, securities, or other financial accounts in a foreign country which exceeds US$10,000 in aggregate value, must report the relationship each calendar year by filing Treasury Department Form 90-22.1 before June 30 of the succeeding year."

If you're a U.S. citizen or permanent resident alien and hold US$10,000 or more in one or more foreign financial accounts, you must report the existence of these accounts each year on your federal income tax return, IRS Form 1040 (Schedule B). You must also file a separate information return (Form TD F 90-22.1) with the U.S. Treasury. "Willful" non-compliance may result in criminal prosecution.

Instructions for Treasury Form TD F 90-22.1 read, in part:

"F. **Bank, Financial Account**. The term 'bank account' means a savings, demand, checking, deposit, loan, or any other account maintained with a financial institution or other person engaged in the business of banking. It includes certificates of deposit. The term 'securities account' means an account maintained with a financial institution or other person who buys, sells, holds, or trades stock or other securities for the benefit of another. The term 'other financial account' means any other account maintained with a financial institution or other person who accepts deposits, exchanges or transmits funds, or acts as a broker or dealer for future transactions in any commodity on (or subject to the rules of) a commodity exchange or association."

The US$10,000 account limit includes the total value of cash, CDs and negotiable securities held personally in your name in any offshore bank accounts. It *excludes* foreign investments held separately from the bank account itself. (If you have any question about these rules, consult with a qualified professional to find out whether or not you need to file these forms.)

Since the US$10,000 reporting ceiling does not apply to separately owned foreign investments, these are a logical alternative to be considered . Under IRS definitions, reportable offshore accounts do not include brokerage accounts or arrangements in which a foreign bank acts as a securities custodian. So, if you find yourself in danger of breaching the US$10,000 ceiling, use the account cash to buy foreign bonds or stocks, and take delivery of the title certificate by registered mail at your U.S. address.

Be careful of the hair-splitting distinctions under the IRS foreign account reporting rules. If you physically place your foreign bond or stock certificate in a safe deposit box abroad, that doesn't mean the certificate value counts toward a reportable offshore securities account.

Be aware: the same rule doesn't hold true with most *foreign mutual funds*. Such funds register evidence of share ownership electronically in the name of the owner's foreign securities account, usually without providing actual certificates of title. Many EU countries have eliminated the issuance of paper stock and bond certificates entirely, evidencing share ownership by an investor only in corporate book entry form. The value of these non-certificate registry shares counts towards the US$10,000 limit for U.S. account reporting purposes.

The Qualified Intermediary Rule

The U.S. Internal Revenue Service, as of January 2001, forced foreign banks and financial institutions into the unwelcome role of IRS informants, a.k.a. "qualified intermediaries" (QI). On that date, U.S. persons holding U.S.-based investments purchased through offshore banks had a choice of either having banks report the holdings to the IRS, or having the bank withhold a 30% tax on all interest and dividends paid. To avoid either, the U.S. investor can, and should, liquidate his or her *U.S.-based investments* made through an offshore bank or financial institution.

Foreign investments held offshore by U.S. persons through an offshore bank or financial institution are exempt from these IRS rules. Bent on crushing possible tax evasion, in effect the IRS imposed extraterritorial tax enforcement burdens on foreign nations and their banks. Both have been forced to meet IRS established anti-money laundering and "know your customer" standards in order to obtain "QI" status. Those banks that qualified got IRS "approved status," meaning the 30% tax on U.S. source income need not be withheld, and reduced tax rates can be applied under mutual double tax avoidance treaties.

"The U.S. investor can, and should, liquidate his or her U.S.-based investments *made through an offshore bank or financial institution.*

But the IRS stamp of QI approval comes freighted with onerous conditions which may end customer confidentiality for U.S. offshore investors who don't know the rules. It also gives the IRS leverage over foreign nations when demanding exchange of tax and other financial information, unless those nations have strict financial privacy laws. Some offshore banks may suffer U.S. financial sanctions if they don't tell the IRS who their U.S. customers are and what they are doing. Under the guise of enforcing U.S. tax laws, the IRS demanded and got imperial approval of foreign nations' banking rules and reporting requirements.

Non-Reportable Foreign Investments

These investments appear to be excluded from reporting when they are purchased without opening a "bank, securities, or other financial account" or using such an account to maintain custody: **1)** offshore real estate; **2)** most insurance policies; and **3)** directly purchased foreign securities.

However, even a mere book entry in a foreign corporation's records is considered an "other financial account" if the corporation transmits or disburses funds or otherwise functions as a bank on behalf of the securities owner.

Direct ownership of real property in a foreign country, including a timeshare arrangement, is not a reportable foreign account

---

Real Estate Investments

Direct ownership of real property in a foreign country, including a timeshare arrangement, is not a reportable foreign account as defined in Form TD F 90-22.1. However, real estate holdings are generally a matter of public record in the jurisdiction in which they are located and they cannot be liquidated easily. If you own the real estate through a holding company or trust, that entity may be required to file its own disclosure forms.

If you wish to purchase and hold real estate in a foreign country without disclosing your ownership, this can be accomplished by placing title in an international business corporation (IBC) located in a nation such as Panama where beneficial ownership does not have to be disclosed. Your IBC does not have to be located in the same nation where the real estate is located.

Safekeeping Arrangements

Valuables or documents purchased outside the U.S. and placed *directly* into a non-U.S. safety deposit or private security vault do not appear to constitute a foreign account. To avoid having to personally visit the box each time you wish to add or remove valuables, you can give a local attorney or other trusted intermediary a limited "power of attorney" allowing them to perform this function.

Many foreign banks offer custodial arrangements, maintaining custody of cash, securities or precious metals for the owner. Some argue such an arrangement may be non-reportable because the bank is merely safekeeping the assets. However, such an arrangement usually exists in tandem with an actual bank account and assets may be conveyed between them upon the owner's instructions. This is unquestionably closer to a reportable account relationship than simply renting and using a safety deposit box or private vault.

Safekeeping is available through companies that offer private vaults, many of them non-financial institutions. As such, they are subject to fewer recordkeeping and disclosure requirements and some permit anonymous vault rentals. Most honor power of attorney arrangements. Three recommended foreign private vault services are:

Mat Securitas, Steinackerstrasse 47, CH-8302 Kloten, Switzerland; Web site: www.viamat.com.

Safes Fidelity SA, 6, Place Chevelu, CH-1201 Geneva, Switzerland.

Das Safe, Auerspergstrasse 1, 1080 Vienna, Austria.

Materials held in a safety deposit box or private vault are not ordinarily insured against theft or other loss. Supplemental insurance can be purchased, but the existence and location of the assets must be disclosed to the insurer.

Foreign Insurance Contracts

Foreign insurance policies appear to be exempted from reporting as "foreign accounts." There is no mention of "insurance companies" in Treasury Regulations pertaining to the reporting requirements. An insurance policy is a contract with the insurer taking on specific responsibilities in exchange for a sum of money, not an account relationship. However, U.S. persons purchasing foreign insurance contracts must file IRS Form 720 and pay a 1% excise tax, unless this tax is waived under a tax treaty.

Avoiding Double Taxation

Governments everywhere love taxes. The government in the nation in which your offshore bank account is located has the power to impose its own withholding taxes on your assets and deposits, and many of them do just that. For example, in Switzerland a 35% tax is imposed on interest income. In many nations, taxes are withheld by the financial institution where the account is located. That's why it's important to check the potential tax liabilities beforehand, then make certain to locate your account in a "no-tax" jurisdiction.

Governments everywhere love taxes.

If you have a bank account in a country that has a "double taxation treaty" with your home country, you may qualify for a credit against your national income tax obligation in the amount of the foreign tax paid. However, claiming that credit means you must disclose the existence of your offshore bank account to the authorities. You may want to skip the foreign tax credit claim, since average credits allowed vary from country to country according to the terms of the treaty in force at the time. In most cases, the tax authorities are unlikely to allow a credit of more than a fraction of the foreign tax withheld.

A word of caution about bilateral tax treaties; these agreements sometimes give home governments access to all kinds of information about the accounts of foreign investors. Normally, the offshore nation governs how much and what kind of information it will disclose to foreign officials. Swiss law, for example, in principle does not recognize non-payment of foreign income taxes as a crime. Accordingly, in the absence of a Swiss court order, most Swiss banks refuse to open their books to foreign tax officials if an account holder is accused only of non-payment of their home country taxes. Other nations will give out such information, however, so before you make a final choice, carefully investigate the bank privacy laws of the nation under consideration and its treaties with the U.S. or your home country.

If you are concerned about this privacy aspect of offshore banking, obtain a copy of the U.S. tax treaty with the nation you are considering for placement of your financial business. Treaties are published by the U.S. State Department in the *Treaties in Force* series, which is available in major libraries worldwide. More recent U.S. treaties also are available on the Internet at: http://www.irs.gov/businesses/corporations/article/0,,id=96739,00. html.

Swiss Bank Compromises U.S. Privacy
The merger of Swiss Bank Corporation and Union Bank of Switzerland creating UBS AG was approved by the U.S. Federal Reserve in 1999 – but only after the Swiss bank agreed to provide the U.S. government with all information "necessary to determine and enforce compliance with ...[U.S.] federal laws." This surrender goes far beyond the financial information required to be exchanged under the U.S.-Swiss Tax Treaty and it may also circumvent Swiss laws that usually require a court order to release private banking information.

UBS caved in after the U.S. government threatened to shut down the bank's extensive American financial operations. The UBS sellout was bad news for financial privacy seekers – and it blows a large hole in the much vaunted Swiss claim of "bank secrecy." U.S. depositors should avoid UBS AG and any Swiss bank with U.S. financial operations.

In these pages and in the Appendix, I list many excellent banks and financial institutions across the globe. You can choose any of these with full confidence your finances will be in good hands. Sovereign Society members have special access to offshore banking arranged for them. If you want to learn more about The Sovereign Society Convenient Offshore Bank Accounts, see page 311.

One more word; in several places in this chapter when describing the meaning and requirements of IRS reporting rules, I have used the phrase *"appear to be."* That's because IRS requirements change almost daily as the agency issues new rules and new interpretations, and as courts rule on tax issues. You should always check with a qualified U.S. tax professional, an attorney or accountant, if you have any questions about IRS rules. See Appendix on page 299 for a list of qualified professionals that I recommend.

Chapter 3
What You Need To Know About Offshore Havens

SUMMARY: Here you learn about tax havens and asset havens, their laws, procedures, how to use them and what methods you can employ for your maximum benefit. I explain the future of offshore havens and why they have been attacked.

A *tax haven* is a country or other jurisdiction, some are colonial possessions of other nations, that promotes and guarantees no taxes or low taxes for foreigners who choose to do business there.

An *asset haven* is a country or jurisdiction that has adopted special laws and established a judicial system that guarantees strong protection for assets, plus a high degree of financial privacy.

The same jurisdiction or place can be both a tax and asset haven and they usually do combine these functions. But a nation may be in just one or the other of these categories.

In this chapter, I explain the differences and similarities of havens, how to use them, and where they are located. Specific and detailed treatment of our choices of the best haven nations can be found in Chapter 4 on page 77.

Understanding Tax Havens

It may be surprising to the over-taxed citizens of the world to learn that many nations can finance their governments while imposing only low taxes, almost no taxes, or by offering special tax concessions to foreigners.

Just as several American states (including Florida, New Hampshire, and Alaska) offer their citizens a chance to escape other state's income taxes, foreign tax havens may be the solution for offshore-minded people seeking national tax relief. You don't have to move your residence to these offshore havens in order to enjoy their benefits – only your cash and/or other assets.

But in spite of what you may have heard, accept this fact: for U.S. persons, haven nations offer only *minimal* tax savings. Always keep this fact in mind: the U.S. government taxes all worldwide income wherever it is earned and wherever the U.S. person may live or have residence(s).

This means U.S. citizens and resident aliens (both groups known in tax law as "U.S. persons") must, by law, report all of their income and pay U.S. taxes accordingly. Unlike individual U.S. taxpayers, many American-owned businesses profit by establishing themselves as foreign corporations in tax havens, since a foreign company owned by Americans pays only limited U.S. taxes on certain types of investment income. If these corporate profits are kept offshore, reinvested or ploughed back into the business, personal income and some other taxes often can be deferred indefinitely.

---

the U.S. government taxes all worldwide income wherever it is earned and wherever the U.S. person may live or have residence(s).

U.S. offshore business ownership is highly complex when it comes to taxes. The very best professional tax advice is needed to assure you are in compliance with the law if you own an offshore business – and to make sure you are eligible for every tax break for which you may qualify.

Tax obligations differ in various nations according to their laws, so before you go offshore, check the tax status of your intended country with advice from a competent professional you trust.

Understanding Asset Havens

What makes a place an "asset haven?"

Asset havens are countries or jurisdictions with established laws that:

1) offer legal entities that provide asset protection, such as trusts, family foundations and international business corporations (IBCs);

2) by law strongly protect financial and personal privacy; and

3) provide and support a judicial system that consistently favors asset protection.

Most asset havens also are tax havens – meaning they do not impose income, capital gains, estate or other taxes on foreigners who choose to open bank accounts or form IBCs or trusts registered in the country.

The U.S. is one of the world's leading tax havens, giving special tax treatment to foreigners (but not Americans).

But not all asset havens are tax-free for foreigners or their business operations, an important factor to be considered in every case.

Different Havens; Different Uses

Remember, an established *tax haven* jurisdiction does not necessarily qualify as an *asset haven*.

Many nations with favorable tax laws do offer strong asset protection as an added incentive to attract foreign money and investments, but some do not. In these pages, I'll tell you which countries or jurisdictions offer the best deals, and how you can employ them to your benefit.

Not all tax havens are *nations*. Many are colonies or territorial possessions of other nations, as Bermuda is a partial self-governing overseas territory (colony) of the United Kingdom. The Cayman Islands falls into this same status.

Historically, many tax havens have spurred economic development by recreating themselves as both tax and asset havens. Some of these countries have never imposed an income tax. Others are countries with special tax legislation or incentives favoring certain types of business.

The U.S. is one of the world's leading tax havens, giving special tax treatment to foreigners (but *not* Americans) who invest in U.S. real estate and securities and commodities markets. The United Kingdom also gives major tax breaks to foreigners, although as this is being written, these existing tax breaks are being reconsidered by the Labour government. In fact, the U.S. and U.K. are leading world tax havens, if one bases that calculation on the total foreign-owned, tax exempt cash and assets located and managed there.

Tax Havens Come in Different Flavors

A tax haven is any country whose laws, regulations, policies, and treaty arrangements make it possible for a foreign national who does business there to reduce personal and/or corporate tax burdens.

Not all foreign tax haven countries are created equal.

This is done by voluntarily bringing yourself – or your trust or corporation – within the country's jurisdiction. This general definition covers all four major types of tax haven nations, each categorized by the degree and type of taxes imposed.

It's important to understand these tax haven differences. Not all foreign tax haven countries are created equal. You must fully understand the tax characteristics of each type before you make any plans or decisions.

No-Tax Havens

In "no-tax" havens, foreign citizens who do business there pay no taxes – no income, capital gains, or wealth taxes.

A foreign citizen can quickly and easily incorporate and/or form a trust, and register to do business immediately. You can expect a few minor administrative taxes, like stamp duties on incorporation documents, charges on the value of corporate shares issued, annual registration fees, or other fees not levied directly as a tax on income. In addition, there will be the non-governmental costs of engaging a local agent and the filing of annual reports.

The government in a no-tax haven nation earns considerable revenue from the sheer volume of foreign corporations and trusts that are registered within its borders, even if these entities conduct most or all of their business elsewhere.

No-tax havens – all of which are located in or near the Caribbean basin – include: Bermuda, The Bahamas, the Cayman Islands, St. Kitts and Nevis, the Turks and Caicos Islands, Belize, and St. Vincent and the Grenadines.

As you will see later in these pages, I do not recommend all of the above havens because of recent changes in their offshore laws, particularly the weakening of financial privacy and bank secrecy laws.

Foreign-Source Income Havens

The second group includes "foreign-source income" tax havens. These countries have a "territorial tax" approach, *taxing only income actually earned within the country*.

Income earned from foreign sources is tax exempt, since it involves no in-country domestic business activities, apart from simple housekeeping chores. Often there is no income tax on profits from exports of local manufactured goods, although there may be a tax on domestic manufacturing itself.

Foreign-source income tax havens are divided into two sub-groups.

The first group allows you or your corporation to conduct business both internally and externally, taxing only the income from in-country sources. These nations include: Costa Rica, Ecuador, Guatemala, Honduras, Israel, The Philippines, Thailand, and Sri Lanka. Since none of these nations qualify as full-fledged tax or asset havens, I won't discuss them further, but I encourage you to research them further if you find them of interest.

The second group of nations, named below, requires corporate organizers to decide at the time of incorporation whether the business will limit itself either to taxable domestic activity, or to foreign tax-exempt business. These nations include: Panama, the Channel Islands of Jersey and Guernsey, and the Isle of Man.

The four jurisdictions named above are particularly attractive as locations for U.S.-owned foreign trading corporations and foreign investment corporations. American tax laws give these two types of offshore corporate entities relatively better tax breaks.

Tax Treaty Nations

The third type of haven is called a "tax treaty nation." While these nations impose taxes on worldwide corporate and trust income, their governments have reciprocal double taxation avoidance agreements with other nations – especially with major trade partners like the U.S., France, Canada, Germany, and the U.K. These mutual agreements significantly reduce the withholding tax imposed on foreign income earned by domestic corporations, and give credit against domestic tax liability for taxes paid by a local business to a foreign government.

Although these nations are less attractive for asset protection, they are suitable for lower taxed international corporate activity. Their main drawback is that international tax treaties permit the free exchange of information between national taxing authorities, allowing far less privacy.

Among leading tax treaty nations are: Cyprus, The Netherlands, Belgium, and Denmark. For more about using tax treaties, see Chapter 2, page 49.

Special Use Tax Havens

The final category of havens features several countries that impose the kind of taxes Americans and citizens of the United Kingdom know and dislike – high taxes. But these high taxes are tempered by a government policy of granting special tax holidays, concessions, or rebates to favored business enterprises they want to attract and promote, usually as a means to increase local employment.

These concessions typically include:

• corporate tax credits for local job creation;

• tax exemptions for manufacturing and processing of exports; and

• special tax benefits for international business or holding companies, offshore banks, or other selected industries.

In the U.S., critics call this kind of domestic business tax break "corporate welfare," but many nations offer these kinds of foreign business inducements in some form or other. Other nations that offer generous special tax concessions to foreign-owned businesses include Chile, Portugal, and Barbados.

For instance, Barbados grants tax exemptions to retired foreigners who settle there. Living conditions are pleasant, with high literacy and educational levels. Special laws favor headquarters of international companies and major banks with income tax exemptions. The government also offers generous tax breaks and subsidies for foreign-owned local companies that increase employment.

Contacts

Chile – Pro Chile New York, 866 United Nations Plaza, Suite 603, New York, New York 10017; Tel.: 212-207-3266; Fax: 212-207-3649; Web site: http://www.chileinfo.com.

National Chamber of Commerce of Chile, Santa Lucia 302, Piso 4, Santiago, Chile; Tel.: +562-639-6639 / -7694; Fax: +562-638-0234.

Portugal – Official government Web site: www.portugal.org/. For an excellent six-chapter outline on the topic, click on "Doing Business in Portugal."

Portuguese Foreign Trade Institute (ICEP), Avenida 5 de Outubro 101, 1016 Lisboa Codex, Portugal; Tel.: +351-1-793-0103; Fax: +351-1-793-5028.

Barbados – Barbados Government Information Service, Bay Street, St. Michael, Barbados, West Indies; Tel.: +246-426-2232; Fax: +246-436-1317; Web site: http://www.bgis.gov.bb.

Tax-Free Zones

Closely akin to special use tax havens are "tax-free zones" established within specified areas of some countries. Often these zones are used as trans-shipment points for finished goods, such as the Colón Free Trade Zone in Panama (www.colonfreezone.com/), or the Hong Kong free zone.

(For more about Panama and Hong Kong, see Chapter 4, page 77.)

Other tax-free zones, however, are major bases for industry, business, and finance, complete with well-developed infrastructure and favorable laws to attract business to the zone. A good example is the Jebel Ali Free Trade Zone in Dubai, one of the United Arab Emirates. The Zone's web site is at http://www.jafza.com/02.html.

Offshore Havens Under Siege

To understand the position in which offshore havens today find themselves, a review of recent world financial history is in order.

For more than a decade, beginning in the 1990s, there has been an ongoing battle, the outcome of which will determine the survival of tax haven and asset haven nations – and with them, the last realistic chance for low taxes and financial privacy anywhere in the world. At this writing in early 2004, the havens are ahead.

Governments of many major nations, along with allied international groups, officially have aimed their biggest political and economic artillery directly at legitimate offshore tax, business, and banking haven nations. If the tax hungry bureaucrats had their way, national sovereignty and independence would suffer. All of this coordinated activity has been a part of a concerted battle being waged against personal and financial freedoms, on both national and international fronts.

Among the main antagonists working against tax haven nations have been the presidential administration of Bill Clinton (1993-2001), the United Kingdom's Labour government under Prime Minister Tony Blair (1995-present), the European Union, the Organization for Community and Economic Development (OECD), the Financial Action Task Force (FATF), and the United Nations. Each of these big spending, high-tax groups, for their own and for common reasons, has joined to try and crush offshore havens.

European Union Demands

The Brussels bureaucrats, under the hypocritical banner of "tax harmonization" (meaning "high taxes for all Europe"), long have demanded an EU-wide withholding tax on interest income earned by foreigners. Alternately, they want a reporting system that informs a nonresident interest earner's home government of any and all income earned in other EU nations. They call this "tax information exchange." The EU argument is that member nations lose millions every year because of tax evasion by their nationals who move cash to other EU nations or to offshore havens.

For years, the EU tried unsuccessfully to force tax information exchange and cross-border taxes on all its nations – and on non-EU member Switzerland as well, the world's leading asset haven. As of this writing, the EU has failed to achieve both objectives.

The best they could do by the end of 2003 was a split deal in which Austria, Belgium, and Luxembourg are allowed to retain their strict financial privacy, but each commits to imposition of a withholding tax on nonresidents' savings. These three nations will then remit 75% of the withheld taxes to the countries of origin of the taxed investors. These taxes are supposedly scheduled to start at 15% in 2004, rising to 20% in 2007 and to 35% by 2010.

Crucially for the EU plan, Switzerland, a non-EU member, and Liechtenstein, both with significant EU depositor bases, have said they may or may not go along with the deal, depending on the exact details.

For years, the EU tried unsuccessfully to force tax information exchange and cross-border taxes on all its nations.

The strict EU savings tax initiative foundered in the face of reality and official opposition from the United States when, in 2002, the Bush administration formally said no to the EU initiative, refusing to cooperate with the EU information exchange demands.

The EU savings tax initiative plan itself has serious flaws, including the fact that neither the United States nor major Asian financial offshore centers, such as Singapore or Hong Kong, have agreed to participate. This means that EU depositors and investors seeking to avoid the EU withholding taxes can transfer funds outside the EU, Switzerland, and/or Liechtenstein in order to escape the new reporting requirements or the alternative taxes.

In addition, the EU deal rightly was called "hypocritical" by leading offshore centers such as Panama. It charged that the EU took a lenient stance on tax havens within its own area, while demanding full cooperation from non-EU states. Several offshore jurisdictions have informed the EU that, given the exemptions provided Austria, Luxembourg, and Belgium, they are no longer legally obligated to abide by their previous promise to dismantle "harmful tax practices." In effect they said: "No level playing field, no agreement from us."

The United Kingdom's Colonies

The U.K. Labour government officially announced its anti-tax haven campaign on March 17, 1999. This held special significance because the colonies and dependencies of the United Kingdom include jurisdictions that were at one time some of the world's leading tax and asset protection havens.

In 1999, then Foreign Minister Robin Cook issued an ultimatum: January 1, 2000 was to be the deadline for financial law reforms in the thirteen U.K. Overseas Territories, which include many well-known tax havens, such as the Channel Islands (Jersey, Guernsey, Sark), the Isle of Man, the Cayman Islands, Bermuda, the Turks and Caicos Islands, the British Virgin Islands, and Anguilla. Cook warned that they had to meet international standards against money laundering and the "transparency" of their financial systems, including cooperating with law enforcement authorities.

The Labour government claimed the power to act unilaterally to change colonial laws, something Cook promised would be done if necessary. The method was to use the arcane royal "Orders in Council" signed by the Queen, which in effect imposes the Labour government's rules on any overseas territory. This explicit threat has been reasserted numerous times since by U.K. government ministers, including Chancellor of the Exchequer, Gordon Brown.

What London really wants is greatly reduced financial privacy, total bank account surveillance, and a general end to the financial freedom that allowed these U.K. dependencies to become tax and asset protection havens.

In that vein, Whitehall bluntly pressured the Crown dependencies of Jersey, Guernsey, and the Isle of Man into writing foreign tax evasion into local law as a criminal offense. Similarly, the U.K. Labour government got Bermuda and the Cayman Islands to enact "all crimes" money laundering laws (including alleged tax evasion). By 2003, these jurisdictions had weakened their strict financial privacy laws under threat of being cut off from the U.K. financial and banking systems.

As long as the U.K. Labour government continues in power, you can expect it will continue its unrelenting efforts to curb tax and asset havens, including those under its colonial domination. Just as an aside, keep in mind that curbing the competition of the British tax havens means more business for the many financial firms in the City of London, most of whom are big donors to Labour's political campaigns.

The United States

The U.S. Internal Revenue Service asserts that there is a host of alleged tax evaders and money launderers whom it presumes guilty, based solely on the financial tools the accused taxpayer uses. High on the prime IRS target list: those who set up and use fully legal IBCs, trusts, and bank accounts located in known tax haven nations – especially those where financial privacy laws are strict. If it's offshore, the IRS presumes guilt.

In 2001, some U.S. politicians took advantage of the September 11 terrorist attacks to get their anti-offshore legislation easily passed. Their catch-all anti-terrorist legislation sailed through Congress with little debate just six weeks after the attacks. This new law, known as the USA Patriot Act, seriously jeopardizes Americans' personal financial privacy.

It is enough to say that the Patriot Act attempts to give U.S.

government financial police the power to confiscate funds and obtain financial information in secret, and even tries to extend police jurisdiction beyond U.S. borders by pressuring foreign banks that do business in America. For the most part, at this writing, these powers remain untested in the courts but they are under legal challenge.

USA Patriot Act

Congress passed the Patriot Act without even knowing what was in it. Less than six weeks after 9/11, Congress rammed through a 362-page law, sight unseen, with few members having the courage to oppose one of the worst attacks on American liberties ever enacted into law. But as four states and nearly 300 local governments have passed resolutions calling on Congress to reconsider the Patriot Act, now maybe they will pause and discover what havoc they wrought with American rights.

The United Nations Attacks "Tax Avoidance"

Fortunately without much success, the United Nations has been trying to impose an expansive redefinition of "tax avoidance" on the world at large. A UN report argued that the common theme in financial crimes is the "enabling machinery" that exists in haven nations. The UN sees these haven nations as "an enormous hole in the international legal and financial system" that must be plugged firmly and fast.

The UN report blatantly demanded an end to what it calls the "proliferation" of offshore trusts and international business corporations, attorney-client privilege, use of free trade zones, and the operation of gambling casinos. For good measure, it demanded an enforceable international financial reporting system in which all nations would be forced to participate. Goodbye national sovereignty!

These UN demands have been little more than a Greek chorus in the background as the other groups described here have led the battle.

The OECD Blacklists Haven Nations

The Organization for Economic Cooperation and Development's (OECD's) "harmful tax competition" initiative began in the late 1990s in a report entitled, *Harmful Tax Competition: An Emerging Global Issue.* The OECD condemned the tax practices of more than 30 "tax haven" jurisdictions. The report in essence was a ploy on behalf of high-tax welfare nations trying to stifle the drain of cash towards tax haven nations.

The report suggested various measures be taken to combat harmful tax competition, including withholding taxes on funds transferred to tax havens, and even the possibility of disconnecting them from the global electronic money network. It also demanded that tax collectors in OECD nations be given access to financial records in low-tax jurisdictions, overriding the statutory guarantees of bank secrecy.

In June 2000, the OECD released its first "blacklist" condemning the "harmful tax practices" of 35 nations. But with the 2000 election of President Bush, the OECD lost the key backing of the United States. (During the Clinton years, former U.S. Treasury Secretary Lawrence Summers was one of the strongest adherents of crushing tax havens and imposing high taxes worldwide.)

In 2001, it appeared that the OECD's assault on low-tax countries was going to be successful. Representing the world's most powerful nations, the OECD asserted that all jurisdictions must participate in a global system of information exchange between tax authorities. Their slogan was a call for an end to "harmful tax competition." To the OECD, that meant imposing uniformly high taxes in every nation, in effect abolishing tax havens and ending tax competition worldwide.

The Paris-based OECD bureaucracy published a blacklist of 41 nations and territories that it considered "tax havens," largely because of their low-tax policies and strong financial privacy laws. These regimes were threatened with unnamed financial sanctions unless they agreed to become vassal tax collectors for OECD nations. Six jurisdictions immediately capitulated, including Bermuda and the Cayman Islands, and it appeared that it would be only a matter of time before the rest surrendered their sovereign rights as well.

This OECD unfair tax competition campaign has been a farce, a publicity front for tax collectors from high-tax nations.

As an inducement to low-tax nations, the OECD asked for signed commitments to weaken their attractive tax and privacy laws, but explicitly stated the commitments were binding only if all OECD nations agreed to the same flawed high tax rules. This was known as the "level playing field" guarantee – all nations would agree – or none would be bound to end tax competition.

This level playing field promise created major problems for the OECD since its member nations, including the U.S., U.K., Luxembourg, and Switzerland, are themselves tax havens. Add to this the European Union's so-called "savings tax directive," which also sought uniform taxes and information exchange, and which fell apart as I indicated above.

In late 2003, the OECD met in Ottawa, Canada. Their stated goal was to reaffirm and step up the OECD anti-tax haven drive, but the OECD minions fell flat on their bureaucratic faces. The OECD finally was forced to concede publicly that many of its own member nations are themselves tax havens; that jurisdictions on the OECD phony blacklist have no real obligation to undermine their market based tax laws, unless and until all countries agree to the same "level playing field" rules. As the Ottawa meeting demonstrated anew, that is a highly unlikely event. (The fact that the European Union savings tax directive exempted several OECD nations from any requirement to divulge private financial data to foreign tax collectors also contributed to the OECD's defeat in Ottawa).

From the beginning a decade ago, this OECD unfair tax competition campaign has been a farce, a publicity front for tax collectors from high-tax nations. Built with smoke and mirrors, it claimed but never proved millions of tax evaders and billions of lost taxes. But it completely ignored the fact that reduced taxes are the best incentive to stay at home; that tax havens would not be needed if governments would cut spending and taxes.

The OECD "tax harmonization" campaign was a farce from the beginning, but one that might have seriously compromised healthy tax competition, had it not collapsed under its own grotesque weight. I think any tax haven that may have committed to the OECD should, as Panama has done, end their past commitment and acknowledge the facts – there is no level playing field and that tax competition is a positive international good to be expanded, not ended.

The American free market community, including The Sovereign Society, consistently has mobilized in opposition to the OECD's proposed global network of tax police. The goal of our coalition has been to convince the Bush administration that tax competition should be encouraged, not condemned. When, in late 2002, the U.S. government decided not to support the OECD, it was obvious that the initiative would collapse – and it will.

What This All Means for You

For those with existing offshore investments and banking arrangements – and those considering going offshore, the trend is in favor of continuing financial freedom. It is a major worry for me and others active in the offshore community that perfectly legal tax avoidance has been rewritten as "tax evasion," wrapped neatly into the all-purpose indictment of "money laundering."

But I firmly believe that tax haven nations will continue to exist and prosper. When the high-tax governments of the world finally realize the best way to maintain the allegiance of their citizenry is to cut taxes to the bone and increase financial freedom to the maximum, only then will tax havens be ready to go out of business.

I can assure you that won't happen any time soon.

Chapter 4
The World's Best Offshore Havens

SUMMARY: This chapter is called "the best offshore havens" because it names the four leading offshore financial centers in today's world. Not only that, but it explains how each of these havens can be best used by you and provides my best contacts in each location.

In choosing the top offshore havens, I reviewed the laws, political stability, economic climate, tax situation and the overall financial "clout" in dozens of different jurisdictions.

Applying all these and other factors, I selected four havens as world leaders – **Switzerland**, **Panama**, **Liechtenstein**, and **Hong Kong**.

I evaluated five factors for each jurisdiction, and rated each on a scale of 1 to 5:

1) Government/political stability: How long has the current system of government been in place? Is the jurisdiction politically stable?

2) Favorable laws, judicial system: How long a tradition has the haven had? Does its legal and judicial system have reputation for "fair play" with regard to foreign investors?

3) Available legal entities: Does the jurisdiction have a large enough variety of legal entities to satisfy the average person seeking an estate planning or business solution?

4) Financial privacy/banking secrecy: Does the jurisdiction have financial secrecy laws? How strictly are they applied? What exceptions to secrecy exist?

5) Taxes: Does the haven impose taxes on foreign investors? How easily can these taxes be avoided legally? Are there tax treaties or tax information exchange agreements in effect?

Switzerland – World's Best Money Haven

Switzerland today still stands as the world's best all-around offshore banking and asset protection haven, despite the many compromises in recent years the Swiss have been forced to make under international pressure.

Factor	Findings	Rating
Government/ political stability	The words 'Swiss' and 'stability' are synonymous	5
Favorable laws, judicial system	Highly protective of personal wealth	5
Available legal entities	All major legal entities may be formed or are recognized under the Swiss legal system	5
Taxes	35% on interest paid, which can be mitigated under bilateral tax treaties; income taxes negotiable for resident foreigners	3.5
Financial privacy/ banking secrecy	One of the world's oldest bank secrecy laws, but with new significant compromises	4
	Final Rating	**4.5**

A Reputation to Uphold

A global survey of private banks, published by PricewaterhouseCoopers, found that the major attraction for any bank's new customers is its reputation. Certainly, Switzerland's solid financial reputation is central to the claim that this mountainous nation serves as "banker to the world."

For 250 years, as European empires and nations rose and fell, Swiss topography and determination have combined to defend this Alpine redoubt, while maintaining more or less strict neutrality towards other nations.

As a safe haven for cash, Switzerland has become something of a modern cliché.

In 1945, after the 20th Century's second "war to end all wars," Swiss voters overwhelmingly rejected membership in the United Nations. It was not until 2002 that a bare majority backed UN membership. In 1992 and 2001 national polls, Swiss voters also rejected membership in the European Union, rightly fearing EU bureaucratic interference with Swiss privacy and banking laws. A few years ago, a national ballot soundly rejected a specific proposal to ease Swiss bank secrecy laws, and polls taken in 2004 echo this position.

After each of these national plebiscites, and during world recessions, ever greater amounts of foreign cash flowed into Swiss banks, confirming the widespread notion that Switzerland is the place to safeguard cash and other personal assets. It is estimated that, currently, Swiss banks manage at least one-third of all assets held offshore by the world's wealthy. As a safe haven for cash, Switzerland has become something of a modern cliché.

Declining Privacy Redefines the Swiss Financial System

But in recent years, the nation's image as bankers to the world's rich has taken some severe hits.

Disturbing to privacy seekers is the major Swiss banks' surrender under pressure to demands of the U.S. Federal Reserve System. The 1998 merger of Swiss Bank Corporation and Union

Bank of Switzerland creating UBS AG was approved by the U.S. Federal Reserve only after the banking giant agreed to provide U.S. regulators all information "necessary to determine and enforce compliance with… [U.S.] federal law." No doubt, that means U.S. tax laws, too. U.S. regulators had threatened to shut down the bank's extensive U.S. operations, and rather than defend their client's privacy rights, the bank compromised.

As a result, U.S. depositors considering Swiss banks should avoid UBS AG and any other Swiss bank with U.S.-based branches, affiliates or banking operations, other than a mere "representative office."

Financial Privacy Still Lives

Despite the privacy setbacks, the Swiss financial system, warts and all, still has plenty going for it. Unless there is a strong suspicion of criminal wrongdoing, under Swiss law it is still a crime for bankers to violate the secrecy of their clients. Most Swiss banks still refuse to expose records to foreign tax authorities, although UBS AG may not be able to resist such demands based on its agreement with the U.S. government.

But success can breed notoriety. Having a Swiss bank account today is a red flag for tax collectors in some countries. This is particularly true within the high-tax European Union. Plainclothes tax police from neighboring France stalk the streets of Geneva, recording French-registered auto license plates. They then call ahead to have the cars stopped and searched at the French border. France also systematically screens mail to and from Switzerland for magnetically striped checks. Two French tax officials were arrested for bribing a Swiss bank employee to provide computer tapes of client account data.

Although the constraints of distance force U.S. IRS agents to be somewhat less zealous than their French counterparts, U.S. nationals who visit Swiss banks regularly or receive business mail with Swiss postmarks may find themselves subjected to IRS audits. Then too, in 2003, a supplemental annex to the existing

U.S.-Swiss tax treaty came into effect, which expands Swiss cooperation with the IRS – although "fishing expeditions" into Swiss accounts by U.S. tax authorities still aren't permitted.

Since 1971, the franc has appreciated nearly 300% against the U.S. dollar.

The Very Special Swiss Franc

Switzerland's currency, the Swiss franc, generally has reflected the state of Swiss banking: strong, valuable and unaffected by inflation and stylish monetary fads.

Since 1971, the franc has appreciated nearly 300% against the U.S. dollar. U.S. owners of Swiss franc denominated assets have profited handsomely as a result. That profit came despite traditionally low Swiss interest rates and the bothersome 35% withholding tax on bank interest. In recent years, the value of the franc has fluctuated against the U.S. dollar, strengthening in the early 1990s, weakening from 1995-2001, and strengthening once again in the last two years.

The 1934 Bank Secrecy Law

The rise of Hitler and Nazi Germany in the early 1930s prompted the famous 1934 Swiss bank secrecy law that remains in force today. That law was an effort to stop Nazi agents from bribing bank employees for information about the accounts of German citizens and expatriates. The law protects foreign depositors from unwarranted intrusions into their bank privacy, although now it has been tempered in many important ways.

Swiss banks are prohibited from responding to inquiries about an individual account, whether from attorneys, credit rating services, or foreign governments. The law punishes violations of bank secrecy with fines up to Sfr50,000 (US$33,000) and six months in prison. In most cases, the Swiss government cannot obtain information about an account without a court order. To obtain an order, investigators must demonstrate the probable violation of Swiss law and that there is reason to believe the particular account at issue is involved in that violation. Non-payment of foreign taxes is not a crime in Switzerland, but "tax fraud" is, and, as you'll soon learn, that can be a rather elastic phrase.

In spite of its reputation for bank secrecy, in 1990, Switzerland was one of the first European countries to make money laundering a criminal offense. That law resulted in the demise of the famous Swiss *compte anonyme*, as the French-speaking Swiss termed it. Previously, it was possible to open a nominee account in which the identity of the beneficial owner need not be revealed to the bank.

Since 1994, a central office in Bern has been devoted exclusively to fighting organized crime. Mandatory "know-your-customer" guidelines are used by Swiss banks to investigate potential clients. Banks are particularly attentive to prospective clients that try to open an account with more than SFr25,000 (US$17,000) in cash or its equivalent in foreign currency.

The Swiss have successfully resisted enormous pressure from the G-7 nations, the OECD, and the European Union to further compromise banking secrecy.

On April 1, 1998, a new and even stricter money laundering law took effect that transformed the face of Swiss banking in a fundamental way. Previously, bankers had the option of reporting suspicious transactions to police authorities. Now, under pressure from world governments pursuing corruption, drug cartels, and organized crime, Switzerland requires banks to report suspicious transactions. Failure to report is a crime; bankers can now go to prison for keeping secret the names and records of suspect clients. Not so long ago, they faced imprisonment for failing to keep such secrets.

Using these new statutes, in a few cases Switzerland has actually released information in circumstances not involving a crime under Swiss law. The Swiss government has proven itself willing to freeze assets before an individual is even charged with a crime if a foreign government can demonstrate "reasonable suspicion" that the accused engaged in criminal conduct. This is especially the case in high-profile drug or political corruption cases such as that involving Swiss bank accounts of the late dictator of The Philippines, Ferdinand Marcos.

Unfortunately for the Swiss, the government's money laundering investigations have become a national political issue. Several officials at the Bern office responsible for investigating money laundering resigned to protest what they charged was lax enforcement of these laws. And outside pressure continues.

But there are limits to how far the Swiss will go. In 2001, the Swiss parliament rejected a new, even stricter anti-laundering bill. The Swiss have successfully resisted enormous pressure from the G-7 nations, the OECD, and the European Union to further compromise banking secrecy.

World-Class Banking System

Although Swiss banking privacy is legendary, secrecy is not the most important reason for Switzerland's success. Of far greater significance are the country's political, financial, and economic stability and strength. Most of the world's largest companies and hundreds of thousands of honest, law-abiding foreigners bank with the Swiss. Indeed, Swiss banks manage over two trillion Swiss francs, approximately US$1.4 trillion! Even the international intermediary banking institution, the Bank for International Settlements, is located in Switzerland.

Switzerland is home to several hundred banks ranging from small private and regional banks to the two giants, UBS AG and Crédit Suisse. These major Swiss banks have branch offices in most of the world's financial centers, from New York to Panama.

Swiss banks combine traditional banking with international brokerage and financial management. To guard against inflation or devaluation, Swiss bank accounts can be denominated in the currency you choose – Swiss francs, U.S. dollars, or any other major currency. An account opened in one currency can be switched to another denomination when the time is right for short-term profits or long-term gains and safety.

You can invest in certificates of deposit, U.S. and other national stocks, bonds, mutual funds, and commodities; buy, store, and sell gold, silver, and other precious metals; and buy insurance and annuities. Swiss banks can act as your agent to buy and hold other types of assets. Of course, Swiss banks also issue international credit and ATM bank cards.

Bank officers speak English as well as many other languages. Swiss banks are equipped for fax, wire, e-mail, or telex and instructions are carried out immediately. Or just phone your own personal banker who handles your account.

To some extent, "know your customer" rules have complicated the process of opening a bank account in Switzerland, and proof of identity and references are required. But, the biggest downside is the high minimum deposits required by most banks. While only a few years ago, many banks were content with initial deposits of only a few thousand dollars, Switzerland's popularity among foreign investors, along with the cost of administering "know your customer" laws, has led to sharp increases in deposit minimums, which now average about US$100,000.

The answer can be found in banks run by the various Swiss "cantons," as the largely self-governing provinces are called. These banks offer full services, have relatively low minimum deposits and each cantonal government insures the deposits.

Swiss banks often require that foreigners applying to open a new account do so in person at a face-to-face meeting. Because of the onerous U.S. government red tape and reporting involving Americans, many Swiss banks simply do not want to do business with U.S. persons.

Strict Control, High Quality

Swiss banks have attained their unique position with financial expertise, honesty, international capabilities, and the high percentage and quality of their reserves, much of it in gold and Swiss francs. The Swiss financial industry is tightly regulated, with banks strictly supervised by the Federal Banking Commission (FBC).

Swiss law imposes stiff liquidity and capital requirements on banks. The complicated official liquidity formula results in some private banks maintaining liquidity at or near 100%, unheard of in other national banking systems. The Swiss reputation also rests on the fact that banks traditionally hold substantial unreported, hidden reserves. Every month, Swiss banks with securities investments must write the value of their holdings to market price or actual cost, whichever is lower. That assures no Swiss banks will have unrealized paper losses, as often happens in other countries.

Swiss banks are also subject to two regular audits. The first audit is to insure compliance with the Swiss corporation law. The second is the banking audit, conducted by one of seventeen audit firms specially approved by the FBC. These exacting audits provide the primary guarantee for Swiss bank depositors. Supervision and regulation of Swiss banking surpasses that of any other nation. Plus, the banks have comprehensive insurance to cover deposits, transfers, theft, or abnormal losses. This means that your funds are insured in the event of a bank failure – but that hasn't happened in Switzerland in many decades.

One popular Swiss account for foreign investors is the fiduciary account.

The Fiduciary Investment Account

One popular Swiss account for foreign investors is the fiduciary account. A Swiss bank investment manager oversees the account, but all its investments are placed outside Switzerland, as the account holder directs. Funds that pass through the account are therefore not subject to Swiss taxes.

The fiduciary account comes in two forms: an investment account and a fiduciary loan account. With the investment account, the bank places the client's funds as loans to foreign banks in the form of fixed-term deposits. In the loan account, the customer designates the commercial borrower. Although the bank assumes no risk, it provides an important service by conducting a thorough investigation of the prospective borrower's credit credentials. Many international companies use fiduciary loans to finance subsidiaries.

There is an element of risk in making such loans, though. In the event of currency devaluation, or the bankruptcy of the borrower, the lender can lose.

Discretionary Accounts

With over 250 years in the international portfolio management business, Swiss banks are among the world leaders in investment management. Experienced money managers constantly analyze world markets, choosing investments with the greatest potential and minimal risk. Swiss banks offer a broad selection of investment plans diversified by industry, country, international, or emerging markets. Outside financial managers can be employed to invest deposited funds and bank loans can be arranged for investment purposes.

These accounts are best managed by a private Swiss bank or by a Swiss portfolio manager. The Swiss invented what has come to be called "private banking." They honed private banking to a fine edge centuries before U.S. "cookie cutter" banks discovered the concept. With a private bank, you get personal contact and individual service. However, most private banks require an initial US$250,000 minimum investment and a personal introduction from a well-known source.

The Swiss Alternative: Insurance

Switzerland is also a world-renowned center for insurance and reinsurance. Many Swiss insurance companies offer a broad range of financial services that, in some cases, approach the flexibility of a bank account. Indeed, many Swiss residents use their insurance company as their only financial institution.

Swiss insurance policies offer other important advantages:

• They generally offer higher interest rates than bank accounts.

• They may be configured to offer significant asset protection, unlike a bank account.

• Insurance accounts aren't subject to the Swiss 35% with holding tax on earned bank interest.

In 1998, amendments to U.S. tax law ended the tax deferral previously allowed on fixed annuity contracts issued by foreign insurance companies. All such annuity income must now be reported as part of taxable annual income. However, income from properly structured foreign variable annuities and life insurance contracts generally remains tax deferred.

Switzerland and Taxes

Switzerland is not a low-tax country for Swiss residents or companies, although tax rates are lower than in the surrounding EU nations. But foreign investors can avoid many local taxes by choosing certain types of investments that escape taxes.

There are many legal ways to avoid Swiss taxes by investing in accounts structured for foreign investors.

By law, Swiss banks collect a withholding tax of 35% on all interest and dividends paid by Swiss companies, banks, the government or other sources. Foreign investors to whom this tax applies may be eligible for refunds of all or part of the tax under the terms of Switzerland's network of more than 50 tax treaties with other nations.

In addition, there are many legal ways to avoid Swiss taxes by investing in accounts structured for foreign investors. These include non-Swiss money market and bond funds, fiduciary precious metal accounts, and other instruments. For instance, Switzerland imposes no taxes on dividends or interest from securities that originate outside Switzerland. For this reason, many Swiss banks offer investment funds with at least 80% of earnings in foreign investments or, even better, in money market funds located in Luxembourg or Ireland.

Tax Treaties Abound

To reduce the possibility that Swiss citizens or companies might be subject to double taxation, the Swiss government has entered into a global network of more than 50 tax treaties.

Tax treaties, however, have the unfortunate side effect of eroding financial secrecy. It is not possible to claim a tax credit under a tax treaty without also revealing the income that was taxed. In addition, tax treaties have a second underlying purpose: they exist not only to help individuals and companies investing or doing business internationally to avoid double taxation, but also to facilitate information exchange between tax authorities.

The 1997 U.S.-Swiss tax treaty, still in effect, is a case in point. While non-payment of taxes is not a crime in Switzerland, Article 26 permits the two governments to exchange information about alleged tax fraud. It also allows authorities to transfer information that may help in the "prevention of tax fraud and the like in relation to taxes." IRS officials claim this expansive definition opens up previously secret Swiss bank information, streamlining Swiss judicial procedures for finding tax evaders. According to alarmists, this gives the U.S. government the right to access Swiss bank information when IRS agents utter the magic words, "tax fraud."

The protocol accompanying the treaty defines "tax fraud" as "fraudulent conduct that causes or is intended to cause an illegal and substantial reduction in the amount of tax paid to a Contracting State."

However, a careful reading of Article 26 negates claims that the Swiss bank secrecy has now yielded to the demands of the IRS. In fact, the official "Comments on Article 26" states, "the New Treaty does not significantly modify the exchange of information clause that was applicable under the 1951 Treaty."

The U.S. undoubtedly presses hard to bend Swiss bank secrecy in specific cases. But this new treaty did little more than codify the Swiss view that bank secrecy should be waived only in extreme cases, and certainly not for unsubstantiated "fishing expeditions" launched by the IRS.

Tax-Advantaged Residency in Switzerland

Although it is not generally known, for those who wish to retire in Switzerland, it is possible to negotiate a lump-sum annual income tax payment (known as a *forfeit*) with cantonal tax authorities. The more populous and popular cantons are likely to charge more, but one of the smallest, Appenzell, will settle for lesser amounts per year, regardless of your actual income. The difficulty comes in obtaining a Swiss residency permit, an extremely scarce commodity. But if you are wealthy and offer proof of sufficient future income, you may qualify.

Contacts

Banks:

Swiss First Bank of Zurich: The Sovereign Society has an agreement with Swiss First Bank of Zurich, Switzerland, to provide a "Convenient Account" for our members through the bank's subsidiary in Vaduz, Liechtenstein. For more information on Sovereign Society membership, please see page 311.

Banque Union de Crédit (BUC), Rue du Mont-Blanc 3, P.O. Box 1176, 1211 Geneva 1, Switzerland; Tel.: +41-22-732-7939; Fax: +41-22-732-5089.

Banque SCS Alliance, 18 rue de Contamines, 1206 Geneva, Switzerland; Tel.: +41-22-839-0100; Fax: +41-22-346-1530. Director of Financiere for SCS Alliance in New York is Elisabeth Cerrone; Tel.: 800-226-5727; E-mail: info@scsalliance.com.

Private Banks:

Bank Julius Baer, Bahnhofstrasse 36, P.O. Box, CH-8010 Zurich, Switzerland; Tel.: +41-1-228-5111; Fax: +41-1-211-2560; Web site: www.juliusbaer.com. U.S. Representative office: 251 Royal Palm Way, Suite 601, Palm Beach, Florida; Tel.: 407-659-4440; Fax: 407-659-4744. Owned and managed by the founding family, this private bank serves clients with the same discretion it has offered for over a century. This is the place for those of great wealth who want a private relationship with sophisticated international bankers.

Banque Piguet & Cie SA, rue de la Plaine, 14, CH-1400, Yverdon-Les-Bains, Switzerland; Tel.: +41-24-423-4300; Fax: +41-24-423-4305; E-mail: banque.piguet.yverdon@bluewin.ch; Web site: www.banque-piguet.ch. Banque Piguet & Cie was founded in 1856 and is owned by Banque Cantonale Vaudoise, the fourth largest Swiss banking group. Throughout its 140-year history, Banque Piguet & Cie has specialized in private banking with the utmost in confidentiality, professionalism, and personal service.

Financial Consultants:

Robert Vrijhof, partner, Weber, Hartman, Vrijhof & Partners, Ltd., Zurichstrasse 110 B, CH-8134 Adliswil-Zürich, Switzerland; Tel.: +41-1-709-1115; Fax: +41-1-709-1113. This asset management company offers a wide range of services including investment counseling, formation of companies and trusts, estate planning, and mergers and acquisitions. Mr. Vrijhof serves on The Sovereign Society's Council of Experts.

Marc Sola, NMG International Financial Services Goethestrasse 22, 8001 Zurich, Switzerland; Tel.: +41-1-266-2141; Fax: +41-1-266-2149; E-mail: marcsola@nmg-ifs.com. Mr. Sola has extensive experience in Swiss life insurance and annuities, and serves on The Sovereign Society's Council of Experts.

Chris Kalin, Henley & Partners, Kirchgasse 22, CH-8001 Zurich, Switzerland; Tel.: +41-44-266-22-22; Fax: +41-44-266-22-23; E-mail: chris.kalin@henleyglobal.com; Web site: www.henleyglobal.com. Henley & Partners are specialists in tax advantaged residency and provide international tax planning services for private clients worldwide. Mr. Kalin serves on The Sovereign Society's Council of Experts.

Panama: Privacy and Profits Offshore

Alone among current offshore tax havens, Panama combines maximum financial privacy, a long history of judicial enforcement of asset protection-friendly laws, a strong anti-money laundering law, plus tax exemptions for foreigners. Thanks to its unique historic relationship with the United States, it also exercises a high degree of independence from outside pressures.

Factor	Findings	Rating
Government/ political stability	Although Panamanian politics remains volatile, it has become a stable democracy	3.5
Favorable laws, judicial system	Panama's offshore laws date from the 1920s, but significant corruption exists	3.5
Available legal entities	All major legal entities may be formed or are recognized under the Panamanian legal system	5
Taxes	Foreign residents and investors exempt from taxes on all income earned outside Panama	5
Financial privacy/ banking secrecy	One of the best	5
	Final Rating	**4.4**

Panama Revisited

In 1999, I returned to Panama for the first time in 20 years.

Since then, I have visited many more times.

It's a very different place than I remember during my many visits in the 1970s when I served in the U.S. House of Representatives as the ranking Republican on the Panama Canal subcommittee. My visits then were made during U.S. legislative implementation of the Carter-Torrijos treaty negotiations.

Upon my 1999 return, I marveled at the modern skyscrapers, first-class hotels and restaurants, excellent digital Internet and other international communications, as well as the reduced U.S. ambiance. Downtown Panama City, the balmy, tropical capital on the southern, Pacific end of the Canal, suggests Los Angeles or Miami, except arguably more locals speak English here than in some parts of south Florida.

Yes, Panama also has a long history of government corruption that continues to this day. This hasn't seemed to affect the loosely regulated banking sector. Nonetheless, bribery, cronyism, nepotism, and kickbacks in government dealings regularly make headlines here. But isn't that true of the United States as well?

The Image of Panama

When most people hear "Panama," they think of the canal. But the country is not so well-known for what it has become in the last three decades – Latin America's second major international banking and business center, with strong ties to Asia and Europe, and a special relationship with the United States that, however contentious, continues apace.

At midnight, December 31, 1999, 96 years of official United States presence in the Republic of Panama ended. Panama finally got what its nationalistic politicians had demanded for much of the last century – full Panamanian control over its famous interoceanic canal.

New Era?

Panama is rapidly attaining world-class tax haven status.

Indeed, in many respects – financial privacy, solid asset protection and freedom from outside political pressures –Panama has moved to the head of the class.

However, Panama remains a third world country, with much of its population living in poverty. Nevertheless, it is in much better shape financially than its Central American neighbors to the north, or Colombia to the south. Although economic growth has slowed in recent years, Panama still receives more than US$2 billion annually in foreign investments. For the last 45 years, inflation averaged only 2.4% per annum; during the 1990s barely exceeding 1% per year. Annual inflation has averaged 1.4% for the past 30 years, much lower than in the United States.

Panama is rapidly attaining world-class tax haven status.

Then there is the wealth represented by the canal, generating nearly US$1 billion in annual revenues. While much of this income must be plowed back into maintenance, profits from the canal represent Panama's largest source of income. And in a move that could turn the current flow of 14,000 annual ship transits into a flood, the government is now planning to invest US$6 billion into widening the canal and building bigger locks.

There are also the thousands of acres of land from former U.S. military installations, prized real estate with an estimated value of US$4 billion. Admittedly, its distribution and privatization has been slow and marked by charges of corruption, but development of this property in the next few decades will undoubtedly bring significant benefits to Panama.

Privacy, Profits and No Taxes

In many ways, the Republic of Panama is ideally suited for the offshore investor who wants to enjoy the increasingly rare privilege of strong, legally guaranteed financial privacy and no taxes, either corporate or personal. Unlike Bermuda and the Cayman Islands, Panama pointedly refused to sign the OECD memorandum of understanding that would have committed it to exchanging information with tax authorities in OECD countries.

According to Canada's Fraser Institute, Panama is near the top of the list of the world's freest economies, ranked eighth with Australia, Ireland, the Netherlands, and Luxembourg. Panama has adopted more than 40 laws protecting foreigners' financial and investment rights, including the Investments Stability Law (Law No. 54), which guarantees foreign and local investors equal rights.

Panama's central location makes it a natural base for world business operations. Most importantly, Panama isn't directly under the thumb of the United States, and unlike the British overseas territories of Bermuda and the Cayman Islands, it isn't under the control of London.

Among the current 80-plus banks, the major players are the 58 multinational banks representing 30 countries that primarily conduct offshore business. They hold 72% of a reported total US$37 billion in total assets. Banking alone accounts for about 11% of Panama's GNP.

Nearly every one of the world's major banks has a full-service branch office in Panama, with representation from Japan, Germany, Brazil, and the United States. Derek Sambrook, a veteran international bank regulator and trust expert based in Panama, points out: "Brass-plate banks represented by a law firm, for example, are not permitted in Panama and the 82 banks that do operate are fully staffed and functional. Compare that with the Cayman Islands, that until recently had nearly 500 banks, but less than ten that are full-service retail banks."

Reasserting Financial Privacy

Panama is one of the world's oldest tax havens, with legislation establishing tax advantages for corporations dating back to the 1920s.

A central part of the long tax haven tradition has been statutory guarantees of financial privacy and confidentiality. Violators can suffer civil and criminal penalties for unauthorized disclosure. There is no requirement to reveal beneficial trust or corporate ownership to Panama authorities and no required audit reports or financial statements. Bearer shares are still permitted.

Panama has no double taxation agreements and no tax information exchange agreements with other countries. Although pressured by Washington to sign a TIEA with the United States, Panama has politely ignored such demands. This fact means that in U.S. government circles, a bank account in Panama raises immediate suspicion about the account holder. But that's also true anywhere else that the IRS can't readily stick its official nose into private financial activity.

Still, Panama has made a significant effort to reform its banking system to minimize corruption and insure that banking secrecy can be lifted in criminal investigations. However, this occurred only after significant pressure from the international community.

Panama has stoutly resisted the OECD's demands for the imposition of taxes on foreign investors.

In June 2000, the FATF placed Panama on a blacklist of 15 countries alleged to be tolerant of money laundering. In October 2000, Panama's Congress unanimously approved a strong anti-money laundering law in line with FATF recommendations. In June 2001, the nation was removed from the FATF blacklist. The new law covers all crimes and brings all financial institutions under the supervision of a government banking agency.

In contrast, Panama has stoutly resisted the OECD's demands for the imposition of taxes on foreign investors. In a ringing speech in late 2002, Panama's foreign minister denounced OECD "imperialism" and said flatly his nation will not bow to such outside pressures. Panama's defense of tax competition has created major opportunities for it. One opportunity comes from the EU decision in January 2003 to impose EU-wide withholding taxes on income from savings. The withholding tax agreement, if implemented as currently construed, will inevitably lead EU funds to non-EU financial centers that don't impose such taxes, and that don't routinely exchange financial information with tax authorities. Panama qualifies on both counts.

The Yankee Dollar

While "dollarization" is debated as a novel concept elsewhere in Latin America, since 1904 the U.S. dollar has been Panama's official paper currency.

Panama has no central bank to print money. And as Juan Luis Moreno-Villalaz, an economic advisor to Panama's Ministry of Economy and Finance, recently noted: "In Panama… there has never been a systemic banking crisis; indeed, in several instances international banks have acted as the system's lender of last resort. The Panamanian system provides relatively low interest rates on mortgages and commercial loans. Credit is ample, with 30-year mortgages readily available. These are unusual conditions for a developing country and are largely achieved because there is no exchange rate risk, a low risk of financial crises, and ample flow of funds from abroad."

Welcome Bankers

Panama grew as an international financial center after the enactment of Decree No. 238 of July 1970, a liberal banking law that also abolished all currency controls. The law exempts offshore business in Panama from income tax and from taxes on interest earned in domestic savings accounts and offshore transactions. In 1999, a comprehensive new banking law was enacted that accelerated Panama's growth as a leading world offshore finance center.

The 1990 law uses the guidelines of the Basle Committee on Banking Supervision, the international oversight group that sets banking standards, requiring all banks with unrestricted domestic or international commercial banking licenses to maintain capital equivalent to at least 8% of total assets. Government investigative powers and tighter general controls were increased, bringing Panama in line with regulatory standards found in European and North American banking centers. Although confidentiality is reaffirmed in the new law, a prima facie case of illicit financial conduct can launch an investigation of possible criminal conduct. The law also permits foreign bank regulators to make inspection visits to any of their domestic banks with branches in Panama.

Panama's growing financial sector also includes an active stock exchange, captive insurance and re-insurance companies, and financial and leasing companies. Another major business and financial attraction at the Atlantic end of the canal is the booming Colón Free Zone (www.zonalibre.com), a major tax-free trans-shipment facility, the second largest free trade zone in the world, after Hong Kong.

IBCs and Foundations

Panama has liberal laws favoring trusts, international business companies, and holding companies. In 1995, it enacted Law No. 25, a new private foundation statute modeled after the popular *Stiftung* family wealth protection and estate planning vehicle long used in Liechtenstein. The law allows the tax-free family foundation to be used for investment, tax sheltering, commercial business, and private activity, with the founder retaining lifetime control. Foundation assets are not counted as part of the founder's estate for death tax purposes, and Panama does not recognize the often restrictive inheritance laws of other nations. This can mean significant estate tax savings for U.S. persons who choose Panama's family foundation as their estate planning vehicle.

The BVI and Hong Kong each have nearly 400,000 registered IBCs, however, Panama is close behind with 350,000.

Some argue that the Panamanian private foundation law is only a relatively untested clone of the Liechtenstein law. While it is true that the Panamanian law is much newer, the costs of operating a foundation in Panama are lower than they are in Liechtenstein. For South American clients and others from civil law backgrounds who are unfamiliar with the concept of an Anglo-American trust, a Panamanian private foundation often represents an ideal estate planning solution, if just for the estate tax savings it allows.

Panama's international business company (IBC) Law 32 of 1927, is modeled after the U.S. State of Delaware's corporation friendly statutes. The BVI and Hong Kong each have nearly 400,000 registered IBCs, however, Panama is close behind with 350,000. A Panamanian IBC can maintain its own corporate bank account and credit cards for global management of investments, mutual funds, precious metals, real estate and trade. Tax-free corporate income can be spent for business purposes worldwide, and using the Panama IBC allows avoidance of home country zoning, labor, manufacturing, warranty, environmental, and other restrictions.

Leading Retirement Haven

Despite its relatively advanced industrial and financial infrastructure, Panama remains an affordable place in which to live. A live-in maid earns about US$120 per month; first-run movies cost US$1.50. Unlike much of Central America, Panama boasts a first-class health care system with low costs compared to the United States – a doctor's office visit costs about US$15.

Because of Panama's geographical diversity, there is considerable climatic variation. Panama City, the historical and financial center, has a year-round tropical climate. Yet, only a few hundred miles away is a sub-tropical forest, with cascading waterfalls, mountainsides covered with flowers, and spring-like weather year-round.

There are also many low-priced buys on condos and other real estate, particularly in Panama City and the surrounding areas, a byproduct, in part, of the U.S. government exodus.

The government makes retirement in Panama easy, and laws provide important tax advantages for foreigners who wish to become residents. The only significant requirements are good health and a verifiable monthly income of at least US$500. There are no local taxes on foreign income and you can import your household goods tax-free.

Where might one live in Panama? There are many choices; two in which Sovereign Society members have expressed an interest are:

1. *Contadora*. A 20-minute plane ride from Panama City, the Pearl Island of Contadora is where many of the country's elite spend weekends and vacations. Because of its beauty and seclusion, it also attracts privacy seekers from all over the world. The exiled Shah of Iran came here in 1980. With 13 nearly deserted golf courses, tennis courts, white sand beaches, giant coral reefs, abundant wildlife, and bright tropical flowers, Contadora offers exclusion and untouched natural beauty few places can touch.

The Sovereign Society's sister organization, *International Living*, has remodeled a small enclave of 20 private one- and two-bedroom villas on Contadora. Prices start at US$137,500, a fraction of what you'd pay for something similar in Florida.

2. *Old Panama City*. With buildings dating to 1673, Panama City has a rich historical heritage. However, many buildings in the Casco Viejo, the Old Quarter, require substantial renovation. To encourage purchase and renovation of these properties, the government offers substantial financial and tax incentives for purchase and rebuilding.

To learn more about residency in Panama, contact the Panamanian Embassy or a Consulate, which are listed at http://www.embassyworld.com. Alternatively, contact International Living (Panama), Greg Geurin, 17 Avenida José Gabriel Duque, La Cresta, Panamá, Republic of Panama; Tel.: +507-264-2204.

Contacts

Banks:

Banco Continental, Banco Continental Tower, 50 Street & Aquilino de la Guardia Avenue, P.O. Box 135, Zone 9A, Panama City, Republic of Panama; Tel.: +507-215-7000; Fax: +507-215-7134.

National Bank of Panama (Banco Nacional de Panama), P.O. Box 5220, Zone 5, Panama City, Republic of Panama; Tel.: +507-263-7901; Fax: +507-263-9514; Web site: www.banconal.com.

Trust company:

Trust Services SA, P.O. Box 0832-1630 World Trade Centre, Panama, Republic of Panama. Edificio Balboa Plaza, Oficina 522, Avenida Balboa, Panama City, Republic of Panama; Tel.: +507-269-2438 / -5252; Fax: +507-269-4922; E-mail: marketing@trust-serv.com; Web site: www.trustserv.com. Licensed in Panama since 1981, this respected firm specializes in offshore corporations and trust formation. Derek Sambrook, a member of The Sovereign Society's Council of Experts, is a director of the firm.

Attorney:

Rainelda Mata-Kelly, P.O. Box 9012, Panamá 6 (Bethania), Panama. Office Address: No. 414, 4th Floor, Balboa Plaza, Balboa Avenue, Panamá 6, Republic of Panama; Tel.: +507-263-4305; Fax: +507-264-2868; E-mail: rmk@mata-kelly.com; Web site: www.mata-kelly.com. Ms. Mata-Kelly specializes in Panamanian administrative, commercial and maritime law and assists clients with immigration, real estate, contracts, incorporation and other legal issues. She is a member of The Sovereign Society's Council of Experts.

Residency & Real Estate:

Greg Geurin, c/o International Living (Panama), 17 Avenida José Gabriel Duque, La Cresta, Panamá, Republic of Panama; Tel.: +507-264-2204. Mr. Guerin directs the operations of International Living in Panama and has excellent contacts in the Panamanian legal and real estate communities.

Henley & Partners (Panama), Galindo, Arias and López, Scotia Plaza,18 Ave. Federico Boyd & 51st St., Floors 9, 10, 11 - P.O. Box 8629, Panamá 5, Republic of Panama; Tel.: +507-263-5633; Fax: +507-263-5335; E-mail: gala@gala.com.pa; Web site: http://www.henleyglobal.com/panama.

On the Web:

List of Panamanian Embassies and Consulates: Web site: www.embassyworld.com.

General Information on Panama: Web site: www.panamainfo.com/english/index.htm.

Panama Tax and Banking Laws: Web site: www.trustserv.com/Panama%20-%20Pathway%20to%20Offshore%20 Protection.htm.

Why Panama? Pensionados for retirees: Web site: www.internationalliving.com/contadora/whypanama.html.

Liechtenstein: The World's Oldest Tax Haven

With asset protection laws dating from the 1920s, a host of excellent legal entities designed for wealth preservation, and strict bank secrecy guaranteed by law, this tiny principality has it.

In the not so distant past, one had to be a philatelist to know the Principality of Liechtenstein even existed. In those days, the nation's major export was exquisitely produced postage stamps, highly prized by collectors. Until the 1960s, the tiny principality, wedged between Switzerland and Austria, subsisted on income from tourism, postage stamp sales, and the export of false teeth.

But in the last 50 years, its lack of taxes and its maximum financial privacy propelled Liechtenstein to top ranking among the world's wealthiest nations. This historic Rhine Valley principality grew into a major world tax and asset haven, posting per capita income levels (US$25,000) higher than Germany, France, and the United Kingdom.

Tiny Liechtenstein (16 miles long and 3.5 miles wide, population 32,000) is nestled in the mountains between Switzerland and Austria and has existed in its present form since January 23, 1719, when the Holy Roman Emperor Charles VI granted it independent status.

Factor	Findings	Rating
Government/ political stability	A popular absolute monarch, whose dictates are subject only to national referenda	3.5
Favorable laws, judicial system	Well-established and respected rule of law	5
Available legal entities	All major legal entities may be formed or are recognized under the Liechtenstein legal system	5
Taxes	Strong, but weakened by recent legislation and agreements	4
Financial privacy/ banking secrecy	Foreign-owned entities are mostly tax exempt	4
	Final Rating	**4.3**

Absolute Monarchy

The government is a constitutional monarchy, with the Prince of Liechtenstein (currently Hans-Adam II) as head of state. Until recently, His Highness' power only extended to sanctioning laws passed by the popularly elected unicameral legislature, the Diet. For the most part, the Diet made the laws, negotiated treaties, approved or vetoed taxes, and supervised government affairs. Proposed legislation was frequently submitted directly to citizen referendum.

This system changed on March 16, 2003, when Hans-Adam II won an overwhelming majority in favor of overhauling the constitution to give him more powers than any other European monarch. Liechtenstein's ruling Prince now has the right to dismiss governments and approve judicial nominees. The Prince may also veto laws simply by refusing to sign them within a six-month period.

Tempering this authority is the fact that the signature of 1,500 Liechtenstein citizens on a petition is sufficient to force a referendum on the abolition of the monarchy, or any other change in the law.

A Leading Financial Center

Liechtenstein's economy is well diversified, and it is one of the most heavily industrialized countries in Europe. Still, financial services provide some 40% of budget revenues, so anything that tarnishes its reputation is a major crisis. Its 16 locally owned banks, 60 lawyers and 250 trust companies employ 16% of the workforce. Its licensed fiduciary companies and lawyers serve as nominees for, or manage, more than 75,000 legal entities, most of them owned and controlled by nonresidents of Liechtenstein.

Liechtenstein was one of the first nations in the world to adopt specific offshore asset protection laws, as far back as the 1920s. Liechtenstein's unique role in international circles is not so much as a banking center, but as a tax haven. The nation acts as a base of operations for foreign holding companies, private foundations, family foundations and a unique entity called an *Anstalt* (i.e., establishment). The banks and a host of specialized trust companies provide management services for thousands of such entities.

Personal and company tax rates are low, generally under 12% for local residents. Any company domiciled in Liechtenstein is granted total exemption from income tax if it generates no income from local sources.

Liechtenstein's unique role in international circles is not so much as a banking center, but as a tax haven.

There is a near total absence of any international treaties governing double taxation or exchange of information with the one exception of a double tax agreement with neighboring Austria, primarily to cover taxes on people who commute across the border for work.

Liechtenstein is independent, but closely tied to Switzerland. The Swiss franc is the local currency and, in many respects, except for political independence, Liechtenstein's status is that of a province integrated within Switzerland. Liechtenstein banks are integrated into Switzerland's banking system and capital markets. Many cross-border investments clear in or through Swiss banks. Foreign-owned holding companies are a major presence in Liechtenstein, with most maintaining their accounts in Swiss banks.

Principality Under Attack

Until 2000, Liechtenstein had an impeccable reputation with government regulators stressing the professional qualifications and local accountability of financial managers.

All that changed in June 2000 when the FATF named Liechtenstein as the sole European country on its list of 15 nations accused of failing to cooperate in the international fight against money laundering. Liechtenstein was forced to defend itself against charges of acting as banker to Central American drug lords, the Russian underworld and the Mafia. The threat of unspecified sanctions against Liechtenstein caused a sharp, but temporary, slowdown in the inflow of funds, as suddenly nervous foreigners avoided one of the world's most secretive tax havens.

In January 2001, Liechtenstein suffered another blow, when Liechtenstein Global Trust Bank (LGT), owned by the family of Liechtenstein's ruling prince, was raided by agents investigating money laundering. Prince Hans Adam II admitted that plucky Liechtenstein was facing its most serious challenge since staving off invasion by Nazi Germany in World War II.

Liechtenstein's reaction to the blacklisting and the LGT scandal was very much in keeping with its history. Rather than overtly contest this designation, the monarchy worked through its own diplomatic and financial channels quietly to be removed from the FATF blacklist. Liechtenstein hired a high-powered expert from Switzerland to see it through a difficult transition period as its banks suffered financial losses and an exodus of assets.

The strategy worked. In June 2001, Liechtenstein was removed from the FATF blacklist. However, the price was steep: it was forced to adopt tough new anti-money laundering laws that cover "all crimes;" create a Financial Intelligence Unit (FIU); impose much stricter "know your customer" and suspicious activity reporting laws; ease its historic, strict financial secrecy; and abolish the rights of trustees and lawyers not to disclose the identity of their clients to banks where funds are invested.

Liechtenstein's longstanding tax haven status was the source of a second major attack by the OECD, which in June 2000 placed the principality on its phony, 35 nation "harmful tax practices" blacklist. There it remains as of this writing, along with the few jurisdictions that have refused to surrender to the OECD. (For more on the OECD by imposing taxes on foreigners. (For more on the OECD, see Chapter 3, page 74.)

But don't let these supposed negatives scare you away. Liechtenstein offers many good and solid reasons for you to consider it as a venue for your offshore banking and investment activity.

Secrecy Guaranteed By Law

Liechtenstein's secrecy statutes have historically been considered stronger even than those in Switzerland. The 2000 amendments to the money laundering laws weaken secrecy significantly, but Liechtenstein still boasts some of the strictest confidentiality statues in the world. While banks must now keep records of clients' identities, such records may not be made public. Secrecy also extends to trustees, lawyers, accountants and to anyone connected to the banking industry. All involved are subject to the disciplinary powers of Liechtenstein's Upper Court.

Liechtenstein is not obliged to honor a foreign court's request for information. Such requests might be approved if it can be shown that a clear violation of Liechtenstein law has occurred.

A court order is required to release an account holder's bank records. Creditors seeking bank records face a time consuming and costly process. Liechtenstein is not obliged to honor a foreign court's request for information. Such requests might be approved if it can be shown that a clear violation of Liechtenstein law has occurred.

Big-Bucks Banking

Liechtenstein's banks have no official minimum deposit requirements, but their stated goal is to lure high net-worth individuals as clients. Opening a discretionary portfolio management account generally requires a minimum of SFr1 million (US$750,000). Trusts and limited companies registered here must pay an annual government fee of either 0.1% of capital, or SFr1,000 (US$750), whichever is higher. Most banks also charge an annual management fee of 0.5% of total assets under their supervision.

If you're considering opening a banking or investment account with a Swiss or Austrian bank, Liechtenstein is worth a comparative look. The principality has all the benefits of the other two nations: a strong economy, rock solid (Swiss) currency, political stability, and ease of access, plus a few added attractions of its own. Unlike Switzerland, it has no double taxation treaties, except with Austria, which means no tax information exchange. The government guarantees all bank deposits against loss, regardless of the amount involved, even though there have been no recent bank failures. Numbered accounts are available for large investors, which also gives an added degree of privacy.

Most observers doubt that Liechtenstein will surrender its financial privacy laws

Until very recently, Liechtenstein also had no information exchange agreements with any nation. But in 2002, bowing to U.S. pressure, it signed a mutual legal assistance treaty (MLAT) with the United States. The agreement, now under consideration by Liechtenstein's parliament (where it has met considerable opposition), covers a broad range of mutually recognized crimes, but does not include foreign tax evasion.

There is concern within Liechtenstein that the MLAT will open the door to "fishing expeditions" by U.S. tax authorities. However, the treaty gives Liechtenstein the right to refuse to disclose information that would require a court order to comply with, if a court order has not been obtained. If Liechtenstein defends its sovereignty by invoking this provision whenever the United States makes unreasonable demands under the treaty, the impact on otherwise law-abiding investors and businesses will be minimal.

Most observers doubt that Liechtenstein will surrender its financial privacy laws to appease the OECD demands for tax information exchange or the U.S. demands for unfettered access to financial records. That, and a certified history of excellent asset protection and banking, makes this tiny Alpine redoubt one of our top choices for offshore financial activity and estate planning.

Rob Vrijhof, senior partner in a leading Swiss investment firm, and a member of The Sovereign Society's Council of Experts, does a lot of business in Liechtenstein on behalf of international investors. He says he has seen a noticeable cleaning up of suspect practices, together with a new willingness to accommodate legitimate banking and investment. Says he: "Notwithstanding some bad publicity, I recommend Liechtenstein unreservedly, if you can afford it."

Foundation/Trust/Corporation Options

Liechtenstein law allows limited liability companies, but does not permit formation of IBCs. But the country has been most inventive when it comes to unusual and useful legal entities fashioned to serve particular financial needs.

Government regulation of the *Anstalt* (see below), foundations, companies, and trusts is extremely strict. This is primarily accomplished through training and regulation of managers, not by prying into the internal affairs of the entity or its holdings. As a result, business management services available in Liechtenstein are excellent in quality, if somewhat slow in execution.

The Anstalt

Liechtenstein is perhaps best known for the *Anstalt*, sometimes described in English as an "establishment" (the German word's closest English equivalent). The *Anstalt* is a legal entity unique to Liechtenstein, and something of a hybrid between both the trust and the corporation with which Americans are familiar.

The *Anstalt* may or may not have member shares. Control usually rests solely with the founder, or with surviving members of his or her family. Both have the power to allocate the profits as they see fit. The law regulating *Anstalt* formation is extremely flexible, allowing nearly any kind of charter to be drafted. Depending on the desired result, *Anstalts* can take on any number of trust or corporation characteristics. You can tailor them to meet specific U.S. tax criteria, then obtain IRS private letter rulings recognizing your *Anstalt* as either a trust or corporation.

The public has access to only very limited information regarding the people involved in individual *Anstalts* or companies. The beneficial owners of a company do not appear by name in any register, and their identity need not be disclosed to the Liechtenstein authorities. On the other hand, diligent inquisitors may discover members of the board of directors by searching the Commercial Register. At least one member of the board must reside in Liechtenstein.

Unlike U.S. corporations, the shares of a Liechtenstein company do not have to disclose the names of shareholders. They can simply be made out to "bearer." While some of the newer tax havens have made a point of promoting the use of bearer shares to provide anonymity, this type of share has long been customary in Europe. Until the 1980s, many U.S. bonds were issued in bearer form, but the custom never caught on. To prevent money laundering and other secret financial transactions, bearer shares are now illegal in the U.S. and many other nations.

The Family Foundation

Liechtenstein's concept of foundation is quite unique. Although Americans associate a foundation with a non-profit, tax-exempt organization, in Liechtenstein a foundation is an autonomous fund consisting of assets endowed by the founder for a specific, non-commercial purpose. The purpose can be very broad in scope, including religious and charitable goals.

One of the more common uses is as a so-called "pure family foundation." These vehicles are dedicated to the financial management and personal welfare of one or more particular families as beneficiaries.

The foundation has no shareholders, partners, owners, or members – it has only beneficiaries. It can either be limited in time or perpetual. The foundation and a beneficiary's interest therein cannot be assigned, sold, or attached by personal creditors. Only foundation assets are liable for its debts. If engaged in commercial activities, the foundation's activities must support non-commercial purposes, such as support of the family. Unless the foundation is active commercially, it can be created through an intermediary. The founder's name need not be made public. Foundations may be created by deed, under the terms of a will, or by a common agreement among family members.

A family foundation can sometimes be more useful than a trust, since it avoids many restrictive trust rules that limit control by the trust creator. If you are interested in exploring the creation of a foundation, I recommend you obtain top quality tax and legal advice, both in your home country and Liechtenstein.

Hybrid Trusts

You can use a Liechtenstein trust to control a family fortune, with the trust assets represented as shares in holding companies that control each of the relevant businesses that may be owned by the family. This legal technique brings together various family holdings under one trust umbrella which, in turn, serves as a legal conduit for wealth transfer to named heirs and beneficiaries.

Liechtenstein's trust laws are practical and interesting due to the country's unusual combination of civil-law and common-law concepts. In 1926, the Liechtenstein Diet adopted a statutory reproduction of the English-American trust system. They even allow trust grantors to choose governing law from any common-law country. This places the Liechtenstein judiciary in the unique position of applying trust law from England, Bermuda, or Delaware (U.S.) when addressing a controversy regarding a particular trust instrument.

Liechtenstein's trust laws are practical and interesting due to the country's unusual combination of civil-law and common-law concepts.

Even though it is a civil law nation, a trust located in Liechtenstein can be useful in lowering taxes, sheltering foreign income, and safeguarding assets from American estate taxes. The law allows quick portability of trusts to another jurisdiction and accepts foreign trusts that wish to re-register as local entities. The trust instrument must be deposited with the Commercial Registry, but is not subject to public examination.

Contacts

Banks:

Swiss First Bank of Zurich (Vaduz Branch Office): The Sovereign Society has an agreement with Swiss First Bank of Zurich, Switzerland, to provide a "Convenient Account" for our members through the bank's subsidiary in Vaduz, Liechtenstein. For more information on becoming a Sovereign Society member, please see page 311.

Centrum Bank AG, Heiligkreuz 8, 9490 Vaduz, Liechtenstein; Tel.: +423-235-8585; Fax: +423-235-8686.

LGT Bank (Liechtenstein), Herrengasse 12, 9490 Vaduz, Liechtenstein; Tel.: +423-235-1122; Fax: +423-235-1522.

Liechtensteinische Landesbank AG, Städtle 44, 9490 Vaduz, Liechtenstein; Tel.: +423-236-8811; Fax: +423-236-8822.

Neue Bank AG, Kirchstrasse 8, 9490 Vaduz, Liechtenstein; Tel.: +423-236-0808; Fax: +423-232-9260.

Verwaltungs-und Privat-Bank AG, Im Zentrum Aeulestrasse 6, 9490 Vaduz, Liechtenstein; Tel.: +423-235-6655; Fax: +423-235-6500.

Vorarlberger Volksbank AG, Heiligkreuz 42, 9490 Vaduz, Liechtenstein; Tel.: +423-237-6930; Fax: +423-237-6948.

Trust Companies:

First Advisory Group, Aeulestrasse 74, FL-9490 Vaduz, Liechtenstein; Tel.: +423-236-0404; Fax: +423-236-0405.

Lexadmin Trust reg., P.O. Box 48, Bahnhofstrasse 7, FL-9490, Schaan, Liechtenstein; Tel.: +423-236-1414; Fax +423-232-1415; E-mail: info@lexadmin-trust.com; Web site: www.lexadmin-trust.com.

Allgemeines Treuunternehmen (General Trust Company), Aeulestrasse 5, P.O. Box 83, FL-9490, Vaduz, Liechtenstein; Tel.: +423-237-3434; Fax: +423-237-3460; Web site: www.atu.li.

Präsidial-Anstalt, Aeulestrasse 38, P.O. Box 583, FL-9490, Vaduz, Liechtenstein; Tel.: +423-236-5555; Fax: +423-236-5399; E-mail: praesidial@praesidial.com; Web site: www.praesidial.com.

Financial Consultants:

Robert Vrijhof, partner, Weber, Hartman, Vrijhof & Partners, Ltd., Zurichstrasse 110 B, CH-8134 Adliswil-Zürich, Switzerland; Tel.: +41-1-709-1115; Fax: +41-1-709-1113. This asset management company offers a wide range of services including investment counseling, formation of companies and trusts, estate planning, and mergers and acquisitions. Mr. Vrijhof serves on The Sovereign Society's Council of Experts.

Marc Sola, NMG International Financial Services Goethestrasse 22, 8001 Zurich, Switzerland; Tel.: +41-1-266-2141; Fax: +41-1-266-2149; E-mail: marcsola@nmg-ifs.com. Mr. Sola has extensive experience in Swiss life insurance and annuities, and serves on The Sovereign Society's Council of Experts.

Chris Kalin, Henley & Partners, Kirchgasse 22, CH-8001 Zurich, Switzerland; Tel.: +41-44-266-22-22; Fax: +41-44-266-22-23; E-mail: chris.kalin@henleyglobal.com; Web site: www.henleyglobal.com. Henley & Partners are specialists in tax advantaged residency and provide international tax planning services for private clients worldwide. Mr. Kalin serves on The Sovereign Society's Council of Experts.

Hong Kong: Special Administrative Region of the People's Republic of China

Even though the Communist government in Beijing controls it, Hong Kong remains relatively free, a reflection of Beijing's need for Hong Kong as its financial powerhouse. Hong Kong retains a strong set of common law based statutes governing banking and finance. If you're doing business in Asia, this is the place to be.

A Far-East Offshore Haven Lives On

In 1996, after 157 years as a British Crown Colony, Hong Kong was unchallenged as the world's richest city-state.

Known as a free-market business haven, in 1996, its 6.4 million residents enjoyed a US$23,000 per capita GDP. In the last year of its independence from Communist China, that GDP figure was higher than in Germany, Japan, the United Kingdom, Canada,

Factor	Findings	Rating
Government/ political stability	Political freedom has diminished, but free market economics still rule	3.5
Favorable laws, judicial system	The rule of law is highly regarded, but courts are susceptible to pressure from Beijing	3.5
Available legal entities	All major legal entities may be formed or are recognized under the Hong Kong legal system	5
Taxes	Traditional financial secrecy strong, but no specific statutory guarantee	3.5
Financial privacy/ banking secrecy	Foreign investors using this as a base can avoid most taxes, and corporate taxes are relatively low	4
	Final Rating	**3.9**

and Australia. At the time, the top income and corporate tax rate of 15% was one of the world's lowest.

However, on July 1, 1997, the United Kingdom surrendered its colonial control of Hong Kong to the sovereignty of Communist China. The peaceful handing over of a democracy to a Communist-controlled dictatorship was unprecedented in history. Unfortunately, the outcome has been far from pleasant in many respects, notwithstanding the widely expressed hope that the transaction would result in a new impulse toward freedom and democracy in China and the rest of Asia.

Uncertainty is now a way of life in Hong Kong. That, despite the fact that Communist Chinese rule has not been as oppressive as feared, and the city's democratic forces have made good showings in legislative elections. But Beijing has systematically clamped down on previously existing civil rights, including free press, the right of assembly, freedom of religion, and many aspects of due process under British common law, both civil and criminal.

The Communist Chinese government in Beijing promised to

honor its 1984 commitment to allow Hong Kong a free, 50-year dual political/economic existence. This was the so-called "one country, two systems" theory.

Once Beijing gained power, it let the world know Hong Kong was no longer the full-fledged democracy it became in its waning British colonial days. The elected legislature was abolished by Communist China, replaced by handpicked agents with a new electoral system rigged to favor Beijing. Instead of its former status as an international financial center, Hong Kong is moving towards a status not unlike other Chinese cities, albeit a very important one.

This anti-democratic trend was accented in 2002-2003 with the introduction of new Beijing-backed laws that appeared to limit further existing civil rights. But political realities suggest that Beijing will restrain itself. As long as China hopes for peaceful reunification with the Chinese Republic of Taiwan, it has to maintain a more or less hands-off policy towards Hong Kong to demonstrate to the world that the "one country, two systems" concept still works.

It's the Economy, Stupid

But in 2003, Hong Kong was still suffering from one of its worst recessions since the city-state began compiling annual economic statistics in 1961 – probably the worst since the end of World War II. In 1998, the local GDP fell 5.1%, and it has declined every year since.

A few years ago, Hong Kong was the world's fifth largest banking and foreign exchange center, seventh largest trading power, and the world's busiest container port. With low taxes and a trusted legal system, international banking and business flowed in, sure of stability and a high degree of financial privacy.

Business was booming then. Today the economy is struggling back to its feet, weighted down with a huge government budget deficit, steep declines in once soaring real estate prices and huge bank loan defaults.

Worse still, this city, once known as the laissez-faire capital of business, is now run by a government beholden to the Communist rulers in Beijing and its own rich cronies among the Hong Kong tycoons who dominate the local economy. Beijing's handpicked government has repeatedly intervened to prop up the failing economy in ways that favored the real property owning tycoons. The worst example was the government purchase of US$15 billion worth of Hong Kong stocks in a vain effort to stem the free fall of the Hang Seng, (the Hong Kong stock market). That did major damage to the city's official reputation as a hands-off friend of free enterprise.

China has long employed Hong Kong as a convenient financial window to the West.

But Hong Kong is proof that "money talks." China has too much invested in Hong Kong to destroy it all in a fit of rigid political ideology. Today, 30% of Hong Kong bank deposits are Chinese and China accounts for 22% of all its foreign trade (including cross-border trade), 20% of the insurance business and over 12% of all construction. More than 2,000 Chinese-controlled entities now do business in Hong Kong, many of them "red chip" stocks, the value of which have declined steeply in the last year.

China has long employed Hong Kong as a convenient financial window to the West. It is their banker, investment broker and go-between in what is now a multi-billion annual trade flow. In the past 15 years, some US$150 billion of foreign direct investment has flooded into China – 60% of which came from, or through, Hong Kong.

But with the coming of the Asian recession, that began to change. For the first time in a decade, 1997 saw direct foreign investment drop to US$30 billion, from a high of US$42 billion in 1996. It declined still further in 1998. But with a potential 1.2 billion Chinese consumers, foreign investment will continue and likely grow again. By 2004 the recession was well in the past and

Hong Kong made an impressive economic comeback.

Despite their wrong-headed attitudes regarding Hong Kong democracy, the leaders of the People's Republic of China realize that they have an enormous vested interest in Hong Kong's economic health. They want Hong Kong to keep running at full steam, but on their own terms.

World-Class Financial Sophistication

In a strange twist of world economic fate, the recent clampdown by the European Union and the OECD on tax havens in the West operates to the benefit of the remaining true tax havens like Hong Kong. Another factor: wealthy account holders from the Middle East started shifting cash towards Asia from Europe and the United States in the wake of the September 11, 2001 terror attacks.

Asian banks, many of them in Hong Kong, were sitting on US$1.7 trillion of reserves in early 2004. Funds have been continuously pouring money into emerging markets and, according to J.P. Morgan's estimates, about US$2 billion (HK$15.6 billion) was pumped into the Asian market during the last quarter of 2003.

A major attraction for offshore business has been Hong Kong's 16% business tax rate, raised to 17.5% in 2003.

Hong Kong is still regarded by foreign firms as a highly advantageous location from which to do business. In 2003, over 77% of foreign firms based in Hong Kong surveyed said they felt that it was an advantageous location for them, due to advanced telecommunications networks, a free trade environment, low taxes and effective regulation. On an industry basis, according to the survey results, the financial services sector was the most positive overall.

A major attraction for offshore business has been Hong Kong's 16% business tax rate, raised to 17.5% in 2003. Faced with recession, years of declining revenue and a major budget deficit, in

2003, the government increased the ceiling for taxes on personal income and unincorporated businesses from 15% to 16%.

Hong Kong's status as one of the world's top trading centers for stocks, bonds, commodities, metals, futures, currencies, and personal and business financial operations long has meant that such transactions could be conducted there with a high degree of sophistication. That's still true, and the city's 154 licensed banks hold nearly US$300 billion in deposits.

But Hong Kong is no longer the free-for-all market of old, where insider trading, self-dealing and other illegal practices were commonplace. After severely tightening financial laws in recent years, local regulators continue to press to meet higher world standards. There have been significant reforms in laws governing stocks, bonds, banking, and mutual and hedge funds. A strict anti-money laundering law is in place and is enforced with vigor. But there is evidence that the widespread corruption that infects mainland China's economy is spreading to Hong Kong.

Hong Kong as a Business Base

In Hong Kong, there is no specific legal recognition of an international business company (IBC). The basic Hong Kong corporate legal principle applied to taxes is "territoriality of profits." If profits originate in or are derived from Hong Kong, then profits are subject to local tax. Otherwise, they are tax-free, regardless of whether the company is incorporated or registered there.

Interestingly, IBCs and all other foreign corporations generally may open a Hong Kong bank account without prior registration under the local business statute. This can save charges for auditing and annual report filing, and removes the annoyance of having to argue with the Inland Revenue Department about the territoriality of the business.

On the other hand, one must be careful not to transact any taxable local business, because doing that without local registration is against the law. In cases where local business does occur, tax authorities generally are lenient, usually requiring local registration and payment of unpaid tax. But in some cases, IBCs have been forced to register as a listed public company at considerable expense.

Hong Kong offshore companies require by law a local resident company secretary, who usually charges about US$500 per year for filing a few documents with the Company Registry. Annual auditing by a CPA starts from about US$500 for companies with few transactions, and can easily reach ten times as much for a mid-size operational offshore trading company.

Financial Secrecy in Hong Kong

Until now, Hong Kong's banking laws did not permit bank regulators to give information about an individual customer's affairs to foreign government authorities, except in cases involving fraud. But Hong Kong has never had specific banking secrecy laws such as many other asset and tax haven nations enjoy including Switzerland, Panama, and Luxembourg.

Hong Kong banks have always requested a judicial warrant before disclosing records to any foreign government.

As a matter of local custom, Hong Kong banks have always requested a judicial warrant before disclosing records to any foreign government. Access is much easier for the local government, but there are no double taxation agreements with countries other than the People's Republic of China. An MLAT with the United States was signed in 1998 and came into force in 2000.

New anti-money laundering laws and "know-your-customer" rules have made the opening of bank accounts for IBCs much more difficult. Account applicants must declare to the bank the "true beneficiary" of an IBC or a trust with supporting documentation. Documentary proof must be shown for all corporate directors and shareholders of the registering entity and any other entities that share in that ownership.

In What Direction?

Many "experts" thought Hong Kong's powerful business taipans would use their financial clout to temper the worst excesses the Communists might impose. Instead, Beijing recruited these money musclemen onto its own team with offers of favorable treatment. One of the business elite's own leaders, Tung Chee-hwa (now in his second term of office) has five years behind him as head of Hong Kong's "Special Administrative Region" government – unhappy years in the view of many locals, since he is viewed as being too subservient to Beijing.

If you do intend to make Asia your business investment target, keep in mind lessons other foreigners have already learned the hard way.

Pick your Asian business partners (and business investments) carefully, avoiding the inefficient Chinese state-owned enterprises. Stick to those with solid basics like marketing, distribution, and service. Guard technology from theft. And remember, a series of small ventures gets less government attention and red tape than big showcase projects that often produce demands for graft. Many foreign business investors have been burned by crooked bookkeeping, few shareholder controls, sudden government rule changes, and systemic corruption.

Only recently, as the nation's economy has become more westernized, has Beijing finally begun to address the need for laws guaranteeing the right for citizens and foreigners to own and transfer private property. So, in dealing with China, remember: "Caveat emptor!

Most important, keep a sharp eye not on the government's hype, but on what's really happening in China.

All this uncertainty means that offshore financial activities by foreign citizens can prosper, but without immediate assurance of success. Unless the "New China" is definitely your sphere of intended business activity, you may want to look elsewhere for your Asian financial haven in places such as Singapore or Thailand.

Communist Connections

For non-Chinese wishing to conduct business in China, perhaps another, more secure option, is to open a bank account at the Hong Kong branch of the Bank of Communications (BC).

Headquartered in Beijing, BC provides good openings to the mainland. Unlike the Bank of China, it has no U.S. branches subject to the kind of U.S. government investigative pressures that have been brought against other Hong Kong banks, such as Standard Chartered.

The Bank of Communications is likely to resist any U.S. pressure to lift bank secrecy practices. There are U.S. banks in Hong Kong, but when you open an account in one of those institutions, they demand a signed waiver allowing secrecy to be lifted at the request of U.S. authorities. That is a good argument for going Communist when banking in Hong Kong, or at least banking non-American.

Hong Kong's best-known bank, Hong Kong & Shanghai Banking Corporation (HSBC), is now much more of a global bank than a Chinese one. It purchased Marine Midlands, a U.S. bank, as part of it's diversification away from Hong Kong and it is now subject to pressure from American authorities. However, with operations in 79 nations, HSBC is able to handle a wide range of banking needs in multiple countries.

Contacts

Banks:

Bank of Communications, Hong Kong Branch, 20 Pedder Street, Central, Hong Kong; Tel.: +852-2841-9611 / -2973; Fax: +852-2810-6993; Web site: www.bankcomm.com.hk/e_index.htm.

Rabobank, 2 Exchange Square, Central, Hong Kong; Tel.: +852-2103-2000; Fax: +852-2530-1728.

Corporation & Trust Services:

Henley & Partners Far East, Ltd., 13/F Silver Fortune Plaza, 1 Wellington Street, Central, Hong Kong; Tel.: +852-2525-7717; Fax: +852-2140-6833; E-mail: jflader@zetland.biz. Managing Director, Jack W. Flader, Jr. can assist will company formation, administration and trust services.

Offshore Incorporations, Ltd., 9th Floor, Ruttonjee House, 11 Duddell Street, Central, Hong Kong; Tel.: +852-2521-2515; Fax: +852-2810-4525; E-mail: info@offshore-inc.com; Web site: www.offshore-inc.com.

OCRA (Hong Kong); Tel.: +852-2522-0172; Fax: +852-2521-1190; E-mail: ocra@ocra-asia.com; Web site: www.ocra-world-wide.com/offices/officespopup/hongkong.html.

Sovereign Trust (Hong Kong), Ltd., Suites 1601-1603, Kinwick Centre, 32 Hollywood Road, Central, Hong Kong; Tel.: +852-2542-1177; Fax: +852-2545-0550; E-mail: hk@SovereignGroup.com; Web site: www.sovereigngroup.com/worldwideoffices/hongkong.asp.

North Asia Corporate Services, Ltd., Suite 1505-6, Albion Plaza, 2-6 Granville Road, Tsimshatui Kowloon, Hong Kong; Tel.: +852-2724-1223; Fax: +852-2722-4373; E-mail: nacs@nacs.com.hk; Web site: www.nacs.com.hk.

On the Web:

Hong Kong official government site; Web site: www.info.gov.hk/eindex.htm.

Hong Kong Economic and Trade Offices; Web site: www.hongkong.org.

Hong Kong Trade Development Council; Web site: www.tdc.org.hk.

Chapter 5
The United Kingdom

SUMMARY: Most Englishmen probably don't know it, but the United Kingdom is one of the leading tax havens of the world – for those foreigners who are not U.K. citizens but who choose to live there. Plus, the U.K. is home to some of the leading private banks and some of the best offshore investments available anywhere. Here I explain what the U.K.'s benefits and possibilities can mean for you as a potential resident or as an offshore investor. And I give you some historical background that will help to understand why, when it comes to finance, "There'll always be an England."

Once an Empire

Despite her descent from empire status in the 20th Century, England still is the home of some of the finest financial institutions in the world. Both in personal service and privacy, the smaller British banking houses often exceed anything comparable U.S. banks have to offer, and private banking itself is practically a British invention. The Bank of England, the nation's official financial arm, has been a pillar of economic stability for as far back as memory serves.

For Americans, banking in England is just one step from home. Since the founding of the Jamestown colony in 1607, America has been linked inextricably to England, politically and financially. The shared experience of the colonial period, the Revolution, the World Wars and the Cold War formed bonds between America and its parent nation that remain strong to this day. The Gulf War and the war for the liberation of Iraq only intensified this feeling.

For much of this history, England was the dominant partner in the relationship. English language, culture, and institutions, mixed with New World influences, helped to produce the distinctly American ethos. And while the United States has clearly surpassed Mother England both militarily and financially, England remains a steadfast ally with which we continue to maintain our "special relationship."

The English Economy

The United Kingdom remains one of the world's great trading powers, and "the City of London" (England's equivalent of Wall Street) is the world's second leading financial center.

Even with its relatively small size and limited resources, the U.K. economy ranks among the four largest in western Europe. During 18 years of Tory rule, ending in 1997, successive Conservative governments reversed the socialist trend, replaced nationalization with privatization, and curbed the welfare state. State-owned sectors such as telephones, railways, airlines, power, water, and gas were sold back to private concerns. The power of unions that held the nation captive with frequent, crippling strikes was greatly reduced. Although the Labour Party finally managed to return to power in 1997, they did so by co-opting a large part of the Tory platform and emphasizing a need for political party change. Since their 1997 takeover, there is little sign of a Labour return to its worst doctrinaire Socialist tendencies.

The U.K. economy, following world trends, has registered steady growth in recent years. Exports and manufacturing output have been the primary engines of growth. Unemployment has fallen and inflation has been tolerably low. The U.K. has large coal, natural gas, and North Sea oil reserves. Primary energy production accounts for 12% of GDP, one of the highest shares of any industrial nation. Services, particularly banking and insurance, account for the largest proportion of GDP by far. Manufacturing continues to decline in importance, now employing only 23% of the work force.

A major economic policy question for the U.K. remains the terms on which it will participate in the financial and economic integration of the European Union. The English view monetary union and other sovereignty issues with extreme caution, and seem unlikely to participate fully in any plan which will unduly limit their control over important internal financial matters. As I go to press, the U.K. is holding out against EU demands that member states surrender the ultimate control over their tax policies.

The Labour government has hinted at U.K.-EU full financial integration by 2005, including monetary union. But the British are reluctant to abandon the long respected pound sterling in favor of the euro. Some observers claim that it will be very difficult for the British to resist monetary union, since refusal might lead to a long-term major loss of business for the City of London. But, an eventual euro acceptance may depend on a promised national referendum, the outcome of which would probably be in the negative, based on 2003 polls.

Overall, the United Kingdom has enjoyed several years of controlled economic growth. For the most part, the British have remained loyal to the renewed economic traditions that made them one of the most prosperous nations on earth. One of these traditions is a high level of service and privacy in their banks, financial and investment institutions.

Banking in the U.K.

One major advantage of banking in the United Kingdom is the language. It is no exaggeration to say that English now has become the *de facto* international language of banking – and almost every other global endeavor. Language facility is certainly a big plus when banking offshore, where local customs can be confusing enough without having to cultivate multilingual capabilities. But the argument can be made: these days everyone, everywhere in offshore banking speaks English.

There is a plus to banking in a major world financial capital where you are only one among many.

For those seeking an offshore bank account with a reasonable degree of privacy and freedom from U.S. withholding taxes, London is the place.

In spite of growing government intervention and demands for financial information, you, as a foreigner, can get lost in the banking client crowd in London. There is a plus to banking in a major world financial capital where you are only one among many. The IRS doesn't raise its eyebrows nearly as high when you report a London bank account, as it does for an account in the Cayman Islands or The Bahamas.

While acceptance as a bank account holder certainly comes only after the closest scrutiny, as a client you will reap the considerable benefits of one of the oldest and most efficient banking systems in the world. In global financial circles, a check drawn on most English banks commands far greater respect than paper from some exotic Caribbean island haven.

U.K. Bank Privacy

A major judicial decision, in 1922, declared four situations in which an English banker could legally compromise a client's banking secrecy: 1) by an order pursuant to law; 2) when a duty to the public exists; 3) in the interests of the bank; and 4) with a client's express or implied permission. Until a few years ago, these principles continued to guide the English banking system's privacy policies.

The general rule used to be that U.K. Inland Revenue agents had no general right to seek the identities of the true owners of shares of stock. In cases where a bank account holder was discovered not to be a British resident, agents used to end their owner-ship inquiry as a matter of policy.

Today, anti-money laundering laws, tax reporting require-ments, and U.S. government pressure have produced seriously diminished banking privacy in England. The U.K. government, in partnership with the U.S., has been in the forefront pushing anti-money laundering "all crimes" laws on British overseas territo-ries, Crown dependencies, and British Commonwealth nations. "All crimes" refers to the expansion of the application of money laundering laws from their original anti-drug targets, to any type of financial offense, including alleged foreign tax evasion.

The Bank of England, long known as "the Little Old Lady of Threadneedle Street," (its ancient London address), supervised all British banks until 1997. The Labour government made sweeping changes, giving the Bank more power in setting short-term inter-est rates, not unlike the U.S. Federal Reserve Board. On the other hand, the Bank's seldom-used supervisory power over the national banking system was handed over to a new, combined agency supervising all financial institutions, the Financial Services Agency (FSA).

The need for revised regulations had been recognized with the passage of the Financial Services Act of 1986. Since then, every individual and institution rendering investment advice has fallen under the jurisdictional umbrella of the Securities and Investment Board, which controls a variety of regulatory organizations. As a whole, SIB was charged with keeping close watch over banking, insurance, commodity investment, stock exchanges, and financial advisory sectors. The FSA took over most of these powers starting in 2002.

U.K. Money Laundering Laws

The 2002 Proceeds of Crime Act gives the U.K. police plena-ry powers to seek financial information related to money launder-ing, terrorism, and many other alleged crimes. Further, it imposes a positive duty on bankers, solicitors and other professionals to report any financial "suspicious activities" to the police. Thus, financial privacy has been diminished to a great degree for anyone who may be the subject of police interest.

As in the U.S., Britain's anti-money laundering laws place the burden of detection on individual banks, their managers, and even clerks and tellers. If a bank fails to establish detection procedures, it may be fined, and uncooperative officials face a two-year prison sentence. British banks have been forced to spy on their own customers, just as their American counterparts have been.

Forfeiture U.S. Style

The Labour government also adopted U.S.-style civil forfeiture laws for the U.K. Well beyond the criminal element, everyone should have serious concern about these broad new police powers. The proposed legislation gives Inland Revenue and the NCIS a virtually free hand to rifle through tax files at will. The official line is that tax file inspections will only be targeted at individuals suspected of crimes. However, this paves the way for police fishing expeditions to look for evidence to build civil forfeiture cases. In 2003, an important House of Lords decision held that anyone investigated for suspected U.K. tax offenses must first be given a warning and explanation of their rights.

Government policy calls for cash confiscation from individuals suspected of criminal activity, even if insufficient evidence exists to convict in a court of law. In theory, if a suspect is judged to be "living beyond his visible means," the police can ask a court to freeze his assets immediately.

The Future of British Banking

Will British bankers open their books to foreign governments? This is an important question, given the close ties between the U.S. and the U.K. Will U.S. federal agents gain access to your English accounts as easily as the ones you hold on U.S. soil? The answer is a bit more complex than a simple 'yes' or 'no.'

While British courts may legally compromise your financial privacy in response to a foreign subpoena, they do so only occasionally – and then under extreme diplomatic pressure. But it is most unlikely that the British system will consider revealing your bank records.

English bankers work hard to provide excellent service in addition to financial security.

The U.S. Treasury and the IRS maintain large staffs at the American Embassy in London's Grosvenor Square precisely because British officials are so unwilling to cooperate. English government officials frown on foreign government agents who demand information or conduct "fishing expeditions" in U.K. bank records. All things considered, your money may be far safer in England than in the U.S. – if the Feds come knocking.

Private Banking in Splendor

Many English "private banks" offer a measure of discretion that American institutions will not (or cannot) approach. But added privacy is not the only advantage of banking in the U.K. English bankers work hard to provide excellent service in addition to financial security.

Americans love convenience and speed, usually at the expense of civility and dignity in everyday life. The British are more willing to provide personalized and traditional services, and while it's not easy to find such care, banking with small, private British banks provides a welcome reminder of gentler, more civilized times.

Of course, there are some trade-offs involved to get this kind of personal service. First, without a formal introduction from a prominent Brit or your American bank manager, you won't be able to open an account with Child & Co. or Rothschild's, for instance.

In truth, these small, exclusive British private banks neither need nor want a large number of customers, so applicants are screened with particular care. To gain entry, it helps to have an existing relationship with a U.S. bank that's affiliated with an international private bank network (such as Brown Brothers, Harriman). Making the necessary connections might take some time and effort, but the rewards are worth it.

U.K. Tax Haven for Foreign Residents

Nearly two million foreigners live in England, and most escape the terribly high income and other taxes which U.K. citizens are made to suffer.

In order to be recognized as a foreign resident in England who can avoid taxes, one must:

- Qualify as a legal resident by investing £750,000 (US$1.3 million) in local stocks or government bonds, and be self-employed or manage your own business with at least £1million (US$1.7 million) in disposable personal assets. Income from these investments is subject to U.K. income taxes;

- Stay four years in the U.K., prove you have local connections such as relatives or business ties, that you're over 60 years old and your annual income is over £25,000 (US$42,400). This allows you to stay in England as a retired person;

- Have a legal passport and evidence of valid citizenship in another country;
- Formally state your intention to make the U.K. your main residence and home;

- Prove you have an established foreign domicile and will maintain it;
- Prove that most or all of your income is earned outside the U.K.; and

- Show proof of your ability to obtain foreign capital from abroad (known as *remittances* in English tax law) sufficient to support you while living in the U.K. These remittances may be from a trust or IBC you previously created just for this purpose.

U.K. tax law does not require payment of income taxes on any foreign-source income, or estate taxes on foreign assets, if you are a resident but not legally "domiciled" in the U.K. If you meet the requirements described above, your "domicile of origin" remains elsewhere.

This cozy arrangement has allowed very rich people from around the globe who make their "home away from home" in England to live there tax-free. Caveat: In recent years, the Labour government has repeatedly threatened to repeal these tax breaks for non-domiciled foreigners. As we go to press, these tax exemptions are again under official review, but no action is expected until at least 2004. If you are interested in possible tax-free U.K. residency, check with a qualified professional listed on page 299.

Big Taxes on Former Residents

The U.K. may be very kind tax-wise to resident foreigners, but it definitely is not kind to its own citizens who go offshore (known in the U.K. as "expats") to avoid high U.K. taxes.

Until 1998, U.K. citizens who lived and worked outside the U.K. for more than a year were exempt from taxes on their earnings, if they were physically no longer than 62 days each year in the U.K. Tony Blair's government abolished this "foreign earnings deduction" in what it called "fairness." Now any U.K. citizen who earns any amount of U.K. *source income* while in the U.K. must pay taxes on *their entire year's earnings*, regardless of where the income was earned.

The results were predictable and swift. In particular, nonresident U.K. athletes and entertainers were forced to modify their schedules to avoid earning even a single shilling of U.K. source income.

Another word of caution: the Labour government may have

plans for more tax increases. Taxing foreign nationals who are U.K. residents is a possibility, so be sure to obtain the latest tax law information before conducting financial activities there.

Avoiding U.K. Withholding Taxes

British bankers do not deduct withholding taxes on interest paid to your nonresident account. That's because the law imposes no taxes on a foreigner's account. When opening an account, a foreigner must state that he is a nonresident and show proof with a passport. Although Great Britain, as yet, does not require citizens to have official identity papers, "know-your-customer" rules impose broad information requirements on all persons opening new accounts.

Special Tax Treatment for Foreign Residents

If you decide to make a long-term home in the U.K., very careful tax plans must be made to avoid the possibility of U.K. *estate taxes* being imposed. British law treats a foreigner who is resident in the U.K. during 17 out of the 20 years prior to death for estate tax purposes, as having been domiciled in the U.K.

These U.K. death taxes can be avoided with the creation of a trust or IBC. When a foreigner purchases shares in a U.K. company, capital transfer taxes (estate taxes) may be payable to Inland

Revenue when the purchaser dies. But purchasing U.K. shares in the name of an IBC completely avoids U.K. death taxes.

I say it again: check with your tax professional before you do anything.

If you have questions about avoidance of U.K. capital transfer or other taxes, I recommend you contact **David Melnik**, QC, 350 Lonsdale Road, Suite #311, Toronto, Ontario M5P 1R6, Canada; Tel.: +416-488-7918; Fax: +905-877-7751; E-mail: dm1976cp@netcom.ca. Mr. Melnik's assistant is Carol Bruce; Tel.: +905-877-3156.

For information on taxation issues for foreign persons resident in the U.K., contact: **James McNeile**, Solicitor, **Farrer & Co.**, 66 Lincoln's Inn Fields, London WC2A 3KG, UK; Tel.: +44-171-242-2022; Fax: +44-171-917-7431.

For assistance with obtaining official U.K. residence status, contact: Head Office, **Immigration Advisory Service**, 190 Great Dover Street, London SEE 4YB, UK; Tel.: +44-171-357-7511; Fax: +44-171-403-5857; Web site: www.iasuk.org.

U.K. Investment Trusts

In the United Kingdom, what Americans call a "mutual fund" is known as a "unit trust." Another U.K. investment entity is an "investment trust," a closed-end financial fund that sells shares to individuals and invests in securities issued by other companies.

Initial purchase of British investment trust shares must be through a brokerage house or bank. The shares are publicly traded on the London Stock Exchange, frequently at a 10-12% discount to net asset value. When you sell or switch between funds, you may face an even bigger discount. In the interval, you will have more money working for you than you are investing.

The accounts of investment trusts also are subject to regulation by the Financial Service Administration. That means these funds are audited periodically by major international accounting firms, but even so, check the facts carefully before you buy.

The British and the Scots pioneered the development of investment trusts and the total number trading in London far exceeds closed-end funds trading in New York. Many specialize in investments in non-British markets, a painless indirect route into European equities for Americans operating offshore.

U.K. investment trusts do not pay tax on capital gains realized within the portfolio, and most dividends are distributed to the trust shareholders.

Unlike U.S. funds, a U.K. investment trust's total investments may exceed 100% of the value of invested shares. Borrowing to buy additional shares is allowed, increasing both leverage and risk.

U.K. investment trusts do not pay tax on capital gains realized within the portfolio, and most dividends are distributed to the trust shareholders. Management charges are low compared to those of unit trusts (mutual funds) in Great Britain. Dealing costs are about the same as for any other entity.

City of London Investment Group was formed in the early 1990s as a subsidiary of a stock brokerage business; **Olliff & Partners (O&P)** was founded in 1987 by City of London's Chief Executive, Barry Olliff. O&P was an agency stockbroker and corporate finance house specializing initially in the U.K. investment trust sector. O&P contact details: 10 Eastcheap, London EC3M 1LX, UK; Tel.: +44-207-711-0771; Fax: +44-207-711-0772; Web site: www.citlon.co.uk.

Friends Ivory & Sime (est. 1898), 100 Wood Street, London EC2V 7AN, UK; Tel.: +020-7506-1100; Fax: +020-7236-2060; Web site: www.friendsis.com.

For investment trusts, smaller is not necessarily better. It is difficult to withdraw money from smaller trusts that may require written withdrawal notices or impose no withdrawal time periods. A good source for up-to-date information is *The Financial Times of London* (www.ft.com/), a respected journal that publishes weekly net asset value figures for all funds. Check before you invest.

Dunedin Independent, plc, 41-42 Charlotte Square, Edinburgh, Scotland EH2 4HQ, UK; Tel.: +44-131-477-8899; Fax: +44-131-477-7787; Web site: www.dunedinifa.co.uk.

U.K. Unit Trusts

The unit trust is the equivalent of an open-ended mutual fund in the U.S.

British banks will hold stocks, bonds, and unit trust shares, and collect dividends and interest for foreign clients, with no withholding taxes levied on investment accounts. There is even a reimbursement of the 40% tax on corporate dividends when you file for relief from the Inland Revenue. This unusual tax credit is payable to U.K. company shareholders as reimbursement for corporate taxes already paid by the company in which they own shares of stock. But keep in mind: Inland Revenue informs U.S. authorities about U.K. tax payments made by Americans.

Some excellent investments can be found in U.K. mutual funds and for more information we recommend you subscribe to Eric Roseman's newsletter, Global Mutual Fund Investor. Contact: 2 Westmount Square, Suite 1802, Westmount, Quebec H3Z 2S4 Canada, Toll Free (877) 989-8027 Phone: (514) 989-8027 Fax: (514) 989-7060, E-mail: enr@qc.aibn.com

Communicating with Shareholders

British banks usually communicate well with unit trust shareholders on behalf of companies. In the U.K., official rolls of corporate shareholders are maintained either by the corporation, the unit trusts, or the bank that holds shares for nominee share purchasers. These institutions routinely keep shareholders aware of any important developments.

Generally, U.K. investment and unit trust managers are more accessible than their American counterparts. In the U.S., heavy institutional investor involvement in the mutual funds market leaves fund managers with little time for small investors. In the U.K., firms customarily deal with masses of small investors and are significantly more forthcoming with information and help.

Borrowing from British Banks

Some U.K. banks offer major credit cards (denominated in dollars, sterling, or the euro) that draw payments from a client's bank account. Great Britain's **Access** cash system provides **MasterCard Gold** and the **Eurocard**, available in all other European countries.

For more information on acquiring an offshore **Visa** credit card, contact **Lloyds Bank**, Ancholin House, 71 Queen Street, London EC4N 1SL, UK; Tel.: +44-171-248-9822; Fax: +44-171-248-2361. In the U.K., a credit card holder must pay monthly bills by check or bank debit transfer. Direct automatic bank account debit cards are not available, as they are in the U.S. or on mainland Europe. (For maximum privacy, and to avoid paper trails, never use an offshore bank or credit card for charges within your home country.)

Profits from Interest Rate Differentials

Some British and continental banks allow overseas investors to simultaneously deposit assets in a high-yield currency, then borrow the equivalent value or more in a low-yield currency, such as the dollar or the euro. The lending bank requires the borrower to deposit the loan with them. The remaining difference between the yield and the fee the bank charges for the loan is credited to your account, which opens another possibility for high interest returns. Of course, the risk is yours; the interest rate is higher on the second currency precisely because there is a devaluation risk.

Gamblers who cover the exchange risk by buying currency

"futures" may lose the interest advantage as well. That's because the price of futures reflects interest rate differentials and because significant transaction fees are charged for small sums. To beat the odds, you must predict currency trends more successfully than even the market can.

This sort of currency speculation loan (and it is extremely risky) is available in the U.K., but the Danish **Jyske Bank** is especially well-known for its Invest-Loan program. Contact the Jyske Bankscheme, Vesterbrogade 9, 1501 Copenhagen V, Denmark; Tel.: +45-3-121-2222.

Another popular U.K. bank plan (also available in other tax haven nations) enables business customers in good standing to borrow against their own deposits, effectively cutting taxable earnings and enabling a build-up in foreign exchange assets even as the loans are repaid. As a foreigner unfamiliar with local bank plans, get a second opinion from an accountant or tax planner before you proceed.

U.K. Banks:

Barclays, 54 Lombard Street, London EC3 P3AH, UK; Tel.: +44-171-626-1567; Fax: +44-171-699-2712; Web site: www.barclays.co.uk.

Coutts & Co., 440 Strand, London WC2R 0QS, UK; Tel.:+44-207-753-1000; Fax: +44-207-753-1050; Web site: www.coutts.com.

Lloyds, Antholin House, 71 Queen Street, London EC4N 1SL, UK; Tel.: +44-171-248-9822; Fax: +44-171-248-2361; Web site: www.lloydstsb.com.

National Westminister Bank, 41 Lothbury, London EC2P 2PB, UK; Tel.: +44-171-606-6060; Fax: +44-171-606-7273; Web site: www.natwest.com.

Scottish Banks:

Bank of Scotland, 38 Threadneedle Street, London EC2B 2EH, UK; Web site: www.bankofscotland.co.uk.

Royal Bank of Scotland, 142-144 Princes Square Street, Edinburgh, Scotland, EH2 4EQ, UK; or 88 Pine Street, New York, New York 10005; Tel.: 212-269-1700; Fax: 212-269-8929; or 67 Lombard Street, London EC3 P3DL, UK; Tel.: +44-171623-4356; Web site: www.rbs.co.uk.

Building Societies:

Abbey National, 419 Baker Street, Abbey House, London W1C 2EF, UK; Tel.: +44-171-935-2121; Web site: www.abbeynational.co.uk.

Catholic Building Society (Catholic Church-related, but accepts other customers), 7 Strutton Ground, Westminster, London SW1P 2HY, UK; Tel.: +44-171-222-6737; Fax: +44-171-222-2922; Web site: www.catholicbs.co.uk.

As you can readily understand, the United Kingdom offers many opportunities for offshore residency, banking, investments and profits. For foreigners, it can be a tax haven and a place to blend into the financial crowd. London is one of the world's greatest cities for much more than just making money.

Chapter 6
The United Kingdom's Offshore Havens

SUMMARY: Even though the U.K. government under the Labour Party has done all it could to curb tax havens worldwide, the historic fact is that some of the world's major tax haven jurisdictions, for many decades, have been England's Crown dependencies, the Channel Islands and the Isle of Man. Here I describe these haven jurisdictions, the impact Labour's policies have had on them, and the possibilities for investment and tax savings still available from them, of which there are many, including life insurance and annuities as investment vehicles.

Only a few miles off the coast of the United Kingdom lay islands that offer even more sophisticated financial services than those found in the fabled City of London.

So unique are these financial centers that tens of thousands of investors and businesspersons worldwide have used the services of investment houses, accountants, lawyers, insurance brokers, and trust and corporation services located there.

To the south of the U.K., in the English Channel off the coast of France, are **the Channel Islands of Jersey**, **Guernsey**, **Sark**, and **Alderney**. To the west, between the U.K. and Ireland, in the Irish Sea, is the **Isle of Man**. While each of these independent islands is associated constitutionally with the U.K., each has remained free of most of the U.K.'s tax and other business restrictions (although that is changing, as you'll read below). This broad financial freedom, coupled with determined self-promotion, made these islands important world business centers in miniature.

Until recently, the British government tolerated this offshore finance industry, because on balance it brought more expatriate and foreign wealth into the U.K. than was lost from the various tax avoidance mechanisms the islands offered. When the Labour government took over in 1997, London's tolerance ended – and this eventually may end the utility of these islands as tax and asset havens.

As you read this, keep in mind that these are offshore havens in transition, so things can change from day to day. Before you act, keep informed of the current situation.

Asset/Tax Haven Status in Doubt

As part of the worldwide campaign to curb the use of tax havens described in Chapter 3, the U.K. Labour government has done much to curtail the financial privacy formerly enjoyed by these islands. Because of their ambiguous constitutional status, the Channel Islands and the Isle of Man are particularly susceptible to pressure from London.

Since 1997, the Labour government's demands were made clear and many are now written into law. These are some of the changes that have occurred: 1) drastic, tighter financial law reforms; 2) "all crimes" money laundering and tax evasion statutes; 3) extensive banking client surveillance; 4) increased cooperation with law enforcement authorities seeking tax and other information about persons and legal entities based on the islands, including disclosure of previously confidential information; and 5) imposition of the EU savings tax directive on the islands, meaning either complete exchange of tax information with foreign governments, or a 35% withholding tax on EU nationals. At this writing, it appears that all of the islands will adopt the EU withholding tax rather than allow full information exchange.

Of concern to U.S. persons is the fact that now the Isle of Man, Jersey, and Guernsey each have signed Tax Information Exchange Agreements (TIEAs) with the United States. This is yet another example of curbs placed on the previously guaranteed financial privacy that has made these islands successful tax and asset protection havens.

When the pressure from London began in 1999, the Labour government stated its willingness to precipitate a constitutional crisis by forcing these changes into law without the approval of the islands' governing bodies. It need not have worried. One by one, each island's politicians have caved in and adopted the changes demanded.

In considering your possible financial activities on these islands, you should compare their reduced privacy guarantees with other jurisdictions in these pages that have not compromised privacy.

To the average offshore investor, these changes don't mean much beyond a greatly reduced guarantee of financial privacy that was once nearly absolute. For those engaged in criminal activity, it means an increased probability of eventually being found out and prosecuted. The danger lies in a middle area of activity in which foreign tax collectors may try to conduct "fishing expeditions" looking for possible tax evasion simply because their citizens are active offshore financially. The TIEA with the United States may lend itself to just this sort of tax overreaching, depending on how the island governments administer its terms, although each has denied that they will allow IRS fishing expeditions.

This means that in considering your possible financial activities on these islands, you should compare their reduced privacy guarantees with other jurisdictions in these pages that have not compromised privacy. Because the islands are under some degree of control by the United Kingdom, they do not have the greater degree of freedom to act as would an independent tax haven nation such as Panama.

The Labour government pressure was formalized in the "Edwards Report," a year long study of the financial activities on the Isle of Man and in the Channel Islands made public in early 1999. It noted that, of the combined £350 billion financial industry in the islands, one-third was from the U.K. By the end of 1999, all of these jurisdictions adopted new laws in three categories demanded by London: 1) "all crimes money laundering" laws; 2) laws easing police access to alleged criminal evidence; and 3) laws guaranteeing "international cooperation" with investigators' requests for information. These laws also forced disclosure of previously confidential information that revealed true ownership of international business corporations registered there.

Island financial officials tried to put the best face on the conclusions of the Edwards Report, which they claimed found the situation generally to be acceptable by Labour government standards. But the clear fact is all the islands were forced to surrender the most attractive privacy features on which their haven reputations had been built .

An informal poll of a select group of leading U.S. asset protection experts produced a consensus: none recommend that their clients choose the Channel Islands as suitable for asset protection or banking purposes. While opinion was divided about the Isle of Man, the majority advised against its use as an asset protection jurisdiction – although it remains an excellent venue for insurance and annuities.

I believe this concern about the islands is well placed, but there are many other financial services that these islands offer which do not require as great a degree of privacy or concern for government intervention. In considering the information that follows, keep in mind these important distinctions as you make decisions about placement of your assets and investments.

Unique Status

These self-ruling British Crown dependencies have the power to set their own corporate and personal income tax rates. Through their U.K. association, the islands also enjoy some of the benefits of EU membership, such as the continental financial ease of doing, without being official EU members.

The islands were all subject to the EU savings tax directive and the Labour government agreed with the EU demand that it force the islands' compliance in one way or another. As a result, the Isle of Man, Jersey, and Guernsey appear headed for adopting a graduated withholding tax rather than agree to complete tax information exchange. The islands would then remit 75% of the withheld taxes to the countries of origin of EU investors. Taxes are scheduled to start at 15% in 2004, rising to 20% in 2007, and to 35% by 2010. These taxes apply only to citizens of the EU nations and do not apply to investment or interest earnings of U.S. persons.

Financial Services Abound

The Channel Islands of Jersey and Guernsey offer full offshore banking, trust, investment, and legal and accountancy services. A few companies operate on their sister islands, Alderney and Sark. Jersey and Guernsey earn 50% to 60% of their GDP from the financial sector, with tourism following at 30%. In the last few years, there has been a marked consolidation and cutback of banks and banking staffs on the islands, a reflection of a slower world economy, plus doubt as to the islands' future tax haven role.

While the offshore finance industry has grown in the last two decades, the Isle of Man has also rapidly expanded its offshore business sector. The island possesses a smaller financial community than Jersey, with less strict start-up controls and more conservative operational attitudes.

Americans enjoy specific benefits when doing business through these islands, such as purchasing non-U.S. mutual funds that typically cannot sell shares in the United States because of SEC regulations. U.S. investors can invest in these funds by using an accommodation address on the islands, thus legally skirting the SEC rules that forbid offshore funds from sending materials or having direct contact with investors in the U.S.

Ancient Origins, Modern Politics

For the most part, both Jersey and Guernsey base their legal systems on the ancient customs and laws of the French province of Normandy. The Channel Islands have also incorporated many common law features into their commercial code and activities, although with a French flavor. The Isle of Man's legal system follows English common law.

In theory, the British parliament lacks power to enact laws for these islands. Technically, they are not considered a part of the United Kingdom. Jersey and Guernsey were originally part of the French Duchy of Normandy, which conquered Great Britain in 1066. Her Majesty, Queen Elizabeth II, is the official head of state, not as queen, but in her separate role and title as "Duchess of Normandy." The Channel Islands are the only part of the original Duchy of Normandy still remaining under Her Majesty's dominion.

The special status of the Channel Islands and the Isle of Man in relation to the United Kingdom means that while they are not actually part of the U.K., the U.K. is responsible for their foreign relations and military defense. In their internal domestic affairs, the islands govern themselves, although laws enacted by the legislative assemblies must be validated by "Royal Assent," until now a *pro-forma* procedure common to all British territories.

Taxes and Immigration

The islands' tax systems have been remarkably free of political manipulation for many years. Successive legislatures have preserved the standard income tax rate at 20% for more than half a century. In 2003, laws were enacted to reduce corporate taxes to zero beginning in 2004. There are no inheritance, gift, or other wealth taxes. The possibility of any increase in the income tax rate or the enactment of new taxes is remote.

Nonresidents are subject to income tax only on locally earned income, but bank interest is exempt. A local trust is treated as a nonresident for tax purposes, provided none of the beneficiaries is an island resident.

Very few wealthy new immigrants are accepted annually by Jersey – only about seven a year. Jersey requires new residents to have annual incomes greater than £500,000 (US$840,000), total assets of £10 to £12 million (US$17 to $20 million), and local property worth at least £1 million (US$ 1.7 million). Guernsey is far less restrictive on newcomers who want to establish residence, but requires work permits for those who want to undertake any form of business. Establishing residency on the Isle of Man is simpler, mainly because it is comparatively spacious, with a land area more than seven times larger than Jersey, and over ten times the size of little Guernsey.

One of the lesser Channel Islands, Alderney, has a small number of financial service companies and places few restrictions on immigration by wealthy foreigners. Sark, an even smaller island, has few residents and tight ownership restrictions, but no taxes.

Jersey: Tiny Island With Big Business

Jersey's financial institutions house an astonishing amount of wealth. The island has over 70 banks (representing 16 nations) holding deposits of over £150 billion (US$247 billion). It is also home to an estimated US$400 billion in mutual funds and trust assets. (It's impossible to quantify the value of trust assets, since their existence need not be reported to island authorities.)

Individuals must be professionally qualified or have years of direct, hands-on experience to set up trust companies.

The Isle of Man

Absent the French influence, the Isle of Man's history and legal system are somewhat different from the Channel Islands, but its advantages for offshore business users are similar.

Located just thirty miles from the U.K. mainland, this island has become an important international tax haven. Its independent parliament, the Tynwald, dates back over a thousand years. The Tynwald is responsible for all domestic legislation, including taxation for its 72,000 citizens. The legal system is based on English common law, currency is the pound sterling, and social and economic links with the U.K. are strong; the island also remains closely tied to the United Kingdom in matters of defense and foreign affairs.

The Isle of Man protects investors with laws such as the 1988 Financial Supervision Act governing activities of financial managers.

The Isle of Man offers an excellent communications network, modern business facilities, and a highly skilled work force. The financial sector is the largest single contributor to GDP, employing more than 20% of the total work force. More than 50 licensed banks (including many international banks) with total deposits exceeding £10 billion (US$17 billion) are present on the island. Their services are comprehensive, discreet, and confidential, comparing favorably with the banking sectors of Switzerland and Liechtenstein. In addition to banking, high-caliber legal, accounting, insurance, and other financial services are available on the island.

It is the only low-tax financial center actively encouraging new residents. Work permits are easily and quickly available. Over 37,000 international business corporations are registered here, and with future government plans for zero business taxes in 2004, more will soon arrive. The 2003 business tax rate was a very low 10%.

The government supports the island's financial sector, yet maintains strict control through a Financial Supervision Commission and Insurance Commission that licenses banks, investment advisors and insurance companies.

The Isle of Man protects investors with laws such as the 1988

Financial Supervision Act governing activities of financial managers. Others laws protect investor rights, outlaw money laundering, and seek to exclude undesirable elements. These tough controls assure financial integrity, and have earned the Isle of Man a reputation for what *The Economist* calls "stuffed shirt probity."

Where the Money Is

Although banks on the Channel Islands and the Isle of Man are not directly supervised by the Bank of England, they apply its standards in practice. In some cases, reporting is even tougher than in the United Kingdom. Authorities take rule compliance very seriously.

In spite of their ancient history, banking on the offshore islands is modern, sophisticated and user-friendly. Total deposits in the Isle of Man banking system exceed £10 billion (US$17 billion).

Far fewer Brits use the islands for tax avoidance or retirement these days. The tradition of U.K.-based banks using the islands as administrative centers for their international business, while policy and strategy were set in London, is fast ending since the islands have weakened their privacy laws, which are now close to those in the U.K. But any financial services one can obtain in the City of London can now be found on these islands, and with the islands giving a lot more personal service and concern to clients.

The investment industry has come into its own, with substantial funds managed on the islands; £10 billion (US$17 billion) on Jersey alone. There are a number of major stock brokerages, such as Jersey's **Le Masurier James & Chinn**, part of the **Banque Indosuez Group**, an international network offering the many benefits world scope can provide. Jersey also has other U.K. stock brokerages, such as **James Capel** and **Quilter Goodison**. You can find banks like **Lazard Brothers** in Jersey, **N.M. Rothschild** in Guernsey, and **Coutts & Company**, part of the National Westminster Bank Group, on both islands. There are also several independent brokerage houses that boast investment track records every bit as good as their bigger City brethren.

Privacy Concerns

All three islands had similar policies against divulging any bank/client information unless compelled to do so by a local court order. Unless criminals' acts such as drug activity or money laundering are alleged, local courts will issue orders to release information only if a fraudulent transaction is shown. Prosecution by a foreign government, including the U.S. IRS, for alleged non-payment of taxes formerly was not sufficient grounds for a local court to order bank records or client information surrendered.

But all this has changed and financial privacy is fading. Jersey now has a law that extends money laundering offenses to cover "all crimes" including "fiscal offenses," just as the U.K. does. The law also allows confiscation of funds and assets alleged to be the product of crimes, as do U.S. forfeiture laws. While illegal drugs are the ostensible target of such laws, most observers believe the true object is to put an end to tax evasion, real or imagined.

I have written before about problems that can flow from having an offshore account in a bank that has direct ties to the United States or any other home country. You should take care in deciding on a Channel Islands or Manx bank for your account, since most of the banks here are associated with major international financial institutions that have some U.S. or other national associations. Look for a smaller institution without connections to your home country. This distinction is very important, especially in view of the spread of new forfeiture and "all crimes" laws in these jurisdictions.

Banks:

Isle of Man

Duncan Lawrie Offshore Services, Ltd., 14/15 Mount Havelock, Douglas, IM1 2QG, Isle of Man, Channel Islands; Tel.: +44-1624-662200; Fax: +44-1624-662878; Web site: www.duncan-lawrie.co.uk.

Jersey

Cater Allen (affiliate of Abbey National Bank), Sovereign House, 16-22 Western Road, Romford RM1 3SP, Channel Islands; Tel.: +44-1708-773333; Web site: www.caterallen.co.uk.

Standard Bank Jersey, Ltd. (division of Standard Bank of South Africa), P.O. Box 583,47-49 La Motte Street, St. Helier, Jersey JE4 8XR, Channel Islands; Tel.: +44-1534-881188; Fax: +44-1534-881199; Web site: www.sboff.com/site/offshore/offshoreJersey.html.

Banque Internationale a Luxembourg, Ltd., P.O. Box 12, 1-3 The Esplanade, Liberation Square, St. Helier, Jersey JE4 9NE, Channel Islands; Tel.: +44-1534-871888; Fax: +44-1534-871999.

Dealing with American Investors

Investment and mutual funds on the Channel Islands and the Isle of Man are not limited to major corporations, insurance companies, and wealthy investors. Middle class, small share investors are also welcome, because volume makes profits. These funds typically allow free worldwide switching between funds that invest in Great Britain, or in money market instruments denominated in sterling or foreign currencies.

Most unit trust (mutual fund) groups will not even mail their literature to a United States address, because they are not registered with the SEC and they don't sell to U.S. citizens. A large number of portfolio management companies accept money from U.S. investors because they are listed on the London Stock Exchange and don't require SEC registration as well. The way to get around these restrictions is to invest through your own offshore-based trust or IBC. (See Chapter 2, pages 32 and 48.) Keep in mind that, under U.S. tax laws, income from these sources must be reported as income annually on IRS Form 1040.

British Expats Do Well on the Islands

The Channel Islands are the preferred place for offshore

money market funds sold to the British expatriate market. Because of a legal quirk, this once was the only place where a single corporate entity could offer money market funds in a variety of currencies, making it easier to offer free switching between currencies to customers investing only modest sums. A few other offshore havens now offer streamlined transactions, but the Channel Islands remain the center for multi-currency money market and bond funds.

The Channel Islands are the preferred place for offshore money market funds sold to the British expatriate market.

The range of business being conducted on the Channel Islands and the Isle of Man is greatly diverse. Mutual funds offer shares that literally span the globe. Major corporate employee pension and benefits programs are headquartered in the islands. This is especially true on Jersey, where one company, **Mourant & Co.**, has carved a niche for itself in this area of business finance. Other corporate business involves debt, securitization plans, financial restructuring, stock and bond issues, captive insurance programs, and leasing. Much of this activity is associated with the many trusts and companies set up under the laws of the three islands.

Equally diverse is the international range of private clients doing business in the islands, attracted by a long history of political stability, absence of exchange controls, reasonable privacy, and good management.

Channel Islands Fund Managers

Gartmore Fund Managers International, Ltd., (Banque Indosuez of France), P.O. Box 278, 45 La Motte Street, Helier, Jersey, Channel Islands; Tel.: +44-1534-886688.

Guiness Flight Fund Managers, Ltd., P.O. Box 188, St. Peter Port, Guernsey, Channel Islands; Tel.: +44-1481-712176.

Hill Samuel Investors, Ltd., P.O. Box 63, 7 Bond Street, St. Helier, Jersey JE38PH, Channel Islands; Tel.: +44-1534-604604.

Isle of Man Bank, 2 Athol Street, Douglas, Isle of Man; Tel.: +44-1624-626232; Web site: www.natwestoffshore.com.

Royal Bank of Canada (Channel Islands), Ltd., P.O. Box 48, Canada Court, St. Peter Port, Guernsey GY1 3BQ, Channel Islands; Contact: Christian Weetman; Tel.: +44-1481-719856; Fax: +44-1481-711370; Web site: www.rbcprivatebanking.com.

There are so many trust, banking, and investment companies in Jersey that it is difficult to know where to start. There are some 200 trust companies alone. **Atlas Trust Company (Jersey), Limited** is a small trust company founded by four professionals, all of whom have considerable experience in the financial field. Atlas will put you in contact with other professionals on the island who might also be able to accommodate your financial goals. Contact Atlas at P.O. Box 246, 11 Esplanade, St. Helier, Jersey JE4 55P, Channel Islands; Tel.: +44-1534-608878; Fax: +44-1534-280808. Ask for Ian R. Swindale, Managing Director.

For more information

Guernsey Income Tax Office, P.O. Box 37, 2 Cornet Street, St. Peter Port, Guernsey GY1 3AZ, Channel Islands; Tel.: +44-1481-724711; Fax: +44-1481-713911.

Guernsey News; Web site: http://www.thisisguernsey.com.

News from the Isle of Man; Web site: http://www.newsmann.com.

Life Insurance and Annuities

The Isle of Man is known worldwide for its excellent insurance and annuity products. Many of these are popular with Americans, since under U.S. tax law life insurance allows four key benefits: 1) Tax-free build-up of cash value, including dividends, interest, and capital gains; 2) Tax-free borrowing against cash value; 3) Tax-free receipt of the death benefit; and 4) Freedom from estate and generation skipping taxes. These benefits are available in any life insurance policy or annuity designed to comply with U.S. tax laws.

For a more detailed explanation of the many benefits of offshore life insurance and annuities, see the description I gave earlier in Chapter 2, page 39 under "Strategy 4: Offshore Variable Annuities" and page 43 under "Strategy 5: Offshore Life Insurance."

For insurance and annuities, contact **Colin G. Bowen** on the Isle of Man at **IOMA Group**, IOMA House, Hope Street, Douglas, Isle of Man IM1 1AP, British Isles; Tel.: +44-1624-681200; Fax: +44-1624-681391; E-mail: colinb@ioma.co.im or info@ioma.co.im; Web site: http://www.ioma.co.uk.

Summary

The Channel Islands and the Isle of Man are tax havens in transition.

Their future depends on their ability to resist the restrictive demands made upon them by the Labour government in London. The chief casualty so far has been greatly diminished financial privacy.

Nevertheless, these havens offer a long tradition and much experience with the creation and management of asset protection trusts and international business corporations and with offshore finance and banking.

My advice is be careful, pick and choose, and you can find some excellent offshore devices, especially in annuities and life insurance as investment and tax deferral vehicles.

Chapter 7
Special Havens in Europe

SUMMARY: Europe has no monopoly on nations that qualify as tax or asset havens, but the history of civilization makes Europe a center of financial development ever since the Middle Ages. Earlier in Chapter 4, I described the attractiveness of Switzerland and Liechtenstein as two of the best financial havens in the world.

Here I describe some of the lesser-known European havens. Some are best for tax-free residency, others for banking or investment. In considering European venues for your cash and investments, keep in mind the ongoing pressure by the European Union to end financial privacy and to impose uniform high taxes on all of its member states.

The Austrian Republic – Unique European Banking Secrecy

Austria is not a haven in the sense of low taxes, but it is a "banking haven." That's because this nation has one of the strongest financial privacy laws in the world. It's written into the constitution and can be changed only by a national referendum of all voters. For the very wealthy, Austria also offers low-tax residency, if you qualify.

The Austrian Republic has long been a bastion of banking privacy. Strategically located on the eastern European border, from

1945 to the Soviet Russian collapse in 1992, while the Soviet Union and the U.S. were locked in constant confrontation, this convenient banking haven served as a willing go-between for West and East.

Secrecy: It's the Law

When Austrian national banking laws were officially codified in 1979, the well-established tradition of bank secrecy was already two centuries old. During this time, Austrian bank secrecy and privacy produced two major types of so-called "anonymous accounts." These accounts usually required no account holder identification, no mailing address and no personal references. Just deposit funds and use the account as you pleased, all anonymously. Both the *Sparbuch* bank account and the *Wertpapierbuch* securities account have now been abolished, victims of the European Union's fixation with destroying financial privacy wherever possible.

Current Austrian bank secrecy laws forbid banks to "disclose secrets which have been entrusted to them solely due to business relationships with customers."

Notwithstanding the demands of the EU, current Austrian bank secrecy laws forbid banks to "disclose secrets which have been entrusted to them solely due to business relationships with customers." This prohibition is waived only in criminal court proceedings involving fiscal crimes, with the exception of petty offenses. The prohibition does not apply "if the customer expressly and in writing consents to the disclosure of the secret."

As an additional protection, the Austrian constitution includes a guarantee of banking and financial privacy. This protection can only be changed by a majority vote in a national referendum, a highly unlikely event. All major political parties support financial privacy as an established national policy of long standing.

No EU Information or Tax Sharing

As a member country, Austria consistently mounted strong official opposition to European Union plans for compulsory withholding taxes and financial information sharing. Defending the banking secrecy behind which its financial sector has prospered, Austria rejected any deal that would force it to exchange information on nonresident account holders. Austrian Finance Minister Karl-Heinz Grasser said his nation would not agree to the proposed information exchange system unless and until other major offshore financial centers accepted similar measures, an unlikely prospect that has yet to come about.

In late 2003, Austria was one of three EU nations exempted from an EU-agreed tax information sharing plan. (Belgium and Luxembourg were the others). All three nations, along with non-EU member Switzerland, declined to share tax information, but did agree in principle to phase in over a period of years a 35% withholding tax on interest paid to nationals of other EU member states. Foreign nationals of non-EU nations, including U.S. persons, are not subject to this withholding tax.

Stocks and Bonds

The Austrian stock market has had one of the world's best performance records in recent years. It has benefited in part from the Eastern European expansion boom in the early 1990s after the Iron Curtain disintegrated.

Nonresidents are not subject to restrictions on securities purchased in Austria: The securities can be transferred abroad without restrictions or reporting. Non-residents can purchase an unlimited amount of bonds and/or stocks, on condition the money used for purchase is in either foreign currency or euros. When securities are sold, the cash proceeds can be freely converted and exported without restrictions.

Taxes

Austrian tax authorities found a way to profit from their attractive banking haven status – the government levies a 25% tax on the total bank interest earned. Foreigners can avoid the 25% tax on bond interest because no tax is withheld if a declared non-resident holds the bank account. Interest paid on investments held in non-bearer form in Austrian banks, such as certificates of deposit, is also exempt from the withholding tax. Interest on convertible bonds, however, is subject to a withholding tax of 20% at the payment source.

Unfortunately, an American citizen bondholder is subject to capital gains tax in the U.S. on the full capital gain, despite the Austrian tax. A double taxation treaty between the U.S. and Austria eases this hardship: if you file a request with the IRS, the Austrian tax will be partly repaid, diminishing the net tax burden to10%. The remaining 10% tax can offset part of the U.S. capital gains tax ordinarily imposed. The double taxation agreement does not apply to Austrian interest and dividends which remain fully taxable in the U.S.

Live in Austria Income Tax-Free

Few people know it, but a wealthy foreigner who takes up residence in Austria can qualify for a unique tax break – 100% of annual income completely free of taxes! This preferential tax treatment, called a *Zuzugsbegünstigung*, is ready and waiting for you at the obliging Ministry of Finance.

As a foreigner who is a new Austrian resident, you can qualify if you:

1. Had no residence in Austria during ten years prior to your application;

2. Don't engage in any business activity within Austria;

3. Prove sufficient income from outside sources;

4. Agree to spend a minimum of US$70,000 in Austria each year; and

5. Have a place to live and intend to stay in Austria for at least six months (183 days) each year.

When you meet all these conditions, you may be able to live tax-free in Austria. All income from foreign pension or retirement funds, dividends and interest from foreign investments, and securities or any offshore businesses outside Austria is tax exempt.

In most cases, officials grant a tax break of at least 75% of potential tax liability – but a good local lawyer may be able to negotiate a 100% reduction. If you have foreign income taxable in your home country, and there is no double taxation agreement between Austria and your country, the Ministry of Finance may grant you a zero tax base, or a special circumstances ruling, but only after you establish your residence in Austria.

Is Austrian residence status for sale? To be frank, yes. If you are a reputable wealthy foreigner, there will be few obstacles to becoming a resident. Residency gives you the best of both worlds: life in an extremely desirable location, but without the high taxes Austrian citizens must pay.

I predict Austrian banking laws will remain secure, at least for the immediate future.

Once in residence, you could apply for citizenship, but that would defeat the purpose. As an Austrian citizen, you'd be liable for full taxation. The only additional advantages would be having an Austrian passport and the right to purchase as much real property as you wish, which is otherwise very difficult for a foreigner merely residing in Austria.

A Secure Future for Privacy

I predict Austrian banking laws will remain secure, at least for the immediate future. The more outsiders try to pressure the government in Vienna, the more the Austrian people resent the inter-ference in their internal affairs. I don't think this "Vaterland First" attitude will change any time soon. As a result, it's wise to keep Austria near the top of your potential banking list, especially if your major area of business interest is in eastern Europe and Russia.

On The Other Hand

Consider the foreigner who uses Austria as his second residence, but not as the "center of his vital interests," (a phrase from Austrian tax law). He goes skiing for three or four weeks each year in Austria. His legal domicile – the place where he lives most of the time, and to which he eventually intends to return – is in another country. In his case, any Austrian source income is taxable in Austria, but all income not earned in Austria is taxable in the country where he lives. His exact tax status and obligations will be determined under the terms of a double taxation treaty that may exist between Austria and his coun-try of domicile.

Contacts

Government:

Austrian Ministry of Finance, Himmelpfortgasse 8, 1010 Vienna, Austria; Tel.: +43-1-5143-30; Web site: www.bmf.gv.at/ministerium/ministerium/englisch/tasks/_start.htm.

Banks:

Anglo Irish Bank, Rathausstrasse 20, Box 306, A-1010, Vienna, Austria; Tel.: +43-1406-6161; Fax: +43-1405-8142; Web site: www.angloirishbank.ie/austria/index.asp. This European bank offers the lowest fees I have encountered for arranging and pur-chasing European government CDs in most currencies.

Creditanstalt, Schottengasse 6-8, 1030-Vienna, Austria; Tel.: +43-153131; Web site: www.ba-ca.com/de/index.html.

Raiffeisen Zentralbank, Am Stadtpark #9, 1030-Vienna, Austria; Tel.: +43-1717070.

Safe Deposit Boxes:

Das Safe, Auerspergstrasse 1, 1080 Vienna, Austria.

The Grand Duchy of Luxembourg

Luxembourg is primarily a business and banking haven, rather than a personal tax haven. It is also a haven for international holding companies and investment funds. Its strong financial privacy laws, which have a long history, are enhanced by the fact that it is one of three EU nations that are exempted from tax information sharing with other EU member states.

Right in the Middle

Little Luxembourg (51 miles long by 34 miles wide) is a hereditary Grand Duchy. The House of Orange-Nassau and its branches have ruled here since 1815. The reign of the present ruler, Grand Duke Jean, began in 1964. Locals commonly speak French, German, English and their own peculiar version of German called *Letzebürgesch*. It's a dialect said to be incomprehensible even to those who have spoken "normal" German since birth.

The pie-shaped country, with a population of 430,000, shares borders with Germany to the east, Belgium to the west, and France to the south. A charter member of the EU, Luxembourg is also a part of the Benelux group along with Belgium and the Netherlands. Since 1922, Luxembourg has had a fully integrated monetary and economic union with its larger neighbor, Belgium. The local currency was the Belgium-Luxembourg franc, but that's been replaced by the euro.

A Mountainous Offshore Haven

Although the nation's international banking activity dates back to the late 19th century, Luxembourg did not hit its stride as an offshore haven until the 1980s. This process developed from forces over which Luxembourg had no control. The causes included:

- The growth of foreign investment in selected European Common Market nations during the mid-1960s;

- The U.S. imposition of an interest equalization tax in the 1980s that drove American corporations to borrow funds abroad;

- German capital flow restrictions and mandatory lending ratios;

- The 35% Swiss withholding tax on bank account and other interest;

- Currency exchange controls in France; and

- Stiff bank account reporting rules in nearby Holland.

Luxembourg is not a tax haven – it's an investment and banking center.

To avoid these circumstances, astute western Europeans and Americans began searching for a safe place to invest their money. They also needed a convenient place to conduct business with maximum freedom and lower taxes. Centrally located in the middle of Europe, Luxembourg and its banks beckoned.

But keep in mind that Luxembourg is not a tax haven – it's an investment and banking center. The effective corporate tax rate is over 30%. Personal income taxes can range up to 38%. Holding companies, which have enjoyed a special status since 1929, do escape most taxes.

Pressure from All Sides

Luxembourg's conservative nature is revealed in a still popular 19th Century local song lyric, *"Wir welle bleiwen wat wir sin."* This simply means, "We want to remain as we are" – a sentiment that easily could be the official national motto. This statement now has broad financial implications, as the European Union (particularly neighboring Germany) continues to pressure this tiny grand duchy for drastic reform of their banking and financial privacy laws.

Unfamiliar to a great many Americans, Luxembourg is an established international financial and banking center. If you want a no-nonsense EU base for business operations and excellent private bank services, this is the place. Offshore banking in Luxembourg has advantages and disadvantages.

Although this tiny country lacks the lure of the Swiss ski slopes or the white sands at Grand Cayman, it more than makes up for its lack of tourist attractions by offering tax-free operations and strict bank privacy.

Business Banking a National Passion

About 60% of all Luxembourg bank activity is now denominated in euros. Another one-third is in U.S. dollars. Roughly 21,000 people are employed directly or indirectly in the Grand Duchy's nearly 200 banks, and nearly 16% of the GDP flows from banking business. German banks, in particular, operate here to escape domestic withholding taxes on interest and dividend loan limitations on corporate customers and they account for over 50% of all banking business. They also use the nation to deal in gold, as Luxembourg imposes no VAT.

Luxembourg's authorities closely watch bank solvency and reserves. Bank accounts are insured against loss in an amount equivalent to about US$15,000 each.

However, the government does not believe it has a duty to ensure that a bank's foreign clients have paid home country taxes. Tax evasion is not as crime here, although the government maintains tax treaties with many nations, including the U.S. and U.K.

Luxembourg, as an EU member state, spearheaded resistance to an EU-wide withholding tax system and to intergovernmental exchange of information – changes that certainly would have disturbed many of this nation's banking system's clients. In fact, as proof of its determination to resist EU pressures, Luxembourg enacted laws enshrining maximum banking secrecy.

Bank assets, liabilities, and other operations must be reported to the Banking Commission. This enables the commission to maintain strict controls on the solidity and honesty of Luxembourg banks. However, banks are strictly forbidden to reveal information about individual accounts and depositors. Doing so is punishable by fines and imprisonment, almost identical to Swiss penalties. Injured clients can sue a bank that violates their privacy rights. The government will provide information only when a crime is related to the bank account itself and the alleged offense is also a crime under local law.

World Connections

Luxembourg's financial picture depends on more than the solvency of its well-supervised banks. The nation is a major transaction center and clearinghouse (Euroclear) for international currency and bond markets. This links its financial health to the state of the entire international banking system. The German and U.S. economies are especially important. Most banking clients in Luxembourg are multinational corporations, not individuals, and their collective fortunes directly affect Luxembourg's financial stability.

Because of this tie to the prosperity of others, those seeking shockproof banking might do better with an account in Switzerland. This is particularly true if you possess sufficiently large deposit sums to command the personal attention of Swiss bankers. For those with less cash, but who still desire privacy every bit as good or better than the Switzerland, by all means, try Luxembourg.

A Neighbors' Complaints

When Germany imposed a 10% tax on interest and dividends in 1989, billions of Deutsche marks poured into Luxembourg almost overnight. Still more money flowed in when Germany sought to enforce collection of the tax in 1993.

The Swiss 35% withholding tax on foreign-owned bank accounts certainly diverted millions of units of various currencies from Switzerland to Luxembourg. So impressive was the Swiss-to-Luxembourg cash flow that many Swiss banks opened branches in Luxembourg in an attempt to hold onto wayward clients. Opening accounts in Luxembourg was the only way these former Swiss banking clients could avoid the tax. That advantage could abate in 2004, if EU withholding taxes begin.

Virtual Tax Freedom for Holding Companies

Since 1929, Luxembourg has been a tax-free haven for holding companies and investment funds. Both are tax exempt except for a relatively small fee at initial registration (1% of subscribed capital) and an annual *taxe d'abonnement*, computed at about 0.2% of actual share value for holding companies, and 0.06% for investment funds.

Holding companies typically own foreign company shares or bonds. They can manage these interests, but cannot engage in local business beyond operational maintenance and staffing. Holding companies are exempt from taxes on dividends, interest and royalties, bond interest, profits from securities sales, or purchases and capital gains taxes. Luxembourg is home to approximately 2,000 holding companies (which include many major multinational holding and finance corporations) and the number is steadily growing. Holding companies are exempt from taxes on dividends, interest, royalties, profits from securities sales, and purchase and capital gains taxes.

The Grand Duchy's stock exchange is used extensively for issues of EU bonds, demonstrating Luxembourg's international importance. Numerous major banks operate there to handle this business. Luxembourg has also passed a series of new laws aimed at attracting mutual funds investment companies.

SICAV Investing

Luxembourg has its own mutual funds, known as *Sociétés d'Investissement Collective à Capital Variable*, or SICAVs. Each Luxembourg bank encourages clients to enroll in its SICAV, unless the investor has an unusually larger sum to invest. Banks earn fees of between 1.5 to 3% annually for managing client mutual fund investments, plus commissions on sales of bonds or stocks in the fund. The Luxembourg government also gets its slice from fees and taxes on the funds.

Luxembourg is the center of ready-made offshore private banking. Your banker alternates as broker and mutual fund salesman. He can help you select one or more SICAV funds to meet your investment objectives, then complete all the necessary paperwork. SICAVs accept relatively modest payments, starting at a US$25,000 minimum at most local banks.

With political and economic stability, no strikes, virtually no unemployment, and the lowest crime rate in Europe, remote Andorra could be your haven from the modern world's problems.

Contacts

Government of Luxembourg, Web site: http://www.gouvernement.lu.

Luxembourg News Online: http://www.news.lu/.

Commission de Surveillance du Secteur Financier, L-2991 Luxembourg, 63 Avenue de la Liberté, Luxembourg; Tel.: +352-4292-9201; Web site: www.cssf.lu/fr/index.html.

Dexia-Banque International à Luxembourg (BIL), 69 route d'Esch, L-2953, Luxembourg; Tel.: +352-4590-2544; Fax: +352-4590-2696; E-mail: contact@bil.lu; Web site: www.bil.lu.

Republic of Andorra

Andorra, nestled between Spain and France in the Pyrenees, is a residential tax haven for very wealth foreigners who enjoy winter sports. It's difficult to become a citizen, but establishing residency is fairly easy. There are no income taxes or other taxes and banking privacy is very strict.

With political and economic stability, no strikes, virtually no unemployment, and the lowest crime rate in Europe, remote Andorra could be your haven from the modern world's problems.

High and Jagged

Andorra is a tiny country with no taxes, no army, and no poverty. The country's standard of living is high, the cost of living low, and the scenery delightful. According to legend, Charlemagne, Emperor of the Holy Roman Empire, named Andorra. Gazing over the mountain region newly wrested from the Moors of Spain, he is said to have exclaimed, "Wild valley of hell, I name you Endor!" (The valley of Endor, at the foot of Mount Thabor in the Holy Land, was the campsite of the Israelites during the war against the Canaanites.) With political and economic stability, no strikes, virtually no unemployment, and the lowest crime rate in Europe, remote Andorra could be your haven from the modern world's problems.

Bargain Isolation

Until the end of World War II, Andorra was a time capsule of traditional European mountain life. Napoleon, declining to invade the diminutive joint principality, said, "Andorra is too amazing. Let it remain as a museum piece." In the last three decades, the country has been transformed from a traditional pastoral and farming economy to one of commerce and year-round tourism. The population is increasing; from 5,500 in 1945 – the same as in the 1880s – to around 63,000 today. Only about 13,500 are citizens. Most of the others have moved there for work opportunities or to escape onerous taxes in their home countries.

As Andorra's economy expands, its banking system has grown to meet the demand. Andorran banks are considered among the safest in the world. Some institutions do have outside shareholders, but the banks remain firmly Andorran in attitude. Under the latest policy dispensation, the country is allowing foreign banks to enter the market, but new entrants are restricted to three new banks annually.

Geography, Government

Andorra consists of 185 square miles, about one-fifth the size of Rhode Island. Andorra's rugged terrain consists of gorges and narrow valleys surrounded by mountain peaks that rise higher than 9,500 feet above sea level. It is an independent nation-state and is governed by 28 elected members of the General Council. Until 1993, the President of France and the Bishop of Seo d'Urgel (Spain), as co-princes, were responsible for Andorra's foreign affairs and judicial system. These "co-princes" could veto decisions by the General Council. They controlled the judiciary and police, but did not intrude into Andorra's affairs, except in 1933, when French gendarmes were sent in to maintain order after the judiciary dissolved the General Council. For the next 60 years, demands for independence were a repeated refrain.

In March 1993, Andorrans voted to sever their feudal links with France and Spain. The country subsequently gained a seat in the United Nations in July 1993 as the third smallest member-state. While citizenship is a daunting prospect – it can only be attained by marrying an Andorran and by staying in the principality for at least 25 years – the number of resident foreigners in Andorra demonstrates just how attractive the country is as a tax haven. Seventy percent of the people who live in Andorra are resident foreigners, and these immigrants are demanding more political rights.

Andorra established formal links with the European Union in 1991. After two years of tough negotiations, Andorra signed its first ever international treaty by joining the EU customs union, the first non-member country to do so. Andorra now applies the common EU external tariff and trade policy. This allows free transit of its goods (except for farm products) within the EU market.

No Income Taxes, Duty Free

Andorra's simple, pastoral life of a half century ago is gone, but it became the shopping mall of the Pyrenees because of its duty-free tax status. Although the duty-free status ended in 1993, the country still is exempt from the EU's value-added taxes, making it a sort of "Mall of Europe." An estimated 10 million visitors a year – mostly day-trippers – invade Andorra. They pour over the border and head for shops along the central valley road. On weekends, traffic jams are a prelude to the jostling, crowd-packed streets of Andorra la Vella, the capital.

Andorra's citizens and residents pay no taxes on personal income, capital gains, capital transfers, inheritance, or profits. There is no sales tax or VAT. Nominal local property taxes are used for municipal services – average annual rental property tax varies from around US$120 for an apartment to US$240 for a house of any size.

Resident or "Perpetual Traveler"

A second residence in Andorra won't alter your domicile of origin for the purposes of home nation inheritance or estate taxes.

But if you're granted a passive residence in Andorra, you have the right to protection under the law, certain benefits from the health and social security systems, the right to a driver's license and the right to own and register resident-plate vehicles. Residence does not confer the right to vote, nor does it allow local commercial activity, such as owning or running a business.

Anyone in Andorra who is not a resident is considered a

tourist – but there's no legal limit on the period of stay. Tourists can even rent or purchase a property for personal use for as long as they wish. So it's easy to live in Andorra, "Perpetual Traveler" style, without an official residence permit.

If you're looking for residence status, there are two categories of permits, both difficult to obtain: those that give the holder the right to work in Andorra and those that don't allow employment. Residence permits are issued for renewable four-year periods.

The annual quota for non-work permits in recent years has ranged from 200 to 500. The earlier you apply, the better your chance of success. Applicants must also show availability of sufficient economic means to permit residence in Andorra without having to work throughout the period of passive residence.

Real Bank Secrecy

Andorran has no exchange controls and bank secrecy is strict. The country allows numbered and coded accounts. Foreigners and foreign legal entities may open and operate bank accounts without the kind of restrictions now imposed even in Switzerland, provided the foreign party can justify the need for an Andorran bank account – establishing residence or buying a condominium in Andorra is sufficient reason. Bank secrecy laws preclude giving bank account information to foreign governments.

Taking advantage of tax freedom and bank secrecy, Andorra is home to thousands of numbered bank accounts. Most belong to prudent Spaniards. Annually, an estimated 10% of the billions of euros that escape Spanish regulation and taxes are thought to be funneled through Andorran accounts. Perhaps 1,500 tax exiles from the U.K. have residences here.

Two or three foreign banks do exist here. All six local banks have a worldwide network of foreign correspondents. With no exchange controls, accounts can be held in up to twenty foreign currencies and traded in any quantity at the rate quoted in Zurich. Exchange rates for clients are some of the best in Europe.

The Economy

There are no accurate estimates of Andorra's gross national product (smart smugglers don't keep records), but tourism is the key factor. The country has developed summer and winter tourist resorts, with more than 250 restaurants and 1,000 shops. There are about 300 hotels, ranging from elegant to simple. Some have double rooms available for as low as US$50 per night. Tourism employs a growing portion of the labor force.

During the winter, skiers flock to Andorra's slopes. High peaks separate six deep valleys, and though the Pyrenees lack the famous Alpine altitudes, they are breathtakingly steep and far less expensive to visit. The Andorran government encourages upscale tourism at its popular ski resorts, attractive because of comparatively low prices. Ski areas are state of the art, and bountiful snowfall guarantees weekend visitors from throughout Europe. Hikers use the lifts in the summer.

Andorra's thriving tourist industry has hastened the country's economic transformation. Former shepherds – now wealthy investors – import cheap Spanish and Portuguese labor to man the building boom, which has transformed Andorra's central valley into a string of shops and condominiums. Don't get the idea, however, that all the land is developed. Only 8% of Andorra's land is both suitable and zoned for development. One can still find small villages in which to live. Many house less than 100 inhabitants, and offer absolute peace and quiet.

Today, locals say that the only poor Andorran is one who hasn't come down from the hills. For those who have made it, a Porsche, Ferrari, or BMW is the vehicle of choice. There are more cars than people in Andorra by far.

Contacts

Government:

Permanent UN Mission of the Principality of Andorra, Two, United Nations Plaza, 25th Floor, New York, New York 10017;

Tel.: 212-750-8064; Fax: 212-750-6630.

Embassy of Andorra, 30, Rue d'Astorg. 75008 Paris, France; Web site: www.amb-andorre.fr/.

Andorra Tourist Delegation, Director: Sra. Maria Rosa Picart, 63, Westover Road, L SW18 2RF, England; Web site: www. andorra.ad/.

Banks:

There are six Andorran banks, with head offices in the capital, Andorra la Vella. All have branches in the other parishes:

Crèdit Andorrà, S.A., Av. Meritxell, 80, Andorra la Vella, Andorra; Tel.: +376-888-888; Fax: +376-888-881; Web site: www.creditandorra.ad.

Banc Internacional / Banca Mora, S.A., Av. Meritxell 96, Andorra la Vella, Andorra; Tel.: +376-820-607; Fax: +376-829-980. Web site: www.bancamora.ad/entrada-fra.php.

Banc Agricol i Commercial d'Andorra, S.A., Centre De Negoci, Av. Fiter i Rossell, 4-bis, Escaldes-Engordany, Andorra; Tel.: +376-873-333; Fax: +376-863-905.

Banca Privada d'Andorra, S.A., Plaça Rebes, 7 Andorra la Vella, Andorra; Tel.: +376-808-400; Fax: +376-867-729.

Banca Reig, S.A., Av. Meritxell 79, Andorra la Vella, Andorra; Tel.: +376-872-872; Fax: +376-872-875; Web site: www. andbanc.com/andbancarsf.htm.

Caixabank, S.A., Plaça Rebes, 3 Andorra la Vella, Andorra; Tel.: +376-874-874; Fax: +376-862-762; Web site: www1.caixabank.ad:8090/webba/wpr0pres.nsf/wurl/bahome_eng.

Real Estate:

Servissim S.L., Roc Escola 3, 1A+B, Avinguda Meritxell 20, Andorra la Vella, Principat d'Andorra; Tel.: +376-860414; Fax: +376-863797; E-mail: servissim@andorra.ad; Web site: www.servissim.com. Servissim is a dependable relocation agent that provides a free newsletter with information about the residency laws and changes that may occur. Servissim not only handles real property sales and quality vacation rentals, but provides the only advice and assistance service for English-speaking foreigners in Andorra.

Campione d'Italia - Back Door to Switzerland

This little bit of northern Italy is completely surrounded by Switzerland, and it's one of the least known residential tax havens in the world. But you have to buy a residence to be a resident. Foreigners who can afford to live here pay no taxes, and foreign-owned businesses are also tax-free. It may be Italy, but everything here is Swiss; license plates, currency, postage and banking.

Although generally it's a well-kept secret, there is a highly unusual enclave – just north of the Italian border, but right inside Switzerland itself. But it's all Italian! Squeezed between snow capped Alpine peaks and beautiful Lake Lugano, this town looks like a scene from a fairy tale. Thanks to a quirk of history, for many years it truly has been a tax-free financial fairyland.

The residence permit allows the holder free movement within Switzerland and Liechtenstein, making Campione a valuable European executive base.

Campione d'Italia, on the shores of beautiful Lake Lugano, is distinguished by its very uniqueness: a little plot of Italian soil, completely surrounded by Switzerland. It has become one of the wealthiest towns in the world per capita, attracting prosperity because of its limbo between two nations.

Since Italy is a half-hour drive and a customs checkpoint away, people here use Swiss money, license plates, and tele-phones, even as they live under Italian law. There are no border controls, so there's complete freedom of travel. Campione, home to about 2,800 people (700 of them resident foreigners), is located in the southern Swiss canton of Ticino, about 16 miles north of the

Italian border and five miles from Lugano by road. Oddly enough, because of its proximity to the Adriatic and Mediterranean Seas, Campione enjoys sub-tropical weather part of the year, and an occasional palm tree can be seen on the lake shore.

Campione is not a tax haven where you can just park your cash. You must establish a domicile in order to benefit from its virtually tax-free status. A local residence permit is comparatively easy to obtain. All you have to do is buy a house or apartment, then spend some time there. The residence permit allows the holder free movement within Switzerland and Liechtenstein, making Campione a valuable European executive base.

Tax Matters in Campione

What attracts so many wealthy foreigners? Campione has no income taxes, as such, and few local taxes. Almost all revenue is derived from the local municipal gambling casino.

Since it's officially subject to Italian law, Italian taxes are levied, but the foreigners resident in Campione pay only a fraction of the full income tax, if any at all. That's because Italian tax authorities make very little effort to impose taxes on Campione's foreign residents. Campione's personal and company tax exemptions do not apply if a resident does business within Italy, however. Since taxes are complicated, discuss your affairs with an international tax consultant before deciding if Campione is right for you. One other point worth noting: profits from transactions from both Swiss and other international sources are excluded for tax purposes, provided they pass through a Swiss bank. Unlike Switzerland or Italy, Campione has no tax treaties with the United States, Canada, nor most other western countries.

Companies Benefit in Campione

Corporations registered in Campione have distinct advantages over Swiss companies. They can use Swiss banking facilities and have mailing addresses that appears to be Swiss, while escaping

Switzerland's relatively high income and withholding taxes. Corporations are governed by Italian corporate law and can be formed with a minimum capitalization of about US$1,000. Corporations can be owned and directed entirely by foreigners, a status Swiss law denies. Corporate registrations are usually handled by Italian lawyers in Milan for modest fees. European Union regulations do apply to business here, as do Italian business taxes.

As a Place to Live

Those are some of the practicalities, but think of the location – of opening your shutters to the splendor of lake and mountains. The joys of living here include easy access to some of Europe's best snow skiing, summer hiking in alpine pastures, and boating on mirrored lakes. For connections to elsewhere, Campione is Europe central. Within 90 minutes, you can be shopping in fashionable Milan.

No crime, no grime. Campione sounds very Swiss, but with lots of anomalies. For instance, the few local police are Italian and electrical power is brought in from Italy.

There are no real residency restrictions, and foreigners don't need special permits to buy property. If you're planning to purchase property and take up residence, just report to the local police within five days of arriving in Campione. A residency permit is issued when you present a notarized property purchase contract and a residency application to the administrative offices in Como, Italy to the south.

The only real restriction in force is that prospective residents must prove they have a proper home, since a mere post office box address is not enough. Residents must spend a certain amount of time living in Campione each year. However, an exact amount of time is not stated specifically so this "rule" isn't too worrisome. But municipal authorities apparently do put great weight on a foreign resident actually being in Campione for at least part of the year. They can and do check to see if a foreign resident's home is occupied and furnished.

Since there is no requirement for new residents to prove a certain level of wealth or annual income, you may wonder why more people aren't flocking to Campione. Simple: very few people can afford the astronomical cost of local property. Even for the tiniest of studio apartments one must pay US$150,000 – it costs more to buy a home in Campione than in Switzerland itself.

Case In Point
Along with the little stretch of its water that belongs to Campione, Lake Lugano is shared by both Italy and Switzerland. Costs on the Italian side of the lake are somewhere between US$800 and $3,000 per square meter. On the Swiss side, they're US$2,000 to $4,000 per square meter. And in Campione d'Italia, the figures jump to approximately US$2,500 to $7,000 per square meter.

Residency:

Henley & Partners, a respected foreign residence and second citizenship service firm, handles establishing residence for foreigners in Campione. Contact: Chris Kalin, Henley & Partners AG, Kirchgasse 22, CH-8001 Zurich, Switzerland; Tel.: +41-44-266-22-22; Fax: +41-44-266-22-23; E-mail: chris.kalin@ henleyglobal.com; Web site: www.henleyglobal.com.

Campione office: Dr. Ernst Zimmer, 2 Corso Italia, CH-6911 Campione d'Italia, Switzerland; Tel.: +41-91-649-3340; Fax: +41-91-649-3129; E-mail: campione@henleyglobal.com.

Real Estate:

Consulting International, 2 Corso Italia, CH-6911 Campione, Switzerland; Tel.: +41-91-649-5510; Fax: +41-91-649-4268; E-mail: consulting@swissonline.ch.

Wetag Consulting, Lugano Riva Caccia 3, Lugano, Switzerland; Tel.: +41-91-994-6851; Fax: +41-91-994-6852; E-mail: info@wetag.ch.

The Principality of Monaco

Monaco is a tax haven for the very wealthy – and great wealth is what it takes to afford living here. It's home to many millionaires, even some billionaires, from around the world, many of them retired and enjoying the good life.

Monaco, in general, is for individuals who have already made their money – people who want to practice the art of living while others mind the store for them; people who want to spend time on the Riviera.

The 1.08 square miles of Monaco on the French Riviera is home to over 33,000 people, but this unique and ancient principality is not for everyone. If you want to make this your permanent home, it helps to have more than a modest amount of money and an assured income for life. It also doesn't hurt to know the Prince and his royal family.

Monaco, in general, is for individuals who have already made their money – people who want to practice the art of living while others mind the store for them; people who want to spend time on the Riviera. If tax avoidance is the only goal, there are cheaper places to do it.

Many residents are just upper-middle class people who have decided to retire in Monaco. They are drawn to the pleasant atmosphere, Mediterranean climate and leisure. Monaco has all the facilities that wealthy people consider necessary: country clubs, health clubs, golf and tennis clubs. Indeed, Monaco may have a small population and area, but it has all the services and cultural activities of a city the size of San Francisco.

Monaco's prices are expensive, but no worse than London, Paris, or Geneva. These days, there are as many Italian restaurants as there are French ones. Long before the euro, money of any kind was the European common currency in this principality.

Monaco is high profile. The world remembers Grace Kelly,

the Hollywood film star, who married Prince Rainier in 1956. The international spotlight followed her until she died in a tragic car accident in 1982. During his long rule, Prince Rainier III has worked hard to expand the economic and professional scope of the country. Few recent monarchs can claim credit for extending their dominions by one-fifth without conquest. But, by land filling the sea, the Prince has managed to expand his tiny principality by 23% in the 50 years since he succeeded his grandfather in May 1949. This land expansion mirrors Prince Rainier's determination to make this a dynamic modern mini-state.

Monaco is stable and any major changes are unlikely to come from inside. In 1997, the Principality celebrated its 700th anniversary of life under the rule of the Grimaldi family. Prince Rainier III is now in his 70s. His children, of course, have wild reputations and the details of their private lives constantly appear in the gossip columns of the European press.

Monaco has also been at the heart of a remarkable economic development based around trading, tourism and financial services in a tax friendly environment. Monaco manages to generate annually over €6.8 billion (US$7.6 billion) worth of business. The state has an annual budget of US$600 million, carries no debts and possesses unpublished liquid reserves of at least US$1.8 billion.

The Principality is no longer just a frivolous playground for the rich, its government is funded primarily through casino gambling proceeds. It is now a modern economy participating at a global level in a diverse range of sectors.

Some people may find Monaco's police presence a little severe. The Principality has the lowest crime rate of any highly urbanized area in the world. This physical security is, of course, one of its great advantages.

Significant Tax Benefits for Residents

Undeniably, there are tax benefits to be gained from a move to Monaco. The authorities do not like the Principality to be known as the tax haven that it in fact is. It's a low-tax area rather than a no-tax area, but still a haven. Since 1869, there have been no income taxes for Monegasque nationals and resident foreigners, one of the main attractions for high net worth individuals. There are no direct, withholding or capital gains taxes for foreign nationals, except for the French, who because of a bilateral tax treaty with Paris, cannot escape the clutches of the French tax system. There are first-time residential registration taxes, but no ongoing real estate taxes.

Banking

There are corporate and banking advantages, too. Confidentiality is good as far as business records go, and the same can be said for the banking services. The Bank of France is responsible for the Monegasque banking system and carries out regular inspections. The banking services in Monaco are not as comprehensive as they could be and attempts are being made to loosen the banking secrecy rules. Since 1993, there has been an anti-money laundering law.

Residency and Citizenship

It is actually much easier to obtain a residency permit here than many might suppose. A clean record, solid bank references and a net worth of US$500,000 should do it. Fees for establishing residency are likely to cost in the US$10,000 to $20,000 range.

The Principality has offered financial and fiscal concessions to foreign nationals for a long time. These have been restricted by the Conventions with France in 1963 and, more recently, by agreements with France after pressure from the EU. And here lies the major concern. Monaco isn't likely to initiate changes. But the rest of Europe, especially France, which has always exhibited a jealous dog-in-the-manger attitude towards the Principality, might pressurize it into getting into line.

If you're on the move already, stability may not be an important issue. However, you might be looking for a base and would do well to consider Monaco. The lifestyle is attractive but is not everybody's cup of tea. If you are contemplating a move purely for financial or fiscal reasons, you might, depending on your specific requirements, do better elsewhere.

Once there, keep a low profile. Foreign nationals who are resident are afraid to make any public criticisms of the country. Why? If the authorities consider you a troublemaker, they can issue a 24-hour notice of expulsion. There's no one to appeal to and you'll be out the door.

Contacts

Henley & Partners, Inc., Kirchgasse 22, CH-8001 Zurich, Switzerland; Tel.: +41-44-266-22-22; Fax: +41-44-266-22-23; E-mail: chris.kalin@henleyglobal.com; Web site: www.henleyglobal.com/ monaco.htm.

Consulate General of Monaco, 565 5th Avenue, New York, New York 10017; Tel.: 212-759-5227. A passport is required for entry to Monaco. A visa is not required for a tourist/business stay up to 90 days. There is no U.S. Embassy in Monaco. Matters are handled by the U.S. Consulate General in Marseilles, France, 12 Blvd. Paul Peytal, 13086 Marseille, France; Tel.: +33-4-9154-9200; Fax: +33-4-9155-0947.

Gibraltar

The Rock, as it is known worldwide, is the United Kingdom's only continental European possession, although it is claimed by Spain. It has fashioned itself into a dual-purpose residential tax haven for high net-worth individuals from around the world – and as a professional base for tax-free international business corporations and trusts.

Ancient Colonial Status

Gibraltar, a colonial possession of the United Kingdom, was ceded to England "forever" under the 1713 Treaty of Utrecht.

Neighboring Spain's 300 years of efforts to recover this British overseas territory, on its southern flank, have been rejected repeatedly by a large majority of the 28,000 citizens of Gibraltar, most recently by 99% in a 2002 referendum.

The famous Rock is tiny – only 2.5 square miles – but boasts a comprehensive banking and financial services industry.

The colony's constitution grants local autonomy in many areas, but reserves strategic decisions to London. Its legal system is based on English common law. Gibraltar has been part of the European Union, by its association with Britain, since 1973.

But hanging over everything in Gibraltar is its uncertain future. The Blair Labour government in London has signaled willingness to "share sovereignty" with Spain, an arrangement that residents of The Rock strongly oppose. In 2003, the U.K. Labour position shifted its approach; a statement that any final agreement with Spain may be years, if not decades away. Prime Minister Blair himself pledged for the first time that no agreement with Spain would be made final unless the people of Gibraltar approved.

The Economy Is Rock-Solid

The famous Rock is tiny – only 2.5 square miles – but boasts a comprehensive banking and financial services industry. Gibraltar has no exchange controls, and offers first-rate communications and infrastructure. The colony's financial services industry is the mainstay of the local economy, providing 30-35% of GDP, with 5,000 jobs depending on the offshore Finance Center.

At the start of 2003, Gibraltar had 22 banks, 19 insurance

companies, 87 trust companies, and 358 licensed financial management and trust companies managing over 2,300 registered trusts.

Gibraltar imposes no capital gains, wealth, or estate taxes.

When the OECD listed Gibraltar on its harmful tax competition "blacklist," the government countered with an "Irish-style" cut in corporate tax rates across the board and said it intended to defend its statutory banking secrecy. But the OECD and the European Union have both attacked Gibraltar's tax haven status, and Spain has joined the critical chorus for its own purposes. As we go to press, the EU has ruled that Gibraltar's offshore favorable tax status is incompatible with EU regulations that apply to the United Kingdom and its colonial dominions. Gibraltar is appealing the EU ruling.

Contacts

Government of Gibraltar: www.gibraltar.gov.gi.

Gibraltar News: www.panorama.gi/.

Financial Services Commission, P.O. Box 940, Suite 943, Europort, Gibraltar; Tel.: +350-40283; Fax: +350-40282; E-mail: info@fsc.gi; Web site: www.fsc.gi.

Corporate formation, trust services:

FORM - A - CO, Suites 41/42 Victoria House, 26 Main Street; Tel.: 79959; Fax: 79894; E-mail: formaco@gibnet.gi.

Trust Management, 4 Leanse Place, P.O. Box 472; Tel.: 40000; Fax: 40404, E-mail: gibraltar@mutrust.com; Web site: www. mustrust.com.

Accountants:

ESV Hassan & Co., Suite 4, ICC; Tel.: 71610; Fax: 70113; E-mail: esvhco@gibnynex.gi.

PricewaterhouseCoopers; Tel.: 73520.

Republic of Malta

Malta offers special tax-free status for foreign retirees. It courts international business and financial firms with tax breaks and subsidies. But as a new member of the EU, it is revising its tax laws and no longer wants to be called a tax haven.

South of the continent of Europe is Malta – a group of islands in the center of the Mediterranean Sea. Malta is well positioned as a cultural and political stepping-stone between Europe and North Africa. About 95% of nearly 400,000 islanders are natives, descendants of the ancient Carthaginians and Phoenicians. Malta offers an excellent climate and quality of life, modern health care and educational systems.

The Maltese government has enacted legislation to increase the islands' role as a leader in international finance services. These provide a variety of tax and financial incentives to banks, insurance companies, fund management firms, trading companies, trusts and investment companies.

In 1530, the Holy Roman Emperor, Charles V, ceded Malta to the governance of the Knights of Malta. They built the fortifications in the harbor of Valetta, the capital, so well that, in 1565, a Turkish siege was repelled largely due to the excellent defenses, which are still in existence today. In 1798, Napoleon invaded Malta and expelled the Knights. At the Congress of Vienna in 1815, Britain was given possession of Malta. With the 1869 opening of the Suez Canal, Malta became an important strategic British base. During World War II, Malta was bombed heavily by the German Air Force since it was a valuable Allied convoy port. In 1947, Malta was granted self-government and in 1964 it became independent.

Business Incentives Are Plentiful

While it is not a tax haven for individuals as such, Malta's government actively courts foreign capital with attractive incentives aimed at investors and entrepreneurs. These include generous tax incentives, soft loans, training grants, and customized facilities at subsidized costs. This pro-business policy seeks to build on Malta's many existing strengths: favorable trade relations with countries around the world; a strategic location on world shipping lanes; and a high-quality, productive, English-speaking workforce.

The Economy

In the last decade, Malta's economy has averaged an annual growth rate of over 7%. The nation has maintained a surplus balance of payments, stable currency, and inflation less than 1%. These factors reflect the overall strength and diversity of the Maltese economy.

Manufacturing, especially high-tech industries, now accounts for over a quarter of Malta's GDP. About 26% of the labor force works in services, 22% in manufacturing, 37% in government, and 2% in agriculture. Major industries now include textiles, machinery, food and beverages, and high-tech products – especially electronics. Tourism is also a growing and increasingly important sector. Other key sectors that provide exceptional investment opportunities include trade, manufacturing, maintenance services, and international financial services.

These sunny Mediterranean islands cater to expatriates looking for a second or retirement home. There are no property taxes and permanent residents pay a 15% income tax on offshore income remitted to the country.

As noted, recent Maltese legislation provides a variety of tax and financial incentives to banks, insurance companies, fund management firms, trading companies, trusts and investment companies. This has increased the islands' role as a leader in international finance services. In 2003, Malta voted to join the European Union. As a new EU member, there will be an adjustment of some of its tax breaks for foreign persons and businesses, so check for the latest facts if you are interested in Malta as a residence or business base.

Residence But Not Citizenship

These sunny Mediterranean islands cater to expatriates looking for a second or retirement home. There are no property taxes and permanent residents pay a 15% income tax on offshore income remitted to the country. Malta has three types of taxes: income, corporate, and estate taxes – the latter applies only to property located on the island. Income tax rates for foreign residents range from 2 to 30%. A permanent resident is not taxed on capital gains paid from offshore, unless the person also is domiciled in Malta.

Foreign nationals are not eligible for Maltese citizenship, but they are welcomed as residents. Maltese residency is of three types:

1) Visitors staying less than three months are counted as non residents;

2) Those remaining over three months are temporary residents; or

3) Permanent residents are granted a permit entitling them to stay.

Those in the latter category must own assets located outside Malta of at least LM150,000 (US$360,000), or have a worldwide income of at least LM10,000 (US$24,000) and demonstrate ability to remit to Malta a minimum annual income of LM6,000 (US$14,400), plus LM1,000 (US$2,400) for each dependent. A residence permit can be inherited by a surviving spouse, but not by other surviving descendants.

Contacts

Henley & Partners, 28 Oratory Street, Mosta MST07, Malta; Tel.: +356-432-364; Fax: +356-418-922; E-mail: marco.griscti@henleyglobal.com; Web site: www.henleyglobal.com/malta. Contact: Dr. Marco Griscti.

Embassy of Malta, 2017 Connecticut Avenue, NW, Washington, DC 20008; Tel.: 202-462-3611; or the Maltese Consulate in New York City; Tel.: 212-725-2345. A passport is required for entry, but a visa is not required for U.S. or other citizens for stays of 90 days or less.

U.S. Embassy in Malta, Development House, 3rd Floor, Saint Anne Street, Floriana, Valletta, Malta; Tel.: +356-235-960; Fax: +356-243-229; Web site: U.S.Embassy@kemmunet.net.mt.

Government of Malta: http://www.gov.mt/index.asp?1=2.

Malta Tourism Board: http://www.visitmalta.com/.

Central Bank of Malta: http://www.centralbankmalta.com/.

The Cook Islands – Far Out and Controversial

Way out in the South Pacific, in the middle of nowhere, are the Cook Islands, home to a very modern set of offshore financial laws that may be just what you need: iron-clad asset protection trusts, IBCs, limited liability partnerships, and a very strict financial privacy law that prevents revealing your personal business. But some people don't like too much distance between themselves and their assets, and these islands are very far out.

If you're researching the world of offshore asset protection, you'll soon hear about the Cook Islands. Since the government first began adopting a series of wealth and asset-friendly laws in 1981, the Cook Islands – though small in population and remote from the rest of the world – have come to play a definite role in offshore financial circles.

A broad net of 15 coral islands in the central heart of the South Pacific, the Cook Islands are spread over 850,000 square miles. The islands occupy an area the size of India, but have a population (19,000 people) no bigger than any small town in America. Indirectly, the islands are part of the British Commonwealth by virtue of their unique association with nearby New Zealand. From 1901 to 1965, this was a colony of New Zealand, and New Zealand still subsidizes the CI government.

The islanders even retain dual New Zealand and Cook Islands citizenship. The New Zealand subsidy has become a sore point in both nations.

The Cook Islands' offshore industry was the result of the government's official collaboration with the local financial services industry. Financial services now rank second only to tourism in the economy. Despite some 50,000 visitors a year to the capital island, Rarotonga, the Cook Islands have remained largely unspoilt. Cook Islanders have their own language and enjoy a vigorous and diverse culture, though most also speak English.

This is a micro-state with macro aspirations, but the grasp may have exceeded the reach. Their checkered history of high finance has been marked by some scandals, sponsored by fast-talking American, U.K., and New Zealand expatriates. It's no secret that certain American asset protection attorneys have played a large role in advising the government on asset protection issues, and actually draft statutes for the island's parliament.

Existing statutes meticulously provide for the care and feeding of IBCs, including offshore banks, insurance companies, and trusts.

Constantly teetering on the brink of bankruptcy, CI government debt exceeds US$100 million – this in a nation with a GDP of only US$101 million. Much of that debt stems from a failed Sheraton Hotel project fiasco involving government officials in the 1980s. Two-thirds of the work force is on the government payroll, financing an old fashioned spoils and patronage system that would make an American big-city political boss blush.

Tailored Wealth Protection

But don't let the distance put you off. There is much here to cheer the hearts of knowledgeable offshore financial enthusiasts; and there are few respected U.S. asset protection lawyers who specialize in offering Cook Island entities. (See contacts below.)

Existing statutes meticulously provide for the care and feeding of IBCs, including offshore banks, insurance companies, and trusts. All offshore business conducted on the Cook Islands must be channeled through one of the five registered trustee companies. A comprehensive range of trustee and corporate services is offered for offshore investors. The government officially guarantees no taxes will be imposed on offshore entities. Thousands of foreign trusts, corporations, and partnerships are registered here, protected by an exceedingly strong financial privacy law.

The Development Investment Act requires all foreign enterprises (those with more than one-third foreign ownership) that want to do business to first obtain approval and register their planned activities with the Cook Islands Development Investment Board. There are various incentives and concessions for tariff protection; import duty and levy concessions; tax concessions by way of accelerated depreciation; allowance for counterpart training; and recruitment of Cook Islanders from overseas.

A highly respected New Zealand asset protection attorney told us that despite the Cook Islands' fiscal problems, the government's tax and asset haven laws are likely to remain in place, even if New Zealand has to retake control.

Updated Laws

In 2003, the Cook Islands adopted a series of new anti-money laundering, financial reporting, and anti-financial-crime laws. These laws were sufficient to get them removed from the FATF blacklist, which was their stated objective.

The laws liberalize the extent to which local financial institutions are obligated to disclose information and override all other laws, making compliance with anti-money-laundering laws and standards paramount. However, the law instituted a procedure which provides due process before any information can be released, including a formal request to the Financial Intelligence Unit showing reasonable grounds to believe that money laundering or criminal activities have taken place. This ensures that any information disclosed is done through proper channels with legal justification.

Conclusion: Don't let those thousands of miles of distance scare you. Your attorney is a lot closer to you and he can be someone who knows how to use the Cook Islands and their asset protection laws to your benefit. See our listed names below.

Contacts

Solicitors:

Clarkes P.C., P.O. Box 123, Rarotonga, Cook Islands; Tel.: +682-24-567; Fax: +682-21-567 / -25-567.

Miller Howard & Lynch, P.O. Box 39, Panama, Rarotonga, Cook Islands; Tel.: +682-21-043; Fax: +682-21-143.

Stevenson Nelson & Mitchell, P.O. Box 552, Avarua, Rarotonga, Cook Islands; Tel.: +682-21-080; Fax: +682-21-087.

Tim Arnold, P.O. Box 486, Rarotonga, Cook Islands; Tel.: +682-23-565; Fax: +682-23-568.

Tony Manarangi, P.O. Box 514, Rarotonga, Cook Islands; Tel.: +682-23-840; Fax: +682-23-843.

Accountants:

Carolyn Short & Associates, P.O. Box 632, Rarotonga, Cook Islands; Tel.: +682-24-530; Fax: +682-24-531.

Deloitte & Touche Tohmatsu, P.O. Box 910, Rarotonga, Cook Islands; Tel.: +682-24-449; Fax: +682-23-449.

KPMG Peat Marwick, P.O. Box 691, Rarotonga, Cook Islands; Tel.: +682-20-486; Fax: +682-21-486.

Banking & Financial Services:

Asiaciti Trust Pacific, Ltd., Level 3, CIDB Building, P.O. Box 822, Rarotonga, Cook Islands; Tel.: +682-23-387 / -24-439; Fax: +682-23-385.

ANZ Banking Group, Ltd., P.O. Box 907, Rarotonga, Cook Islands; Tel.: +682-21-750; Fax: +682-21-760.

Westpac Banking Corporation, P.O. Box 42, Rarotonga, Cook Islands; Tel.: +682-22-014; Fax: +682-20-802.

Cook Islands Development Bank, P.O. Box 113, Rarotonga, Cook Islands; Tel.: +682-29-341; Fax: +682-29-343.

Cook Islands Savings Bank, P.O. Box TX, Rarotonga, Cook Islands; Tel.: +682-29-471; Fax: +682-20-471.

Southpac Trust, Ltd., Centrepoint, Raratonga, Cook Islands; Tel.: +682-20-514; Fax: +682-20-667.

TrustNet Group (Cook Islands), Ltd., CIDB Building, Avarua, P.O. Box 208, Raratonga, Cook Islands; Tel.: +682-21-080 / -801; Fax: +682-21-087 / -088; Contact: John G. McFadzien, Manager.

U.S. Contacts

Attorneys:

Michael G. Chatzky, JD, Chatzky & Associates, P.C., 888 Prospect Street, La Jolla, California; Tel.: 619-456-6085; Fax: 619-456-6099; E-mail: MGChatzky@aol.com.

Barry S Engel, JD, Engel Reiman & Lockwood, The Quadrant, 5445 DTC Parkway, Suite 1025, Englewood, Colorado 80111; Tel.: 303-741-1111; Fax: 303-694-4028; E-mail: bse@ erl-law.com.

Chapter 8
The Atlantic and Caribbean Havens

SUMMARY: The wide arc from Bermuda in the mid-Atlantic to Panama in Central America, including the adjacent Caribbean, is home to several tax and asset havens. Many of these are British colonies and, as such, are under heavy pressure from London to curtail or end their tax haven status. In the past, these small jurisdictions built a record of protecting the wealth of offshore persons from many nations. But because circumstances are changing rapidly in this area, you must be wary.

Park Your Money in a Sunny Tropical Clime?

High finance generates far more money than agriculture, tourism, and fisheries combined – especially among the Atlantic and Caribbean havens.

Over the last half of the 20th Century, many of the sunny islands of the Caribbean realized this economic fact and purposefully transformed themselves into international tax and asset protection havens. Some of them, as British colonies, did so with encouragement from their colonial masters in London. At the time, the U.K. Foreign Office saw this transformation as a way to reduce the need for colonial subsidies from the British Treasury. In a far freer international atmosphere decades ago, London was not much bothered by far-off colonies where foreigners were made to pay no taxes and bank accounts could be opened in fictitious names.

A Basic Change in Policy

By the end of the 20th Century, the tax collectors at the U.K. Inland Revenue began to imagine that vast sums of unpaid taxes were hidden in these British overseas territories. The socialist welfare states of Europe, joined by the United States, also saw tax havens, in general, as a vast sink of tax evasion. As I noted in Chapter 3, tax havens came under siege from a diverse group of leftist antagonists including the European Union, the Organization for Economic Co-operation and Development, the Financial Action Task Force, and even the United Nations.

The "war on drugs" played right into the hands of the tax collectors, since much of the illegal drug traffic originated in Latin America. Caribbean jurisdictions, where banking secrecy had always been a positive selling point, now found themselves accused of hiding illicit drug money. Anti-money laundering laws became the new standard of international finance. It mattered little to the major nations that their own domestic banks laundered most of the criminal cash in the world. The drug war became an excellent public relations ploy and an easy, shorthanded way for politicians to accuse tax havens of being criminal cash conduits.

This anti-tax haven campaign only intensified after the terrorist attacks in New York and Washington, D.C. on September 11, 2001. In the confused aftermath of these earth-shaking events, leftist politicians raised the false accusation that haven nations had been hiding places for terrorist cash. That this proved untrue mattered little to the major nations who saw an opportunity to push their anti-tax evasion plans. These plans called for an end to financial privacy, automatic tax information exchange, and abolition of haven tax exemptions for foreigners.

The high-tax Labour government that took over in London in 1997 was among the strongest proponents of this new onslaught against tax havens, even though many of the leading havens were British. Labour had strong allies in the City of London, where financial firms viewed far off tax havens as a drain on their business. That this sharp reversal of policy harmed the British overseas territories in the Atlantic and Caribbean seemed to matter little to the Labourites.

The "war on drugs" played right into the hands of the tax collectors, since much of the illegal drug traffic originated in Latin America.

This recent U.K. history means that London now views its own colonial offshore tax havens with disfavor. To protect yourself, you must be very careful in dealing with any of these faltering havens. In every one of these jurisdictions, financial privacy and banking secrecy has been seriously diminished. Where foreign tax evasion was not formerly considered a crime, it is now. There are new pressures from London on these havens to impose taxes on foreign investors and bank account holders. Many of these jurisdictions now have signed Tax Information Exchange Agreements with the United States, a crucial step they had resisted strongly for decades.

Nevertheless, in my opinion, several of these haven nations remain well-developed offshore financial centers that still offer good professional, legal, banking, trust, and corporate services. Insurance and annuities are also specialties. As an added attraction, some offer attractive, tax-free residential retirement programs for foreigners. But if financial privacy is your major concern, you must move carefully in this area.

These definite pluses must be weighed against the rapidly changing political and legal climate in these havens, but I warn you that you must obtain the latest facts before you make any decisions.

Atlantic-Caribbean Havens

In a broad arc stretching southward from the mid-Atlantic to Central America are countries and some British overseas territories that specialize in offshore banking and finance. Each offers varying degrees of financial privacy and, so far, friendly, no-tax or low-tax special programs designed for foreigners.

Each of the sovereign nations in this group is a member of the United Nations and the Organization of American States (OAS). Some are also members of the British Commonwealth, and others, by their U.K. association, enjoy special participation rights in the European Union. Most are members of the Caribbean Community (CARICOM), an area-wide economic and trading group of fourteen nations.

As I have said, anyone with investments, banking or offshore entities located in the United Kingdom's overseas territories – **Bermuda**, the **British Virgin Islands**, the **Cayman Islands**, **Anguilla** and the **Turks & Caicos Islands** – should have serious concerns about the direction in which these havens are headed. And for the same reasons, if you're thinking of doing business here for the first time, think again.

In late 1998, the U.K. Foreign Office ordered these territories to amend local laws to permit the enforcement of foreign tax judgments, something none of them previously allowed. Since the U.K. clearly has ultimate colonial jurisdiction over the territories, their only alternative to compliance with the U.K. demands is to declare independence from the U.K., a step none of them has been willing to take. Although independence groups developed in some of these places, most never got off the ground. Very few local political leaders were willing to push for cutting the ties to London.

There were rumblings about possible independence in Bermuda but they faded fast. At least one territorial head of state minced no words: "You have one option; independence or serfdom." The Chief Minister of Anguilla, Hubert Hughes, made this blunt statement in a letter to all Anguillan citizens in direct response to the U.K. Foreign Office demands. Hughes said London was bestowing dictatorial powers on the official Crown-appointed governor who, with agreement of the U.K. Foreign Secretary, may now amend, veto, or introduce legislation without consulting the Anguillan legislature. Similar directives now are in place in Bermuda, the Cayman Islands, British Virgin Islands, and the Turks and Caicos Islands.

Nor does independence seem to be a real option for the smaller U.K. dependent territories, some of which, like the Turks and Caicos, would find it difficult to survive without ties to the "mother country" and the subsidies that brings. That cannot be said of places like Bermuda and the Cayman Islands that can stand on their own considerable financial feet, just as The Bahamas has done more or less successfully since they became independent from the U.K. in 1973. What seems to be lacking in the Caymans and in Bermuda is both the leadership and the collective political will to act. Colonial chains apparently have become too comfortable.

Rationalized Justification

Defending this fundamental change in its attitude towards its offshore financial centers, the U.K. claimed it was acting to meet its obligation to comply with the European Union's anti-money-laundering directives. More recently the excuse has been a need to fight international terrorism. As expected, the result has been to dampen foreign interest in using these places as offshore havens. The resulting outflow of millions, possibly billions, in funds from places such as the Cayman Islands has benefited other haven nations such as Switzerland. Other major beneficiaries have been Far Eastern financial centers such as Hong Kong, Singapore, and Labuan, in Malaysia.

The written constitutions provided to overseas territories pursuant to the U.K.'s Statute of Westminster (1931) allow the British Crown (i.e., New Labour, the government of the moment) to bypass local legislatures by declaring an emergency and imposing its own rules. These extraordinary powers were invoked in the Caribbean area dependent territories in January 1998 after they initially refused London's demand to enact "all crimes" anti-money laundering statutes that would enforce foreign tax claims. Until this threat loomed, these havens traditionally had imposed no taxes on income and did not recognize foreign tax avoidance or tax evasion as a criminal matter.

All four territories, Bermuda, the British Virgin Islands, Anguilla, and the Turks and Caicos Islands already had adopted tough money laundering laws modeled on the 1996 Cayman Proceeds of Criminal Conduct Law that permitted enforcement of foreign confiscation orders in money laundering cases from "designated countries" – only the U.S. and the U.K. at the time. However, contrary to U.K. demands, they all included in their statutes a "fiscal offense" exemption that precluded enforcement in case of tax and customs violations alleged by a foreign government. In 1998, the Cayman Islands government removed the fiscal offense exemption. London said it expected all the territories to follow orders and each did.

Of course, once these anti-privacy demands of London were met, the U.K. overseas territories had diminished greatly their highly valuable status as asset havens. As I write this, they are now being pressed by London to repeal laws allowing a tax-free status for foreign investors. When and if that comes to pass, they will be tax havens no more.

Bermuda: Still the "Cadillac" of Offshore Banking?

This mid-Atlantic island is the world's leading place for "captive" self-insurance used by businesses and for re-insurance, and it offers excellent asset protection trusts and IBCs. Its three respected banks have worldwide branches and investment services. But Bermuda has greatly diminished its haven status by signing a TIEA with the U.S., making foreign income tax evasion a local crime, and by curbing its former financial privacy laws. Of equal concern, as a U.K. colony, it takes orders from London and British Labour.

Bermuda is located in the mid-Atlantic, 750 miles southeast of New York City, 3,445 miles from London. The island (57,000 people, 21 square miles) has a long history as a tax and banking haven. This is a world-class financial outpost, not to mention a very pleasant place to visit or live in any season.

A self-governing British overseas territory, Bermuda is a major international financial center. In the early days, the focus was based largely on re-insurance companies. In fact, Bermuda still ranks right behind the U.S. and England in the field. There are now over 1,300 "captive insurance companies" registered in Bermuda with capital exceeding US$29 billion, and total assets over US$76 billion.

More than 8,000 international business corporations call Bermuda home. They are drawn by the island's friendly, tax neutral environment, established business integrity, and minimal regulation.

Bermuda imposes no corporate income, gift, capital gains, or sales taxes. The income tax is extremely low – 11% on income earned from employment in Bermuda. More than 8,000 international business corporations call Bermuda home. They are drawn by the island's friendly, tax neutral environment, established business integrity, and minimal regulation. Over 60% of these companies operate as "exempted," meaning their business is conducted outside Bermuda (except for the minimal contacts needed to sustain an office on the island).

Bermuda is also home to more then 600 "collective investment schemes" (mutual funds), unit trusts and limited partnerships. Under the strong protective umbrella of the U.K. Copyright Act of 1965, also applicable in Bermuda, many collective investment schemes with intellectual property and software interests use the island as a legal homeport. With a statutory structure for protection, Bermuda also has become a center for offshore trust creation and management. The island offers a wide variety of trusts to meet every need, including offshore asset protection.

The "jewel of the Atlantic" is also a great place to live, but be aware of tough real estate restrictions. Demand is high and supply short. In general, non-Bermudians are permitted to own only one local property. Acquisition is allowed only after careful background checks (at least one bank reference, and two or more per-sonal references). Out of 20,000 residential units on the island, only 250 detached homes and 480 condominiums qualify for non-Bermudian purchasers based on government set values. The price for a single home starts at US$1.5 million, US$375,000 for con-dos. Purchase licenses come from the Department of Immigration and take six months or more for approval. A fee based on pur-chase price is payable at settlement – 20% for homes, 15% for condominiums.

Bermuda Banking

Such extensive worldwide finance and insurance activity requires a highly sophisticated banking system. Bermuda provides this with up-to-date services and fiber-optic connections to the outside world. The three local banks clear over US$3 billion daily. In accordance with the Banking Act of 1969, no new banks can be formed or operate in Bermuda unless authorized by the legisla-ture. The chances of that happening are slim to none. However, international banks may form exempted companies engaged in non-banking activities, and many have done so. Perhaps the biggest local banking news in years occurred in 2003, when the world's second largest bank, HSBC, announced plans to purchase control of the Bank of Bermuda.

Bermuda's three banks follow very conservative, risk-averse policies. They hold an average of 85% of customer liabilities in cash and cash equivalents. For example, the Bermuda Commercial Bank recently had a weighted "risk-asset ratio" of 32%. Eight percent is the minimum required by Basle International Banking Agreement standards.

Bank of Bermuda, founded in 1889, has assets exceeding US$5 billion and offices in the Cayman Islands, Guernsey, Hong Kong, the Isle of Man, and Luxembourg, and an affiliate in New York City. Butterfield Bank (founded in 1859) also has offices in all of those havens, except the Caymans. During 2003, Butterfield expanded by purchasing existing banks in Barbados and The

Bahamas. In 2004 the island was the scene of a temporary financial controversy when the global banking conglomerate, HSBC, bought the controlling interest in the Bank of Bermuda. In spite of some local opposition, shareholders approved the sale.

The Bermuda dollar circulates on par with the U.S. dollar. U.S. currency is accepted everywhere. There are no exchange controls on foreigners or on exempt companies, which operate freely in any currency, except the Bermuda dollar.

Unlike the Cayman Islands or The Bahamas, Bermuda has no bank secrecy laws officially protecting privacy, but bank and government policies make it difficult to obtain information in most cases. To do so requires judicial process. A 1988 tax treaty with the U.S. allowed for governmental exchange of limited information in certain cases, but a more recent Tax Information Exchange Agreement (TIEA) with Washington opened the door to free exchange of information with the IRS. On a comparative 1-to-10 international banking privacy scale, Bermuda now ranks about five or less.

For your personal and business purposes, a Bermuda bank account can offer a tax-free means for global financial activity and vast investment possibilities. If you have need for an offshore based business locale, Bermuda, with its IBC creation laws and its modern digital Internet connections, may be a good bet.

Foreign Tax Evasion a Crime

In the last five years, Bermuda has adopted proposals to toughen the provisions of the U.S.-Bermuda tax treaty. It also upgraded anti-money laundering laws, as well as financial management laws governing the chartering and operation of banks and trust companies. These new laws were seen as Bermuda's calculated response to demands from the Foreign Office in London, and of the OECD and FATF. In late 2003, another round of upgrades to these laws was enacted.

The rewrite of the U.S.-Bermuda tax treaty toughened the

existing agreement at Washington's request. It clarified and expanded the types of information that Bermuda can now give the IRS "relevant to the determination of the liability of the [U.S.] taxpayer." For the first time, Bermuda also permitted on-site inspections of records by foreign tax authorities. The Proceeds of Crime Act fiscal offences list was broadened to include tax fraud. In effect, this meant that by proxy, American tax laws and their enforcement mechanisms were adopted by Bermuda.

Most importantly, the fraudulent evasion of foreign taxes was a made a crime, a major reversal of prior Bermuda policy and law. This made Bermuda the first major tax haven (and the first British overseas territory) to adopt such legislation. Together, these laws allow the U.S. IRS and the U.K. Inland Revenue (as well as other nations' tax collectors) to pursue their alleged tax-evading citizens with the assistance of Bermuda prosecutors and courts.

In 2000, Bermuda became an approved jurisdiction of the U.S. IRS for tax reporting purposes. That meant that the island's banks, investment advisors, and other financial services which deal in U.S. securities agreed to disclose to the IRS the names of their U.S. clients, or to impose a 30% withholding tax on investment income paid to such U.S. persons. This was said to show IRS approval of Bermuda's stricter know-your-customer and suspicious activity reporting rules.

Bermuda Business

Because of the large number of international companies that conduct insurance operations from Bermuda, the island does not rely as heavily on personal offshore services and banking as do most other havens. In 2003, over 12,000 international businesses maintained registration in Bermuda, and nearly 3,000 locally. Total income generated by international companies was nearly US$2 billion. The number of business permits surged as the island promoted itself as an e-commerce haven and opened its shores to licensed investment services providers for the first time. Bermuda has long been a haven for offshore businesses. There is no income tax in Bermuda and international companies pay vastly reduced corporate taxes compared to the United States and Europe.

Under U.S. tax law, a corporation pays 30% or more in taxes. Once that company changes its corporate registration to Bermuda, its profits from foreign operations are tax-free and can be kept offshore.

In my opinion, this makes Bermuda a prime candidate if you are looking for a tax-free offshore base for your business operations. An IBC registered here allows worldwide activity, even though you may live elsewhere. The IBC law allows great flexibility in operation with minimal reporting requirements. IBCs and their profits are tax exempt locally. Another plus for Bermuda incorporation – the island's squeaky clean reputation.

In recent years, Bermuda has become an object of attack for American politicians who loudly denounce U.S. companies who re-incorporate there. The reason companies do this is easy to understand. Under U.S. tax law, a corporation pays 30% or more in taxes. Once that company changes its corporate registration to Bermuda, its profits from foreign operations are tax-free and can be kept offshore. It isn't Bermuda that should be attacked; it's American tax laws that should be changed so as not drive corporations away. But it's a lot easier for U.S. politicians to deliberate the issue, rather than do the hard work of reforming stupid U.S. tax laws.

By the way, you too can benefit from this tax-free Bermuda situation, once you have your own IBC registered there.

Early Surrender to the OECD

Bermuda was one of only six offshore financial centers which gave a written pledge to the OECD before publication of its June 2000 blacklist of "harmful tax competition" nations. Each promised to meet OECD tax requirements in the future. Even after the 1999 adoption of criminal tax evasion and tax information exchange laws, Bermuda's tax agreement with the OECD was still a surprise. In essence, this means that Bermuda eventually might impose taxes on presently tax-exempt foreigners who do business there. But this commitment was based on the OECD guarantee that all nations would adopt the same tax laws, the so-called "level playing field" rule. That this has not happened is hardly surprising.

Essentially, the Bermuda government pledged to the OECD to exchange all tax information with other nations; to require local and international companies to file publicly audited annual accounts; to maintain its current tax system and to implement unspecified recommendations from an advisory committee of local persons by 2003 for the financial sector, and by 2005 for other businesses.

Clean Money

Not only did Bermuda evade the OECD "tax harmonization" hit list but it escaped the FATF list of jurisdictions alleged to indulge dirty-money laundering through banking secrecy and lack of "transparency." Bermuda's three banks all work diligently to maintain clean reputations, although several money laundering cases have occurred, but without any overt bank complicity.

The former Bermuda Financial Secretary, Peter Hardy, argued that endorsement from the FATF and OECD "enables those major companies that want to set up in Bermuda to demonstrate they are, in fact, able to move to jurisdictions where international standards are upheld. We are able to say Bermuda is an upstanding and clean jurisdiction." That may be true, but in my opinion, it is also a jurisdiction no longer able to guarantee strict financial privacy for those who do business on the island.

Bragging Rights

This entire financial housecleaning and its strict new laws led to a government claim that the island was now "the business leader among the British overseas territories," ready to meet and exceed international financial standards and regulation.

Making the best of the end of Bermuda's much vaunted financial privacy, the local office of Lines Overseas Management surrendered with a statement to clients "that in today's global, interdependent economic world 'no island is an island.' Sooner or later, all offshore jurisdictions will accept G-7 dominance over global financial affairs. In the interim, further stratification is expected between legitimate 'white-list' countries and illegitimate 'black-list' jurisdictions." Naturally, Lines saw Bermuda at the head of the "white list."

The British Westminster system confers an immensely important constitutional right on each U.K. overseas territory, that of declaring independence. Until 2004 most local political leaders avoided the issue of Bermuda's possible independence from the United Kingdom. But a new Prime Minister, Alex Scott, called for a national debate on the subject, looking towards the possibility of ending London's control over the island. It is too early to predict the outcome, but independence is a possibility.

Conclusion

Bermuda remains a good, basic, no-tax asset protection jurisdiction for the location of offshore trusts and IBCs. Its banks are also first-class. But its willingness to cooperate with tax-hungry governments in Washington and London has seriously diminished what was formerly a policy of strict financial privacy.

Contacts

Government:

Bermuda Monetary Authority, Burnaby House, 26 Burnaby Street, Hamilton HM 11, Bermuda; Tel.: +441-295-5278; Fax: +441-292-7471; Web site: www.bma.bm.

Banks & Finance:

Bank of Bermuda, 6 Front Street, P.O. Box HM 1020, Hamilton HM DX, Bermuda; Tel.: +441-299-5288; Fax: +441-299-6519; Web site: www.bankofbermuda.com.

Bank of Butterfield, 65 Front Street, P.O. Box HM 195, Hamilton HM AX, Bermuda; Tel.: +441-299-3826; Fax: +441-292-4365; Web site: www.bankofbutterfield.bm.

Bermuda Commercial Bank, Ltd. (est.1969), 43 Victoria Street, P.O. Box HM 1748, Hamilton HM GX, Bermuda; Tel.: +441-295-5678; Fax: +441-295-8091; Web site: www.bermuda-bcb.com.

Royal Trust (Bermuda), Ltd., P.O. Box HM 2508-HM GX, 37 Church Street, Hamilton HM 12, Bermuda; Tel.: +441-292-4400; Fax: +441-292-4070.

LOM Group, The LOM Building, 27 Reid Street, Hamilton HM 11, Bermuda; Tel.: +441-292-5000; Fax: +441-295-3343; Web site: www.lom.com/bermuda/index.htm.

Attorneys:

Gordon L. Hill, QC, Cox, Hallet & Wilkenson, Milner House, 18 Parliament Street, P.O. Box HM 1561, Hamilton HM FX, Bermuda; Tel.: +441-295-4630; Fax: +441-292-7880; E-mail: cw@cw.bm.

Appleby, Spurling & Kemp, P.O. Box HM 1179, Hamilton HM EX, Bermuda; Tel.: +441-295-2244; Fax: +441-292-8666.

Real Estate:

Sinclair Realty, Ltd., 2 Reid Street Penthouse, Hamilton HM LL, Bermuda; Tel.: +441-296-0278; Fax: +441-292-5932.

Castles Realty, Ltd., Somers Building, 15 Front Street, Hamilton HM AX, Bermuda; Tel.: +441-295-6565; Fax: +441-295-2323.

Rego, Ltd., P.O. Box HM 169, Hamilton HM AX, Bermuda; Tel: +441-292-3921; Fax: +441-295-7464.

The Cayman Islands

A few years ago, the Cayman Islands could claim that its financial institutions stood fifth in the entire world in the total billions of dollars of assets under management. For decades, it was the premier jurisdiction of choice for tax-free international banking and business that wanted (and got) iron-clad secrecy guaranteed by law. But a series of highly publicized cases involving drug and other criminal money laundering, plus a major case in which a local bank was used for wholesale U.S. tax evasion, contributed to ending this haven's secrecy.

In recent years, this U.K. colony, under extreme pressure from London and Washington, has shredded its financial and banking secrecy laws. The result: an outflow of billions in assets to other, more privacy-oriented, havens. But the Caymans are still a tax-free haven for offshore bank accounts, trusts, and international business corporations, as well as hedge funds, mutual funds, insurance, and annuities. Its name also is a red flag for foreign tax collectors everywhere.

Let's face it: the major reason the Cayman Islands became a world renowned tax-free haven was its strict financial privacy – not just privacy, but near absolute secrecy. Guaranteed by law and zealously enforced by local courts, any foreigner doing business here was shielded from scrutiny – unless he was engaged in overtly criminal acts. Even then, a lengthy judicial process often was needed to pierce this wall of secrecy.

That was the old Cayman Islands before it was forced, over the last few years, under orders from its colonial masters in London, to compromise its bank and financial secrecy, to become a potential proxy tax collector for other nations.

Many Caymans residents do not agree with what has happened here. Michael Alberga, a Caymans lawyer with a long list of foreign clients accuses the world's richest nations of practicing "economic terrorism" against the Caymans. We are simply "practicing pure capitalism; few or no taxes and little regulation," he claims, asking to be left alone.

Mr. Alberga was not the only one of the 33,000 residents of this British overseas territory who were disturbed by these drastic changes. In the 2000 elections, the Leader of Government, Truman Bodden, was defeated along with another minister who, with Bodden-led negotiations led to compromises with the OECD. Voters ousted both in apparent anger over the government's weakening of the financial privacy laws that made the islands wealthy. But the new government, while it has complained a lot, has changed almost nothing, and in fact, has usually done London's bidding.

Government & History

The Cayman Islands is a parliamentary democracy with judicial, executive, and legislative branches. The present 1972 constitution provides for governance as a British Dependent Overseas Territory.

The Cayman Islands is an English-speaking common-law jurisdiction with no direct taxation on income, profits, wealth, capital gains, sales, estates, or inheritances.

The territory consists of three islands: Grand Cayman (76 sq. mi.), Little Cayman (10 sq. mi.), and Cayman Brac (14 sq. mi.). Administered by Jamaica from 1863, they remained a British dependency after 1962, when Jamaica became independent. Grand Cayman is located directly south of Cuba, approximately 500 miles south of Miami, Florida. The capital, located on Grand Cayman, is George Town, which serves as the center of activities for business and finance.

The Cayman Islands is an English-speaking common-law jurisdiction with no direct taxation on income, profits, wealth, capital gains, sales, estates, or inheritances. Described as being "one of the more mature jurisdictions...in terms of regulatory structure and culture," the traditional impenetrable confidentiality of the Cayman Islands ended finally, in November 2001, when it signed a second Exchange of Tax Information Treaty with the United States. Among other things, that treaty gave the U.S. Internal Revenue Service permission to examine accounts of Cayman financial institutions.

Offshore Business Leader

Shrouded in secrecy, capitalism thrived here, to be sure.

The Caymans is home to nearly 60,000 international business companies (IBCs), 464 financial institutions, including 47 of the world's 50 top banks, 2,621 mutual funds, 114 trust companies, 541 insurance companies, and thousands of closed-end funds, plus the latest financial schemes dreamed up by lawyers and savvy investors (as the Enron scandal showed). At present, the world hedge-fund industry comprises more than 6,000 funds with assets of more than US$600 billion. Cayman dominates offshore hedge funds with approximately a 65% market share. It has excellent communications facilities and extensive professional services.

At one time, the Caymans ranked as the world's fifth-largest financial center behind New York, London, Tokyo, and Hong Kong. Offshore business accounts for roughly 30% of the territory's gross domestic product of US$1.4 billion. Many of the world's most reputable companies, including many American companies, do business through subsidiaries registered in the islands, to take advantage of the favorable, tax-free laws. (This has made the Caymans, like Bermuda, a target for U.S. politicians). And until a few months ago, all these financial operations were conducted in statutorily guaranteed secrecy.

OECD-appeasing changes in financial laws and rules made here may not have hurt the islands' immediate financial standing. According to 2002 information from the Monetary Authority, total assets of Caymans banks stood at US$747.6 billion, a 50% growth over a 1996 figure of US$497 billion. But later figures may show a loss reflecting all these radical new policy changes.

Talking Surrender

In early 2000, the Cayman Islands government, at the insistent urging of London, began secret negotiations with the OECD and FATF. Discussion centered on demands to stop alleged foreign tax evasion and to increase transparency in the islands' financial institutions. The government was threatened with OECD/FATF blacklisting plus possible undefined "sanctions."

Demands also included expansion of existing mutual legal assistance treaties (MLATs) with the U.S. and the U.K. to include, for the first time, criminal tax evasion. The U.S. MLAT, which was signed in 1986 and ratified by the U.S. in 1990, already had been used 170 times to exchange information. Traditionally, the Caymans had not viewed foreign tax evasion as a crime since its law imposed no income taxes.

Under pressure in 1998, the Caymans already had repealed a specific exemption in law that had until then prevented bank account freezes and forfeiture based on foreign government tax claims. London and Washington long had demanded repeal of this legal exemption for "tax offenses." Since non-payment of taxes is not a crime in the Caymans, and local law had applied the principle of "dual criminality," that meant MLAT requests were honored only for alleged acts that were clearly criminal under Caymans law.

As the law stands now, a Caymans court can confiscate all assets of a convicted person up to the amount by which he benefits from the crime. While the law requires the government to have *prima facie* evidence of a crime in order to seize cash or property, there is little recourse for a falsely accused person. An innocent defendant is ineligible for compensation unless he can prove "serious default" on the part of prosecuting authorities. Some Cayman legal experts said this lack of restraint could result in the law being used oppressively for "fishing expeditions." The legal situation now is virtually identical in the other U.K. overseas territories.

Money Laundering Crackdown

Before this, the Cayman Islands had viewed themselves at the forefront of the fight against money laundering in the Caribbean. Drug money laundering was made a serious crime in 1989, and so-called "all-crimes" anti-money laundering legislation took effect in 1996.

In March 2000, the Cayman Islands government issued a new code of conduct for financial institutions aimed at further curbing money laundering, supplementing the 1996 landmark law that had criminalized money laundering in all serious crimes. The new code encouraged reporting of suspicious transactions by providing a safe harbor from liability for those who reported suspected crimes.

The new code underscored existing money laundering laws, proper procedures to identify new clients, how to document evidence, methods for staff training, and how to keep records based on international standards. The code applied to all financial service providers and anyone involved in related transactions, including real estate and financial managers, and trust companies.

FATF Delivers Blow

In spite of all these new laws, in 2000, the Financial Action Task Force listed the Caymans along with15 other "dirty money" nations as being uncooperative in fighting criminal money laundering. Cayman's government officials, who had been quietly negotiating with FATF and the OECD for months, were vocal in their condemnation of the FATF blacklisting. They said it was unfair and inconsistent with past OECD and FATF praise for their efforts to clean up any dirty money problems.

Within days of the FATF blacklisting, undoubtedly by pre-arrangement, the U.S., U.K., and Canadian governments issued "advisory warnings" to their respective banking and financial institutions about dealings with the newly accused dirty-money Caymans.

Surrender of Financial Secrecy

Undeterred by the FATF blacklisting, in June 2000, the government proudly announced what its politicians repeatedly had said they would never do. They had reached an agreement with the OECD on the issue of future "transparency."

Thus, the government officially embraced the OECD's demand for an end to the Caymans' traditional bank and financial secrecy, guaranteeing it would provide financial information about Caymans' clients to foreign tax collecting authorities. This Caymans "advance commitment" said that effective exchange of information on tax matters would begin by January 1, 2004 (that did not happen) and be fully implemented after December 2005 (also highly unlikely). In return for this major surrender, the OECD promised the Caymans would not appear on the OECD blacklist of tax havens allegedly engaged in "harmful tax practices" which was published in June 2000.

Within three weeks of the FATF report, all the primary legislation necessary to address every one of the FATF's concerns was on the statute books. Within a further few weeks, more anti-money laundering rules were introduced to complete the legislative framework. The Islands now have a regime considerably tougher than that which exists in many of the FATF's 29 member countries.

The new laws allow the Cayman Islands Monetary Authority to obtain information on bank deposits and bank clients without a court order and ended existing restrictions on sharing information with foreign investigators. A new provision made it a crime to fail to disclose knowledge or suspicion of money laundering. Previously, it had been a crime for financial sector workers to disclose any private financial information without a court order. The Caymans government even went so far as to guarantee that it would stop island financial services providers from "the use of aggressive marketing policies based primarily on confidentiality or secrecy."

One crucial OECD demand was not addressed. That would require the Caymans (and all other blacklisted haven nations) to abolish any preferential tax treatment accorded foreign business and investment. The OECD demands that everyone, domestic and foreign, must be taxed the same. Of course, that would effectively end the tax advantages and thus the existence of all tax havens! Fortunately, this commitment was based on the OECD's "level playing field" promise; that until all OECD nations imposed uniform taxes, each could preserve its own tax system.

At a London meeting in January 2001, the Cayman Islands government representative in the U.K. admitted the Cayman government made commitments to the OECD in exchange for assurances "that gave us some protection," chiefly the right to retain a zero income tax rate. She did not explain why the non-governmental Paris bureaucrats of the OECD should be given the power to make financial policy for the Caymans Islands.

The 2000 election ouster of appeasement politicians came as many Islanders began to question their status as a U.K. overseas territory and their future association with the British. The written constitutions of U.K. overseas territories (OSTs) sprang from the 1931 Statute of Westminster that allows colonies to opt for independence. But that requires a degree of courage OST politicians so far seem to lack.

In 2004 the local government caved into demands from the U.K. Foreign Office in London and agreed to apply full tax information exchange with all EU nations under the terms of the EU tax directive.

The Caymans Spy Affair

The lengths to which London will go in subjugating its colonies were revealed in early 2003 and the Cayman Islands was the unwitting target.

In January 2003, a major anti-money laundering trial was abruptly aborted by the Cayman Islands Chief Justice, who revealed that the head of the Caymans Financial Reporting, Brian Gibbs, was a paid "mole" for MI-6, the British CIA. Gibbs, a former London police detective, had been paid monthly for 10 years to report to London whatever his spy masters demanded, under a supposedly secret intelligence operation, code named "Victory." It turned out that Gibbs, on London's orders, had destroyed evidence concerning the money laundering trial and may have wiretapped the Chief Justice's telephone. The chief justice said the territory's British appointed governor, its attorney general, and the police chief were aware that Gibbs was a U.K. mole since the early 1990s, but elected Cayman Islands government ministers were kept in the dark.

Regardless of the end of financial secrecy here, enormous amounts of money have flowed through these islands over many years. That has created an impressive financial and professional community from which you and your businesses can benefit.

The Leader of Government, McKeeva Bush, was livid at the revelations, calling the U.K. government's secret conduct "shocking and reprehensible behavior." Bush charged that "the UK has a plan to destroy us" and that London had been waging "a cold war" against the islands' financial sector. Bush and four cabinet colleagues demanded that Gibbs and the islands' attorney general resign. Shortly thereafter, Gibbs and his family fled by plane to Miami, then to London. Baroness Amos, Under-Secretary for U.K. Caribbean Overseas Territories, rejected resignation demands, but said nothing about the Labour government's exposed spying.

The islands' leader, Mr. Bush, said these developments had "shaken the very foundation of our partnership" with the United Kingdom.

Recommendation

Regardless of the end of financial secrecy here, enormous amounts of money have flowed through these islands over many years. That has created an impressive financial and professional community from which you and your businesses can benefit. These professionals can provide first-class investment advice, a variety of offshore legal entities, trusts and IBCs, annuities and life insurance. There are many mutual and hedge funds in which to invest.

If you value financial privacy and are considering or have financial dealings in the Cayman Islands, as with any British overseas territory haven, plan accordingly. But don't overlook what they have to offer – even if everything these days is out in the open.

Contacts

Government:

Cayman Islands Monetary Authority, P.O. Box 10052 APO, Elizabethan Square, Grand Cayman, Cayman Islands; Tel.: +345-949-7089.

Banks:

Cayman National Bank, P.O. Box 1097, George Town, Grand Cayman, B.W.I.; Tel.: +345-949-4655; Fax: +345-949-7506. Cayman National issues its own MasterCard.

Cayman Securities, Ltd., P.O. Box 275, George Town, Grand Cayman, B.W.I.; Tel.: +345-949-7722; Fax: +345-949-8203; E-mail: d.markiuk@candw.ky; Contact: Dan Martiuk.

Midland Bank Trust Corporation (Cayman), Ltd., P.O. Box 1109 GT, Midland Bank Trust Building, Mary and Fort Streets; Tel.: +345-949-7755; Fax: +345-949-7634; Web site: www. midban@candw.ky.

Attorneys/Investment Advisors:

Portfolio of Finance & Development, Government Administration Building, George Town, Grand Cayman, Cayman Islands, B.W.I.; Tel.: +345-949-7900; Fax: +345-949-9538; Web site: www.businessmonitor.co.uk.

Goldman Sachs Trust, Ltd., Harbour Center, North Church Street, P.O. Box 896, George Town, Grand Cayman, Cayman Islands, B.W.I.; Tel.: +345-949-6770; Fax: +345-949-6773.

International Management Service, Ltd., Box 61G, 3rd Floor, Harbour Court, Grand Cayman, Cayman Islands, B.W.I.; Tel.: +345-949-4244; Fax: +345-949-8635.

Citco Fund Services, Ltd., Corporate Center, West Bay Road, P.O. Box 31106 SMB, Grand Cayman, Cayman Islands, B.W.I.; Tel.: +345-949-3977; Fax: +345-949-3877.

Truman, Bodden & Co., George Town, Grand Cayman, Cayman Islands; Tel.: +345-949-7555; Contact: Andrea R. Williams.

The British Virgin Islands

BVI, as it's known, has 21,000 people – but over 400,000 registered IBCs, second only to Hong Kong in total number. That's because the BVI specializes in creating, servicing, and promoting offshore corporations for every purpose. The BVI can truthfully say, "IBCs 'R' Us." Don't overlook their asset protection trusts, international limited partnerships, and insurance.

The British Virgin Islands, with about 21,000 people, consists of more than 60 islands, only 16 inhabited, at the eastern end of the Greater Antilles in the Caribbean. Its economy is closely integrated with the nearby (to the west) U.S. Virgin Islands. The currency, since 1959, has been the U.S. dollar. First settled by the Dutch in 1648, the islands were annexed in 1672 by the English.

The economy, one of the most stable and prosperous in the Caribbean, is highly dependent on tourism, generating an estimated 45% of the national income. An estimated 350,000 tourists, mainly from the U.S., visit the islands annually.

Since 1984, a special BVI law has allowed quick and cheap formation of tax-free corporations to hold assets and execute offshore transactions. In excess of 64,000 new IBCs were licensed annually in recent years, bringing the total number of registered

IBCs to about 400,000 in 2003. Indeed, the total number of BVI offshore corporations is second only to that of Hong Kong. These corporations are used as holding companies, for consultancies, royalty income, foreign real estate, equipment leasing, and ownership of moveable assets such as airplanes and yachts.

Since 1984, a special BVI law has allowed quick and cheap formation of tax-free corporations to hold assets and execute offshore transactions.

The adoption of a comprehensive insurance law in 1994, which provides a blanket of confidentiality with statutory provisions for investigation of criminal offenses, made the British Virgin Islands even more attractive to international business.

One of the major attractions for BVI corporate registration was that true ownership was not a matter of public record. That has now changed. Under pressure from the Labour government in London the BVI colonial government enacted numerous new laws that compromised this former strict corporate privacy. In 2002, the BVI also signed a Tax Information Exchange Agreement with the United States. Anti-money laundering laws have been enacted as well, covering suspicious activities, and know-your-customer rules. The use of bearer shares was restricted in 2003, so much so that they remain "bearer shares" in name only.

BVI companies still are not subject to withholding tax on receipts of interest and dividends earned from U.S. sources. There are no capital gains or asset taxes. Use of a standard BVI corporation can be more profitable than an IBC, particularly if one wants to take advantage of the BVI double tax treaties in effect with Japan and Switzerland. The U.S. canceled a similar BVI tax treaty over a decade ago.

Conclusion

The BVI is suffering as an offshore center because of its status as a U.K. offshore territory under the control of the Labour government in London. That's where its orders come from and it follows them. But if you need an IBC to conduct your worldwide business, the British Virgin Islands will provide it – and all the service and maintenance you will ever need. They also offer trusts and limited partnerships.

Contacts

Ministry of Finance, Financial Services Inspectorate, Road Town, Tortola, B.V.I.; Tel.: +284-494-6430; Fax: +284-494-5016; Web site: www.bvi.org.

VP Bank (BVI), Ltd., 3076 Sir Francis Drake's Highway, P.O. Box 3463, Road Town, Tortola, B.V.I.; Tel.: +284-494-1100; Fax: +1-284-494-1199; E-mail: info.bvi@vpbank.com.

ILS Fiduciary, Ltd., P.O. Box 3085, Suite 6, Mill Mall, Wickhams Cay 1, Road Town, Tortola, B.V.I.; Tel.: +284-494-2999; Fax: +284-494-5076.

The AMS Group, Creque Building, Upper Main Street, P.O. Box 116, Road Town, Tortola, B.V.I.; Tel.: +284-494-3399; Fax: 284-494-3041.

Cloverdale Trust Services, P.O. Box 961, 30 DeCastro Street, Road Town, Tortola, B.V.I.; Tel.: +284-494-5808; Fax: +284-494-5811; Web site: www.owomfg.com/.

O'Neal, Webster, O'Neal, Myers, Fletcher, & Gordon, P.O. Box 961, 30 DeCastro Street, Road Town, Tortola, B.V.I.; Tel.: +284-494-5808; Fax: +284-494-5811; E-mail: admin@owomfg.com.

Nevis: Air-Tight Privacy and Fast Service

While it is not well known outside offshore circles, Nevis is one of the best tax-free asset haven jurisdictions in the world. That's because it has had in place, for over two decades, asset protection friendly laws allowing trusts, IBCs, and limited liability companies. Its courts have assembled an enviable record of support for offshore business and its government is a strong offshore supporter as well. It has few banks, but you bank elsewhere;

and any entity you need can be set up in a matter of a few days at minimal cost.

If there is any one haven country that has all the things you need for smooth offshore financial operations, it's Nevis (pronounced KNEE-vis). Best of all, Nevis has a no-nonsense banking and business privacy law that even the U.S. government can't crack. Its pro-offshore laws have existed for two decades – so there is plenty of experience and precedent in the local courts – and the legislative assembly keeps the applicable laws current. There are well established service companies that can do what you want, and many have U.S. offices for your convenience.

The "sovereign democratic federal state" of St. Christopher-Nevis (as its 1983 constitution ceremoniously describes it), has a governmental form and name almost larger than its population (45,000), and total land area (103 sq. miles).

Nevis has a no-nonsense banking and business privacy law that even the U.S. government can't crack.

But this tiny West Indies two-island nation, known to the natives as "St. Kitts-Nevis," has become very prominent in certain exclusive international financial circles. That's because Nevis has no taxes, extremely user-friendly incorporation and trust laws, and an official attitude of hearty welcome to foreign offshore corporations and asset protection trusts.

The islands are located 225 miles east of Puerto Rico and about 1,200 miles south of Miami. Until their September 19, 1983 declaration of independence, both were British colonies. They are still associate members of the British Commonwealth and recognize Her Majesty, Elizabeth II, as the titular head of state. She still appoints a local Governor General. The elected unicameral parliament sits in the capital of Basseterre on St. Kitts (population 35,000).

Very Independent Nevis

St. Kitts & Nevis suffer under none of the restrictions inflicted by London on British overseas territories. Their national sovereignty allows them to enact their own laws and make their own policies, free from outside pressures.

Nevis also has its own Island Assembly, and retained the constitutional right of secession from St. Kitts. For years, there were heated editorial demands for separation. Then in August 1998, defying international pleas, residents of the seven-mile-long island of Nevis voted on whether to secede from St. Kitts and become the smallest nation in the Western Hemisphere. Approval of two-thirds of the island's voters was required for secession. The vote was 2,427 for secession and 1,418 against, falling just short of two-thirds.

The vote was the culmination of a struggle that began with Britain's colonization in 1628. In 1882, Britain stripped Nevis of its legislature and wed it to St. Kitts. When the islands became independent in 1983, Nevis reluctantly joined in a federation with neighboring St. Kitts, but Nevisians insisted on a constitutional clause allowing them to break away. After years of complaining they are treated like second-class citizens by the federal government on St. Kitts, they invoked that right with the failed referendum.

St. Kitts and Nevis is already the smallest nation in the Western Hemisphere. The 15-member Caribbean Community (Caricom) had suggested that an independent Nevis could have problems joining the trade bloc. That stung in Nevis, where residents wondered how the Caricom could embrace Communist Cuba's Fidel Castro while condemning their right to freedom and independence. The United States also had urged against secession.

Nevis retains the right to secede, and proponents vow they will try again.

An Offshore Corporate Home

Based on the Island Assembly's adoption of the Business Corporation Act of 1984, Nevis has an established record of catering to foreign offshore corporations. The statute contains elements of the American State of Delaware's extremely liberal corporation laws, along with English commercial law. As a result, both U.S. attorneys and U.K. solicitors have no fear about navigating its provisions.

The corporation statute allows complete confidentiality for company officials and shareholders. There is no requirement for public disclosure of ownership, management, or financial status of a business. Although they must pay an annual fee of US$450, international business corporations are otherwise exempt from taxes – no withholding, stamps, fees, or taxes on income or foreign assets. Individually negotiated, government guaranteed tax holidays are available in writing, provided the IBC carries on no business locally. Official corporate start-up costs can be under US$1,000, including a minimum capitalization tax of US$200 and company formation fees of US$600. These low government levies compare very favorably with those imposed by other corporate-friendly havens like the high-profile, high-cost Cayman Islands.

Nevis corporation law's "re-domiciling provision" allows the smooth and instantaneous transfer of an existing corporation from any nation and retention of its original name and date of incorporation.

There are no exchange controls and no tax treaties with other nations. As a matter of official policy, the government of Nevis does not exchange tax or other information with any other foreign revenue service or government. Principal corporate offices and records may be maintained by Nevis companies anywhere in the world.

Nevis corporation law is somewhat unique in that it contains a very modern legal provision. It allows the international "portability" or transfer of an existing foreign company from its country of origin to the island. Known as the "re-domiciling provision," this allows the smooth and instantaneous transfer of an existing corporation from any nation and retention of its original name and date of incorporation. This is all done without interruption of business activity or corporate existence. The only requirement is the amendment of existing articles of incorporation to conform to local laws.

New company creation and registration is fast in Nevis. It's accomplished simply by paying the capitalization tax and fees mentioned earlier. Using Nevis corporate service offices in the U.S. (see the list below), your corporation or limited liability company can be registered and ready to do business within a few hours. You can do everything by phone, fax or wire. Your confirmation papers can be sent to you overnight from Nevis. Formal incorporation documents must be filed within ten days of receiving the confirmation papers. Corporate service firms will assist you with ready-made paperwork.

Small wonder that in ten years since the law's original adoption, thousands of foreign corporate owners have established their companies in Charles Town, Nevis.

Asset Protection Trusts

Building on their reputation for statutory corporate cordiality, in 1994, the Island Assembly adopted the Nevis International Trust Ordinance, a comprehensive, clear, and flexible asset protection trust (APT) law. This law is comparable – and in many ways superior – to that of the Cook Islands in the South Pacific, already well-known as an APT world center.

The new Nevis law incorporates the best features of the Cook Islands law, but is even more flexible. The basic aim of the law is to permit foreign citizens to obtain asset protection by transferring property titles to an APT established in Charlestown, Nevis.

Nevis simply is taking advantage of the worldwide growth in

medical, legal, and professional malpractice law suits. Legislative and judicial imposition of no fault personal liability on corporate officers and directors has become a nasty fact of business life. A Nevis trust places personal assets beyond the reach of foreign governments, litigious plaintiffs, creditors, and contingency-fee lawyers.

Under the 1994 law, the Nevis judiciary does not recognize any non-domestic court orders regarding its domestic APTs. This forces a foreign judgment creditor to start all over again, retrying in Nevis courts, with Nevis lawyers. A plaintiff who sues an APT must first post a US$25,000 bond with the government to cover court and others costs before a suit will be accepted for filing. The statute of limitations for filing legal challenges to a Nevis APT runs out two years from the date of the trust creation. In cases of alleged fraudulent intent, the law places the burden of proof on the foreign claimant.

All these factors combine to create an atmosphere in which a claimant confronted with a Nevis APT will settle for cents on the dollar, rather than attempt to fight an entire new battle in Nevis at great cost. This is especially useful to American doctors or other health providers who can shield their personal assets in an APT and may even decide to use the trust as a substitute for high cost malpractice insurance.

Nevis APT Formation

Nevis has a small international bar and local trust experts who understand and can assist in furthering APT objectives. The APT act has proven very popular, as a considerable number of trusts have been registered in Nevis.

Under the statute, the Nevis government does not require the filing of trust documents. They are not a matter of public record. The only public information you need to establish an APT is a standard form or letter naming the trustee, the date of trust creation, the date of the filing, and the name of the local trust company representing the APT. The only government fee is US$200 upon filing, and an equal annual fee to maintain the filing.

Much Broader Trust Powers

Under the provisions of the Nevis International Trust Ordinance, the same person can serve in the triple role of grantor, beneficiary, and protector of the APT. This allows far greater control over assets and income than U.S. domestic law permits. Generally, American law forbids you to create a trust for your own benefit. The basic structure of a foreign asset protection trust differs little from an Anglo-American trust.

The grantor creates the trust by executing a formal declaration describing the purposes, then transferring assets to be administered, according to the declaration, by the named trustees. Usually, there are three trustees named, two in the grantor's country and one in Nevis, the latter known as a "protector." Named trust beneficiaries can vary according to the grantor's estate planning objectives, and under Nevis law, the grantor may be the primary beneficiary. However, from the point of view of American courts and law, it's far better that a grantor not serve as a protector or trustee. That's because U.S. law (and the IRS) view a grantor in that capacity as having such a large degree of control over the assets as to call into question the validity of the trust. In many such cases, U.S. courts have ruled the entity to be an invalid "sham trust."

One device that a trust grantor can use to retain some control of trust assets is to form a limited partnership, then make the Nevis trust itself a limited partner.

Nevis requires the appointment of a trust protector who, as the title indicates, oversees its operation and ensures legal compliance. A protector does not manage the trust, but can sometimes veto actions. Nevis also allows a beneficiary to serve in the dual role as protector.

Tax and Legal Advantages for Americans

Under U.S. tax law, foreign asset protection trusts are tax neutral, as are domestic trusts. This means income from the trust is treated by the Internal Revenue Service as the grantor's personal income and taxed accordingly. Because the grantor retains some control over the transfer of his assets to any foreign trust, including those established in Nevis, U.S. gift taxes can usually be avoided. Although Nevis has no estate taxes, U.S. estate taxes are imposed on the value of trust assets for the grantor's estate, but all existing exemptions for combined marital assets can be used.

One device that a trust grantor can use to retain some control of trust assets is to form a limited partnership, then make the Nevis trust itself a limited partner. This arrangement allows you, as trust grantor, to retain active control over the assets you transfer to the Nevis trust/limited partner. It also adds further protection to the trust from creditors and other legal assaults.

Aside from the undoubted protection offered by the new Nevis International Trust Ordinance, this is a small nation with great economic and political stability, a highly reputable judicial system, favorable local tax laws, no language barrier, and excellent international communication and financial facilities.

Nevis also has enacted comprehensive anti-money laundering laws which are enforced. This has kept Nevis off the FATF blacklist of "dirty money" jurisdictions.

Contacts

Nevis Services, Ltd., 125 Half Mile Road, Suite 200, Redbank, New Jersey 08830; Tel.: 212-575-0818; Fax: 212-575-0812.

Morning Star Holdings, Ltd., Main Street, P.O. Box 556, Charlestown, Nevis, West Indies; Tel.: +869-469-1817; Fax: +869-469-1794.

Nevis Trust, Ltd., Springate, Suite 100 West, Government Road, Basseterre, St. Kitts, West Indies; Tel.: +869-469-1017.

Nevis Ministry of Finance, Offshore Service Center, Charlestown, Nevis, West Indies; Tel.: +869-469-0038; Fax: +869-469-0039.

Life Offshore Group, Charlestown, Nevis, West Indies; Tel.: +869-469-3774; Fax: +869-469-3776; Web site: www.life-international.com/.

AFM Services Group, Box 281, #22 Cayon, Basseterre, St. Kitts, West Indies; Tel.: +869-465-4459; Fax: +869-465-5893; Web site: www.boncamper.com/.

Belize: Polishing a Caribbean Gem

Belize, the only English-speaking nation in Central America, has had in place, for a decade, a series of offshore laws allowing asset protection trusts, IBCs, maritime registration, insurance – plus maximum financial privacy. Its parliament, courts, and government are very pro-offshore and regularly cultivate foreign business. An unusual feature is a special, tax-free retirement residency program for foreigners. But having said all that, this is definitely a Third-World country, with all the problems that entails.

In the Caribbean area after Panama and Nevis, Belize is a close third for banking privacy, low and no taxes and a business-friendly government. It should be on everyone's list of possible offshore financial bases.

Belize is the only English-speaking country in Central America. Its mixed population of 200,000 includes descendants of native Mayans, Chinese, East Indians, and Caucasians. Independent since 1981, its language came from its colonial days when it was known as "British Honduras." Situated south of Mexico and to the east of Guatemala, Belize is on the Caribbean seaboard. It has the largest barrier reef in the Western Hemisphere and great deep-sea diving. To the east, there's a sprinkle of Caribbean tropical islands included within the nation's borders. A few years ago, American television viewers discovered Belize as the locale for one of the first reality TV shows, "Temptation Island."

Belize retains many of the colonial customs and features familiar in places such as the Cayman Islands and Bermuda. The first settlers were probably British woodcutters, who in 1638, found the valuable commodity known as "Honduran mahogany." Bananas, sugar cane, and citrus fruit are the principal crops. Like many small countries dependent on primary commodities, Belize recently recognized the benefits of introducing tax-haven financial services to boost its income.

Clean Money

American government officials have had a case of nerves over Belize. Some feared that the sleepy little capital town of Belmopan would become a prime site for U.S. tax evasion and money laundering. But more recently, the Belizean government has cooperated with the U.S. in several drug and money laundering cases, although extradition from Belize is still difficult. The nation's clean money reputation was also boosted by adoption of a strong anti-money laundering law that has been enforced vigorously.

There are no local income taxes, personal or corporate, and no currency exchange control. Belize is also home to major growth in the shipping registry business.

In 1992, the Belize National Assembly enacted up-to-date legislation seeking to make the country a competitive offshore financial center. Drafters combed tax haven laws worldwide and came up with a series of minimal corporate and tax requirements that could well fit your business needs. The new laws include the Trust Act, which allows a high level of asset protection, great freedom of action by the trustee, and no taxes on income earned outside Belize. There is also a statute allowing the creation of international business companies, corporations that can be formed in less than a day for about US$700. You only need one shareholder and/or director, whose name can be shielded from public view.

Since 1990, when the International Business Companies Act

became law, foreigners have registered about 4,000 IBCs. That's a relatively small number compared to a place like the Cayman Islands, but the number is growing. There are no local income taxes, personal or corporate, and no currency exchange control. Belize is also home to major growth in the shipping registry business. Other laws favor offshore insurance companies, limited liability partnerships, and banking.

BHI Corporation – A Big Presence

VISA credit cards are issued by Belize Bank, Ltd., owned by Belize Holdings Incorporated (BHI), a holding company with banking and financial services in Belize. BHI also has major stakes in local Belizean telecommunications, electricity, hotels, citrus, and other industries.

The principal owner of BHI is Lord Michael Ashcroft, a sometimes Brit (he has homes in London, the U.S., and Belize City) multimillionaire described by the *Wall Street Journal* as an "unconventional and sometimes controversial deal maker." BHI stock is publicly traded in the U.S. on the NASDAQ stock exchange. The Belize Bank is the largest commercial banking operation in Belize, and is a correspondent of the Bank of America.

Over the last decade, the government of Belize has carefully and systematically established the nation as an offshore haven that welcomes foreign investment and foreign nationals. It has enacted a series of laws crafted to protect financial privacy and promote creation of offshore trusts and international business corporations (IBCs). It has an attractive special residency program aimed at retirement bound foreign citizens.

Having visited Belize twice, I can attest that it's definitely "Third World," but people are amazingly friendly and even oceanfront real estate is still relatively cheap. Belize is one of the few remaining independent nations proud to hold itself out as a tax and asset protection haven.

London Pressures

A member of the Commonwealth and a former British colony, independent since 1981, Belize still has strong ties with London and is thus susceptible to U.K. Foreign Office pressures. In June 2000, shortly after the OECD "harmful tax competition" blacklisting of Belize, London made known that future aid of all kinds, including debt forgiveness, would depend in part on Belize's willingness to cooperate in modifying some of its tax-haven attractions. The U.K. Labour government pointedly objected to certain tax breaks Belize had granted to billionaire Lord Michael Ashcroft, also a controversial British Conservative Party peer and former Tory treasurer. As noted, Ashcroft has extensive business holdings in Belize where he makes a second home away from London. At one point, London suspended debt relief to Belize in response to Ashcroft's alleged tax breaks and those of other favored offshore investors in Belize.

Belize bowed to the pressure by promising to somewhat tighten its offshore regulations. This subsequently included repeal of the Belize instant economic citizenship program and limitations on the issuance and use of bearer shares.

In 2004 the Belize government went along with requests by the U.S. IRS to freeze bank funds belonging to Internet gambling operations based in Belize owned by Americans. The Belize Supreme Court reversed the cash freeze, ruling that no charges had been filed against the parties by the U.S. government.

Offshore Industry Expands

In spite of OECD's and London's carping, Belize's offshore industry continues to grow, providing offshore financial services to a largely nonresident clientele. These services include international business company and offshore trust formation and administration; international banking services, including foreign currency bank accounts and international VISA cards; fund management, accounting and secretarial services; captive insurance; and ship registration.

A sympathetic government continues to work closely with the Belize Offshore Practitioners Association in drafting future legislation. Areas under consideration include offshore banking, captive insurance, limited duration companies, protected cell companies, limited partnerships, as well as other legal entities to expand further Belize's role as one of the few remaining independent nations offering complete offshore services.

So far, Belizean banking is tiny, but secret by force of law. There are only three banks. Deposits have not soared as quickly as expected and this subtropical paradise has not become the "hot" international tax and asset haven some expected it would be. Nevertheless, privacy protection here rivals even that of airtight Nevis. Some banking clients here complain of a third world attitude on the part of Belize bankers, with slow service and failure to protect client privacy due to sloppy work.

Tax-Free Residency

A good example of a Belize welcome of offshore persons is the Retired Persons Incentive Act that came into effect in 2000 and is implemented by the Belize Tourism Board. The program, which resembles the popular pensionado program in Panama, is designed to attract foreign retirees and foreign capital.

Known as the "qualified retired persons" (QRP) Program, the law offers significant tax incentives to those willing to become permanent residents, but not full citizens. The program is aimed primarily at residents of the U.S., Canada, and the U.K., but is open to all.

A "qualified retired person" is exempted from all taxes on income from sources outside Belize. QRPs can own and operate their own international business based in Belize exempt from all local taxes. Local income earned within Belize is taxed at a graduated rate of 15-45% and QRPs need a work permit in order to engage in purely domestic business activities. For QRPs, import duties are waived for personal effects, household goods and for a motor vehicle or other transport, such as an airplane or boat. There is no minimum time that must be spent in Belize, and QRPs can maintain their status so long as they maintain a permanent local residence such as a small apartment or condo.

To qualify for the QRP Program, an applicant must be 45 years of age or older and prove personal financial ability to support oneself and any dependants. A spouse and dependents (18 and younger) qualify along with the head of household at no extra fee. Initial fees for the program are US$700, plus US$100 for an ID card upon application approval. Minimum financial requirements include an annual income of at least US$24,000 from a pension, annuity, or other sources outside Belize. By the 15th of each month, at least US$2,000 must be deposited in the QRP's Belize account, or by April 1 annually, US$24,000 must be placed in deposit.

For more information about the QRP Program, contact the following agencies:

Belize Tourist Board, New Central Bank Building, Level 2, Gabourel Lane, P.O. Box 325, Belize City, Belize; Tel.: +501-231-913; Fax: +501-231-943; E-mail: info@travelbelize.org.

Ministry of Tourism, Constitution Drive, Belmopan, Belize; Tel.: +501-823-393; Fax: +501-823-815; E-mail: tourismdpt@btl.net.

Conclusion

In spite of British, U.S., and OECD pressures, Belize is not about to enact income or corporate taxes that would drive away foreign investors and residents. In this relatively impoverished third world country, the offshore sector is a needed and highly valued source of foreign capital that has strong government support. Any modifications to offshore laws are likely to be minimal and mainly window dressing to mute foreign critics.

The offshore professional sector in Belize certainly is not comparable to the highly developed Cayman Islands as an offshore haven, but neither has it sold out to outside pressures. Its laws offer a full array of well-developed offshore entities for asset protection and as investment vehicles, trusts, IBCs, and limited liability companies. Its one weakness is its small banking community, but you can just as easily locate your Belize IBC bank account in Vienna or London, where private banking is an art.

Contacts

Belize Bank, Ltd., Belize City, Belize; Tel.: +501-227-7132; E-mail: bblbz@belizebank.com. Largest full service bank in Belize with information and services for international and local clientele.

BHI Offshore Financial Services, Belize City, Belize; Tel.: +501-27-7018; E-mail: bblbcsl@btl.net. Investment management, brokerage services with Belize Bank, information, and offshore banking.

Atlantic Bank, Ltd., Freetown Road, Belize City, Belize; Tel.: +501-227-7301; E-mail: atlantic@btl.net. Full range of offshore investment and banking services.

Avalon Trust Co., Ltd., P.O. Box 1113, Northern Highway, Belize City, Belize; Tel.: +501-2-33338; E-mail: mscba@catsa.com.bz.

Barclays Bank, PLC, Belize City, Belize; Tel.: +501-227-7211; E-mail: barclaysbz@btl.net. Offers a wide range of services and products for both international and domestic clients.

Belize Corporate Services Center, Ltd., 60 Market Square, P.O. Box 364, Belize City, Belize; Tel.: +501-2-72390; Fax: +501-2-77018. Official Registrar of IBCs.

Central Bank of Belize, P.O. Box 852, Belize City, Belize; Tel.: +501-2-77216; Fax: +501-2-70221.

Belize Offshore Center, 35 Barrack Road, Belize City, Belize; Web site: www.belizeoffshore.com.

KPMG Corporate Services (Belize), Web site: www.kpmgbelize.com.

Emerald Futures Real Estate, Great House Inn, #13 Cork Street, #7, P.O. Box 1442, Belize City, Belize; Tel.: +501-223-6559; Mobile: +501-614-6818 / -1600; Fax: +501-223-6087; E-mail: realgem@btl.net.

The United States Virgin Islands

It's not generally known, but under a unique special federal income tax arrangement applying only to the U.S. Territory of the Virgin Islands, it is possible for U.S. nationals and others who make the islands their main residence to enjoy substantial personal and business tax benefits. These lower taxes make the islands an offshore tax haven option for very wealthy U.S. citizens, U.S. entrepreneurs, and foreign nationals seeking U.S. citizenship.

Little Known U.S. Tax Haven

The U.S. Virgin Islands – St. Croix, St. Thomas, and St. John – have been territorial possessions of the United States since they were purchased from Denmark in 1917. The Virgin Islands are administered by the U.S. Department of the Interior under a legal code called the Organic Act. The Naval Service Appropriations Act of 1922 (48 USC 1397), provided in part that: "The income tax laws in force in the United States shall be likewise in force in the Virgin Islands of the United States, except that the proceeds of such taxes shall be paid to the treasuries of said islands."

U.S. Virgin Islands residents and corporations pay their federal taxes on their worldwide income to the Virgin Islands Internal Revenue Bureau (IRB), not the U.S. Internal Revenue Service. Persons who are legal residents of the islands, who are born in the V.I., or those people who become naturalized U.S. citizens in the V.I., for purposes of U.S. federal gift and estate taxes, are treated not as *nonresidents of the U.S.* Since the V.I. has no estate or gift taxes, this means that upon death the estates of such persons owe zero federal or state estate or gift taxes.

In an attempt to attract investment, the Industrial Development

Commission of the government of the V.I. grants generous tax relief packages which include a 90% exemption on corporate federal income taxes. This tax grant package, which is usually offered for a period of 10 to 15 years (with possible 5 year extensions), is available to V.I.-chartered corporations, partnerships and limited liability companies on their worldwide income.

As an example, I will establish a V.I. corporation called Worldwide, Inc. Worldwide, Inc. has a ten million dollar portfolio with investments in a wide range of activities. Last year, Worldwide, Inc. did so well that it ended up with net taxable income after all possible deductions of US$2,000,000.

Tax computations: (Based on US$2,000,000 taxable income)

15% x $ 50,000	US$ 7,500
25% x $ 25,000	US$ 6,250
34% x $ 25,000	US$ 8,500
37% x $1,900,000	US$ 703,000
Total tax liability without exemption	US$ 725,250
90% Exemption	US$ 675,000
Worldwide, Inc. net taxes owed	US$ 50,250

If the principals of Worldwide, Inc. are V.I. residents, the tax laws of the V.I. government apply a 90% exemption to individual residents on income derived from dividends of the beneficiary corporation. If Worldwide, Inc. is a subchapter S corporation, owned by a single individual, the total income tax liability on US$2,000,000 at the maximum U.S. (39.6% x 90% exemption) tax rate would be US$79,200. Because the V.I. has no state or local income tax, the individual would get to keep US$1,920,800. If our investor was a regular U.S. resident living on the mainland, he or she would owe the IRS US$792,000, plus state and local taxes which could amount to close to US$200,000.

For over 40 years, a few U.S. investors, with business activities ranging from petroleum production, aluminum processing, hotel and other tourism activities, banking, insurance, and other financial services, have taken advantage of V.I. tax laws and enjoyed income with very little taxes.

In an attempt to attract investment, the Industrial Development Commission of the government of the V.I. grants generous tax relief packages which include a 90% exemption on corporate federal income taxes.

The U.S. Virgin Islands offers three types of entities that are either fully or partially exempt from V.I. taxes and U.S. federal income taxes. One type of entity is a V.I. corporation that obtains the benefits of the Virgin Islands Industrial Development Program for its business activities in the V.I. These companies are fully exempt from most local taxes and receive a 90% exemption from V.I. income taxes. They also enjoy a special customs duty rate of 1%. These companies are generally not subject to U.S. federal income taxes on their V.I. operations. In 2003, nearly 100 V.I. corporations, with over 3,500 employees, enjoyed benefits from this V.I. tax provision.

Another tax-free entity is a V.I. foreign sales corporation (FSC) that pays no local taxes except for a nominal annual fee. Thousands of Virgin Islands FSCs have been set up by U.S. exporters as a means to reduce U.S. federal income taxes on their export sales by about 15%. For foreign persons, even more generous exemptions are available through the use of the third type of tax-free entity: a V.I. exempt company. The Virgin Islands is the only jurisdiction in the world where a non-U.S. person can establish a tax-free entity under the U.S. flag. Virgin Islands exempt companies are often used as holding companies for portfolio investments, for the ownership of aircraft that are registered with the U.S. Federal Aviation Administration, or as captive insurance companies. There are a number of other offshore tax-planning structures that can take advantage of V.I. exempt companies.

The Virgin Islands government also has established tax benefits to financial management companies. The investors or partners of this entity established a V.I. corporation to manage their worldwide assets. Each investor established bona fide V.I. residence by renting or buying a home or condo, registering to vote in the V.I., and designating their stateside home as their secondary residence.

These investors took legal steps to confirm their new principal residence by canceling their stateside voter registration and their state and county homestead exemptions, and moving their business and personal affairs to the V.I.

This arrangement allows the investors to live in their second home anywhere in the U.S. for the spring, summer, and fall, then come home to the Virgin Islands for the winter, where they play golf and tennis, sail and swim, all under the protection of the U.S. flag. These exceptional people enjoy the unique legal privilege of paying 10% of their federal income taxes and no state or local taxes.

Moving your residence to the V.I. is no more difficult than moving from one U.S. state to another. The V.I. has a well-developed infrastructure. The V.I. legal system is subject to the U.S. constitution. The U.S. court system, postal service, currency, and customs and immigrations laws serve the islands. There is no restriction against maintaining a second home elsewhere inside or outside of the U.S., as long as you maintain principal residence in the V.I.

This little known tax "loophole" gateway certainly is worth considering for any wealthy, high net-worth person considering U.S. naturalization, or any current U.S. citizen willing to relocate to a warmer climate to legally avoid burdensome taxes. If you have a net worth of US$1 million or more, this may be for you.

Obviously, the U.S. Virgin Islands tax exemptions are unique in that they require a foreign or U.S. person to reorder their personal and business lives in a major way. It means moving and establishing a personal residence and/or business headquarters in the Virgin Islands. But this is a comparatively small price to pay to gain the substantial tax savings that can result from such a move. In 2004 the need to reorder one's personal life in order to qualify for this tax break was emphasized when the IRS prosecuted a Massachusetts resident who had failed to establish USVI residency, but tried to claim its tax benefits using a local IBC.

It's not surprising that the OECD has denounced the U.S. Virgin Islands as America's own version of "unfair tax competition."

Contacts

U.S. Virgin Islands Government Web site:
www.usvi.net/usvi/tax.html.

Attorneys:

Marjorie Rawls Roberts, PC, LLB, JD, AB, P.O. Box 8809, St. Thomas, U.S. Virgin Islands 00801; Tel.: +340-776-7235; Fax: +340-776-7496; E-mail: jorieroberts@worldnet.att.net; Web site: www.lawyers.com/robertslaw.

Denis Kleinfeld, JD, CPA, The Kleinfeld Law Firm, Suntrust International Building, One SE 3rd Avenue, Suite 1940, Miami, Florida 33131; Tel.: 305-375-9515; Fax: 305-358-6541; E-mail: denis_kleinfeld@kleinfeld.com.

Commonwealth of The Bahamas

During the 20th Century, these islands off the southeast coast of the U.S. blossomed into a major tax and asset protection haven, especially for citizens of the nearby U.S. It offered tax exemption for foreigners and a series of well-crafted laws allowing IBCs, trusts, offshore banks, and insurance – all wrapped in maximum financial privacy protected by law.

Because so many Americans used The Bahamas as their favorite offshore haven, the islands came under heavy pressure from the U.S. government and the IRS because of suspected tax evasion. Then, there is the issue of drug smuggling and money laundering. Starting in 2000, a former Bahamian government adopted a series of U.S.-demanded laws that largely disrupted these cozy arrangements but seriously diminished the islands role as an offshore haven. These changes were topped off with a Tax Information Exchange Agreement with the U.S. Goodbye, financial privacy!

It's still a nice place to retire, vacation, or have a second home, but other, more secure banking, investment, tax, and asset havens can be found elsewhere.

Geography Determines History, Then and Now

Geography has always played a major part in determining Bahamian history. Located at the northern edge of the Caribbean, this chain of hundreds of islands lies in the North Atlantic Ocean, southeast of Florida and northeast of Cuba. The Bahamas archipelago at its nearest point is about 50 miles east of the United States.

Arawak Indians inhabited the islands in 1492 when Christopher Columbus made his first landfall in the New World on the island of San Salvador in the eastern Bahamas. After observing the shallow sea around the islands, it is reported that he said "baja mar" (low water or sea), and thus named the area The Bahamas, or The Islands of the Shallow Sea. (By the way, this nation's official name is two words – "The Bahamas," and that's with a capital 'T'.)

English settlement began in 1647 and the islands became a British colony in 1783. Its population now is about 280,000. Since attaining independence from the U.K. in 1973, The Bahamas have prospered through tourism, international banking, and investment management. But because of its geography, the country is a major transshipment point for illegal drugs to the U.S. and for smuggling illegal migrants into the U.S. And, as you will see, having the United States as your immediate neighbor has not been easy for The Bahamas.

The Bahamas – An Offshore Powerhouse No More?

Start with these facts. The Bahamas grew from a tiny offshore tax haven comprising a few branches of foreign banks in the mid-1960s to a world banking powerhouse by the year 2000. The country's legislation and regulatory structure, comparatively highly skilled workforce, and its friendly, pro-business government attracted some of the most prestigious financial institutions from around the globe.

The Bahamas is a tax haven. There are no business or income taxes, although various registration and transfer fees amount to a tax estimated by some to approach 20%, depending on the nature of the transactions.

The Bahamas is, and has been for several decades, home to a well-developed offshore financial center. Until a few years ago, it had more than 400 banks and trust companies, 580 mutual funds, and 60 insurance companies operating here. It also had registered approximately 100,000 IBCs, most for nonresidents.

The asset base of The Bahamas' banking center was in excess of US$200 billion, positioning it among the top ten countries in the world, behind Switzerland, the U.S., the U.K., Japan, and the Cayman Islands, among others. Private banking, portfolio management, and mutual fund administration are important. Until recently, banks from 36 countries were licensed to conduct business within or from The Bahamas. Licensees included about 100 euro-currency branches of international banks and trusts, as well as 168 Bahamian incorporated banking institutions. Sixty percent of all licensed banks offer trust services in addition to their regular banking operations.

Of the 120,000-strong Bahamian work force, about 5,000 work in offshore banking and trust companies, accounting for an estimated 20% of the gross domestic product. (Largely due to increased offshore financial activity, the Bahamian economy grew by 40% from US$3.2 billion in 1992 to US$4.5 billion in 2000.)

The Bahamas is a tax haven. There are no business or income taxes, although various registration and transfer fees amount to a tax estimated by some to approach 20%, depending on the nature of the transactions.

Since 2000, 200 of 223 private banks in The Bahamas have closed and 30,000 international business companies have been stricken from the official register. In 2003, in one three-month period, Bank of Scotland, Coutts & Co., Lloyds Bank, McDermott International, Citibank's commercial banking operations, and MeesPierson and Fortis Fund Services (The Bahamas), Ltd. all announced they intended to leave The Bahamas. The local news media attributed these departures, at least in part, to stricter money laundering legislation and a weakening of banking and financial secrecy.

Drastic, Unnecessary Change

So, until the year 2000, The Bahamas stood out as one of the world's premier asset and tax haven nations.

But in June 2000, the former Free National Movement (FNM) government (which was defeated for re-election in May 2002) systematically began to dismantle and dilute the islands' offshore legal framework that had been carefully designed to protect financial privacy and offshore wealth brought into the islands.

This signaled retreat from tax haven status by the FNM government was a defeatist response to the double "honor" of being listed on two blacklists issued by the FATF and the OECD. These outsiders charged The Bahamas with damaging "international financial stability," being uncooperative in combating money laundering, and engaging in "harmful tax competition," meaning levying no taxes on foreigners. They were threatened with undefined "stern countermeasures" if they failed to open bank and other financial records to foreign tax and criminal investigators and to make numerous other changes in their offshore laws.

Washington Pressure

Instead of fighting back and telling these outsiders to "buzz off," the FNM government rapidly pushed through Parliament, over strong minority opposition, a host of statutory changes that substantially weakened the very financial privacy and asset protection that had attracted to the islands tends of thousands of offshore bank accounts, international business companies, and asset protection trusts. These new laws admittedly were drafted with the direct assistance of "financial experts" from London and Washington. The government also said it had accepted "a generous offer" of technical assistance from the U.S. Treasury Department.

This capitulation to Washington's demands echoed a crisis in the early 1980s when the late Prime Minister, Lynden O. Pindling, accused of drug dealing, was confronted by an angry U.S. government that threatened sanctions against The Bahamas. Although Pindling was cleared, he was forced to grant U.S. law and drug enforcement officers diplomatic immunity and free passage through the archipelago, plus some limited access to secret offshore banks of some accused criminals.

At one point, the executive director of The Bahamas Financial Services Board told the press the government did not want the islands to be known as an "offshore tax haven" any longer, but rather as a "highly competitive, low-tax international financial center." But the chairman of that board, Ian Fair, warned The Bahamas blacklisting was "a smoke screen for rich countries' concerns about competition from small offshore banking industries." Fair cautioned, "I think we have to be careful that we don't go too far."

The Progressive Labour Party (PLP) parliamentary opposition rightfully argued that repeal or change of most of the offshore laws that brought huge investments and assets to The Bahamas would indeed result in capital flight, as individual offshore bank accounts were closed and financial activity fled elsewhere. Dr. Peter Maynard, president of The Bahamas Bar Association charged that what the OECD and FATF demanded "would be disastrous, a total devastation of the financial sector. It will have an affect on the entire financial services sector and will mean many jobs lost." (Several months later, the Bar association endorsed the government's actions.)

Subsequently, many private banks and offshore financial firms announced their departure, citing the new laws as reason for their exodus. In parliament, Prime Minister Ingraham admitted that the crackdown would cause a loss of millions of dollars in annual revenue from the incorporation, registration and operation of international business corporations alone.

PLP opposition members of parliament called on the government to resign over the OECD and FATF debacle, claiming that the blacklisting was directly related to the government's prolonged inability to deal with drug trafficking. Privately, Bahamian sources said government figures were implicated in numerous questionable, but highly profitable, financial activities, a situation the U.S. was holding over their heads unless they acted as Washington demanded. Throughout this drama, U.S. government representatives hovered over Bahamian officials in Nassau, pressuring them with Washington's point of view.

In May 2002, the PLP opposition won control of parliament and a new PLP Prime Minister, Perry Christie, took office. All these new laws became a major political issue with the PLP, charging they had damaged the offshore financial community. Although Perry and the PLP promised to review and reverse many of these laws, they have failed to do so. Indeed, they went ahead with the U.S. Tax Information Exchange Agreement initiated by the defeated Ingraham and his FNM government.

New Laws, Amendments to Old Laws

Among the many new laws, the "Evidence (Proceedings in Other Jurisdictions) Act 2000" removed the requirement that requested evidence could not be released to another country until a court proceeding had begun in the requesting nation. Evidence can now be released for foreign preliminary investigations. This new law appears to permit Bahamian enforcement of U.S. civil forfeiture orders for the first time. The government also forced through another law allowing it to confiscate cash and assets under a U.S.-style civil forfeiture procedure that permits freezing of bank and other accounts. Still another law empowers Bahamian courts to extradite criminal suspects during investigations before trial. It should be noted that The Bahamas already had in force mutual legal assistance treaties with the U.S., U.K., and Canada.

Money Laundering

Existing anti-money laundering laws were toughened to make violations punishable by a possible sentence of 20 years in jail and/or a US$100,000 fine for each instance. A new "Currency Declaration Act" requires reporting of all cash or investment transfers, in or out of the islands in excess of US$10,000. The Central Bank also was given broad new powers to regulate off-shore banks, their registration, operation, and reporting. In a radical move, for the first time, the law allows foreign bank inspectors to conduct on-site and offsite examinations of the accounts in bank branches or subsidiaries located in The Bahamas.

The Bahamas also created a new police "financial intelligence unit" modeled on the U.S. Treasury Financial Crimes Enforcement Network (FinCEN). Opposition members of parliament criticized the FIU's powers as far too broad, charging there are no provisions to prevent political "fishing trips" or "witch hunts" by government police. This unit can request ("order" might be a better word) a bank to freeze any funds suspected of being part of criminal activity for up to 72 hours, while a secret "monitoring order" is sought by police to confiscate money or block transactions. In such cases, all other financial confidentiality laws are waived. The FIU issued U.S.-style rules requiring "suspicious activity reporting" by all financial institutions.

Still other laws require all banks to verify the true identity of customers for whom Bahamian intermediaries open accounts. Since 2000, Bahamian banks have been using special U.S. cash flow analysis software to detect possible money laundering. Offshore financial trustees and attorneys are now required to maintain records of beneficial owners of offshore trusts and international business corporations. Previously, professional attorney-client privilege rules prevented revealing such information.

IBCs Under Fire

Until 2002, IBCs had not been required to disclose the identities of shareholders or other detailed business information unless forced to do so by a court order. Now, the right of IBCs to issue and use bearer shares has been repealed and all IBCs are required to submit to the government the true identities and addresses of directors. There are currently more than 106,000 international business corporations in The Bahamas, with about 16,000 added each year. Secrecy of ownership undoubtedly was a large factor in attracting these IBCs, and now that has ended.

Conclusion

In spite of pledges to reform some of the harsh laws adopted, the PLP government has not moved to make any major changes. There has been a continuing exodus of banks, IBCs and offshore professional service firms due to the restrictive impact of the new laws.

Even though The Bahamas remains in name, and in fact, an offshore tax haven, it remains in considerable internal governmental and political turmoil. The mass exodus of so many Bahamian financial community members speaks volumes about those who judged events first hand. The best financial and investment climates are those that enjoy some degree of predictability, and that's not The Bahamas today.

My advice for now is to scratch The Bahamas off your list of offshore tax and asset haven nations. Things may change someday but if you were thinking of using the islands as a base of offshore operations, forget it. If you have financial accounts or other interests located there, consider moving them to a safe place. But there may be some attractive real estate deals in The Bahamas soon, as the exodus of the offshore community continues in earnest.

Contacts

Government:

Securities Commission of The Bahamas, Charlotte House, Charlotte Street, P.O. Box N-8347, Nassau, The Bahamas; Tel.: +242-356-6291.

Central Bank of The Bahamas, P.O. Box N-4868, Nassau, The Bahamas; Tel.: +242-322-2193/6; Fax: +242-323-7795.

Investment & Banks:

Alliance Investment Management, Ltd., Suite 304, Beaumont House, Bay Street, P.O. Box SS-6545, Nassau, The Bahamas; Tel.: +242-326-7333; Fax: +242-326-7336; E-mail: info@ allianceinvest.com; Web site: www.allianceinvest.com; Contact: Julian Brown.

International Trade & Investments, Limited, Tel.: 800-370-8921; Fax: +242-356-2037.

Pictet Bank & Trust, Charlotte House, P.O. Box N-4837, Nassau, The Bahamas; Tel.: +242-302-2222; Fax: +242-323-7986; Contact: Yves Lourdin.

Attorneys:

Higgs & Johnson, Sandringham House, 83 Shirley Street, P.O. Box N-3247, New Providence, The Bahamas; Tel.: +242-322-8571/9; Fax: +242-328-7727; E-mail: nassau@higgsjohnson.com; Web site: www.higgsjohnson.com/.

McKinney, Turner & Co., Attorneys at Law, Oakbridge House, West Hill Street, Nassau, The Bahamas; Tel.: +242-322-891475; Fax: +242-328-8326; Contact: Michael Turner.

Chapter 9
Emigrate to Canada, Leave Taxes Behind

SUMMARY: Canada is not an offshore tax or asset haven. But in combination with several other factors, Canadian law offers the possibility, especially for Americans, of ending having to pay U.S. income and other taxes for the rest of your life.

The process by which this can be accomplished is called "expatriation" and many consider this drastic and extreme. It is. Here I explain how expatriation can be accomplished, legally and consistent with U.S. and Canadian law. Expatriation requires professional advice and lots of careful pre-planning. It also requires determination, will, and a lot of courage. Read on.

First, I must apologize for the lawyer-like nature this chapter.

Much of what you will read here is rather dry and legalistic. But that's because the process described must be done very carefully and completely in accordance with the laws of two nations. I am going to walk you through all the steps required, so that you will understand exactly what must be done and how to do it.

Also keep in mind an absolute must – you must obtain competent professional advice to guide you every step of the way. Check the end of this chapter for professionals in whom you can have confidence. I know them and I recommend them.

Expatriate to Canada

Canada is one of the premier nations in the world for exercising the most effective wealth protection strategy – *expatriation*. But for a U.S. citizen (or anyone else), expatriation means eventually renouncing U.S. or other national citizenship, then becoming a foreign national – becoming a Canadian.

Radical? You bet.

---

*Canada is one of the premier nations in the world for exercising the most effective wealth protection strategy – **expatriation**.*

Expatriation is an extreme measure meant for those who have the most to lose in continuing to pay high taxes in their home country.

First, understand that Canada is not a tax haven like the many tax havens described in these pages. Except in this one instance of enticing new immigrants to Canada, as I explain in this chapter, it doesn't offer tax breaks to foreigners. But this one instance can be very important in saving, instead of paying, taxes for you.

Wealthy Americans stand to lose millions to the IRS. The U.S. government could take up to 55% of the estate assets you wish to leave to your children – and that's after having paid up to 40% of your earnings in federal income taxes every year – all your working life. Throw in state and local income and sales taxes, and you stand to lose in taxes well over half your earnings during your lifetime. For those with estates worth millions, the prospect of having their money enrich the bloated coffers of the IRS should be enough to force them to take drastic avoidance measures.

One of the options wealthy Americans are increasingly turning to is expatriation. Perhaps surprising, they are expatriating to Canada. Some immigrants are welcomed more than others for a variety of reasons – and you may be just the type of new citizen Canada welcomes with open arms.

Expatriation is a drastic measure, but it may be the only escape for the wealthy. This is definitely not a strategy for everyone, but it may make sense for you. There are certain trade-offs involved, and each must be researched and considered carefully. Most importantly, you must do it correctly to make it work – so make sure you get qualified professional help if you choose to make this radical change.

Why Canada?

Canada and the United States have long been staunch, if somewhat uneasy, allies. These friendly neighbors share the largest undefended border in the world, although post 9/11 anti-terrorist measures have made border crossing slower and more cumbersome.

Every day, thousands choose Canada as an excellent place to visit, do business, even to live – and with good reason. Economists at the United Nations researched the best nations in which to live and work. They judged Canada number one. Japan came in second, the United States only sixth, and the United Kingdom tenth. Canada has a high standard of living, minimal social class divisions, low crime rate, clean environment, beautiful scenery, economic opportunities, government support services, extensive infrastructure, comprehensive shopping and sports facilities, affordable housing, and the generous hospitality of the Canadian people.

A distinct advantage that comes with this new citizenship is the international official acceptance of the Canadian passport, one of the most respected in the world. And as citizens of a member nation of the British Commonwealth, Canadians are allowed to enter Britain without obtaining a prior visa, and entry to Britain allows travel access to all the nations of the European Union.

The downside: long harsh winters and a continuing English-French problem in the Province of Quebec.

But the major reason to choose Canada is because its laws allow its new citizens, those who have a certain level of wealth, legally to escape Canadian income and estate taxes.

Immigration in Canada

The virtues of Canada as the place to live are known around the world. Recent immigration figures attest to the fact. In recent years, for example, Canada's population of 30 million has increased annually by about 200,000 immigrants. A modern nation built by European settlers, Canada has increased its flow of immigrants by three-fold since 1985. The top sources of immigrants have been the United States, India, Vietnam, Poland, the United Kingdom, the Philippines, Guyana, and El Salvador. The increasing numbers have also included many wealthy Asians, especially residents of Hong Kong, although many of them have gone home as dual citizens since 1997 when Hong Kong was returned to Chinese control.

About Canadian Taxes

Before I get to the good news – the big tax break for new immigrants – you should know that the Canadian tax system is tough and comprehensive. Combined Canadian federal and provincial personal income taxes range from 45 to 54%, depending on the province. The Canadian tax burden has been a direct cause of capital flight, which is relatively unrestricted.

Although residents get hit with stiff taxes, unlike the U.S., Canada does not tax the worldwide income or foreign assets of its *nonresident* citizens. Canada taxes only the worldwide income of its *resident* citizens and resident aliens who live in Canada at any time during the calendar year. "Residents," by law, include individuals, corporations and trusts located in Canada.

Tax-Free New Resident Loophole

However tough taxes may be for the average Canadian citizen, wealthy, new immigrants can take advantage of a huge loophole available only to them. This major tax saving was deliberately written into law in order to encourage wealthy new arrivals. This preference for new citizens with substantial investment capital can translate into huge tax savings and far-reaching financial gains for you and your business. Here's why:

1) A qualified immigrant accepted for eventual Canadian citizenship is eligible for a *complete personal income tax moratorium* for the first five calendar years of residence in Canada – you pay no taxes if the source of your income is an offshore, non-Canadian trust or corporation. You can easily create such offshore entities (in any of the many offshore havens I describe in this book) before you move to Canada and become a citizen. (As a general rule, Canada has a three-year residence requirement after immigrant admission before citizenship is granted, but a five-year residence is required in order to be eligible for this very special tax break).

2) Canadian citizens and resident aliens employed by certain "international financial centers" are forgiven 50% of all income taxes.

3) Canada has abolished all national death (estate) taxes.

4) After living five years tax-free in Canada as a new citizen, you can move your residence to another country and you then pay taxes only on income earned or paid from within Canada. *You pay no taxes on your worldwide income.*

A qualified immigrant accepted for eventual Canadian citizenship is eligible for a **complete personal income tax moratorium** *for the first five calendar years of residence in Canada*

But be aware: a naturalized Canadian citizen who lives ten consecutive years or more outside Canada can be stripped of citizenship at the discretion of the government, although this is very rare.

How Americans Can Stop Paying U.S. Taxes

Let's suppose you, as an American citizen (or resident alien), wish to sell an established business, or convert fixed assets into liquid cash for investment or other purposes.

Depending on how long you have held the property and how the liquidation deal is structured, you may face U.S. capital gains taxes at the current maximum rate of 20%. Depending on your tax bracket, income taxes can be 40% or more. In either case, a major part of the cash proceeds from the sale or conversion will be devoured by the U.S. Internal Revenue Service and state tax authorities – before you ever see a thin dime.

How can you avoid this enormous tax burden?

What if you transfer the title of the U.S. business to a foreign trust (with the property owner – you – as the beneficiary) or to a corporation you control, conveniently located in a low or no-tax offshore jurisdiction?

What if, after the trust or corporation receives title, you apply for and receive Canadian citizenship, later voluntarily end your U.S. citizenship, and become a legal resident of Canada for at least five years?

As a new Canadian, that offshore trust or corporation can pay you benefits and income for five years – tax-free – if you carefully follow the regulations that govern this incredible tax break. You can be a free spirit with absolutely no income or capital gains tax liability in either the U.S. or Canada.

It sounds too good to be true? Read on.

Testing the Waters

Maybe you would like to test the northern waters before making any major decision about a future in Canada. Fortunately, Americans thinking about emigrating can explore life north of the border for an extended period. The U.S.-Canadian Free Trade Agreement allows reciprocal extended stays of up to one year, with no requirement to obtain a special visa. Plus, the number of one-year extensions is unlimited. Tourists are allowed to stay for at least 90 days without special permission.

Americans employed in certain occupations can enter, live, and work in Canada without a permit and with no prior approval. Those welcome to work in Canada include Americans involved in research and designing, purchasing, sales and contract negotiation, customs brokering, financial services, public relations and advertising, tourism, and market research, and professionals paid by U.S. sources.

Until 2003, neither country required a special visa or passport, only proper personal identification, such as a state or provincial motor vehicle operator's license or a voter card or birth certificate. At this writing, that remains the case. As of late 2003, Canadian citizens are exempt from a U.S. plan to tighten border security through increased screening of foreign visitors. Canadians so far are not included in the Visitor Immigrant Status Indication Technology (VISIT) system, adopted after the terrorist attacks on New York and Washington on September 11, 2001. The VISIT screening process is intended to increase security along the world's longest undefended border without obstructing commerce and traffic worth more than US$1 billion a day. The system is scheduled to take effect at U.S. airports and seaports in 2004 and at land border crossings at the start of 2005.

Open Door for Immigrant Investors

Before obtaining Canadian citizenship, you should first explore any family ties you might have in the country. The Canadian government will help you learn if you are eligible for citizenship based on ancestry. Any Canadian Consulate will provide a personal history information form to be completed and submitted with copies of relevant birth records to the Registrar of Canadian Citizenship in the capital city of Ottawa. A "Certificate of Canadian Citizenship" is automatically issued to anyone who qualifies for citizenship by family descent. If you are lucky enough to qualify, this is the least complicated basis on which to establish a new legal residence in Canada.

Independent applicants for permanent residence are rated on a point system that takes into account age, education, fluency in English and French, financial standing, occupational or professional experience, local demand for certain types of workers, geographic destination, and a personal assessment of the applicant. These factors comprise a 100 point scale. Seventy points and over is passing.

Completely separate from the point system for admissions, Canadian law favors a special independent class of preferred immigrants including investors, entrepreneurs, the self-employed and those who will add to the "cultural and artistic life" of the nation. With minor variation in each of the provinces, investor-immigrants generally must have a net worth in excess of C\$500,000 (US\$378,000) and be willing to invest at least C\$250,000 (US\$188,000) in some Canadian business for a minimum three to five-year period. Purchase of a residence usually does not qualify as an investment, although it may if you work from home.

Independent applicants for permanent residence are rated on a point system that takes into account age, education, fluency in English and French, financial standing, occupational or professional experience, local demand for certain types of workers, geographic destination, and a personal assessment of the applicant.

With proof of sufficient assets and an attractive business plan (especially one creating new jobs for Canadians) your permanent resident status and eventual citizenship is almost assured. Government loan guarantees and other assistance may be available for immigrants willing to invest larger sums of C\$750,000 (US\$567,000) or more.

For potential investor visa applicants, the government rolls out the proverbial red carpet, officially known as the "Business Migration Programme." Business experience, marketing skills, contacts within Canada, an adequate credit rating and available funds all greatly increase your chance of success. Applicants are usually required to submit detailed business proposals or general business plans, which must accompany the application for permanent residence. Such plans must detail the nature of the business, operating procedures, key personnel (which may just be the applicant), a marketing plan, and a financial strategy.

Canadian Immigration Process

The immigration process begins with a visit to the Canadian Embassy. It is located at Fourth Street and Pennsylvania Avenue NW, Washington, D.C. You can also try a Canadian Consulate, located in New York and other major U.S. cities.

There, you receive an "Immigration Questionnaire" requiring basic personal information about you, your spouse and family. Within a few weeks, a more detailed questionnaire will be presented if the applicant is initially found acceptable. After this second document is reviewed, a personal interview and medical examinations are needed.

If all goes well, you will shortly receive a visa for entry into Canada as a landed immigrant: "Welcome, *Bienvenue à Canada.*"

It is worth noting that Canada recognizes the principle of dual nationality. They allow successful applicants for citizenship to retain their nationality of origin. For reasons that will become obvious in a moment, that choice is not a viable option for an ex-American expatriating to Canada.

The Big Change – U.S. Expatriation

The potential immigrant from America will eventually have to give up United States citizenship, formally ending his or her U.S. status in a way that carefully avoids identifying the purpose as avoidance of U.S. taxes. If the U.S. government thinks you skipped just to avoid taxes, under U.S. law, the IRS can pursue you and any U.S. income or assets you may have left south of the border.

The difficulty in the IRS proving an individual's intentions makes these recent anti-expatriation laws so much political hot air. By the time someone at the U.S. Department of Justice thinks they know what your intent might have been, you will have come and gone from the United States – along with your liquid assets and wealth.

Do It the Right Way

Here's how to expatriate from the U.S. and avoid pitfalls along the way:

It is crucial to obtain proper legal advice on expatriation in order to be effective in surrendering citizenship. The worst outcome is to wind up with ambiguous dual nationality status. In this case, you go through an extended period retaining not only U.S. citizenship, but citizenship in another country as well. You may then find yourself within the potential grasp of two government taxing authorities.

Generally, an ex-American who properly surrenders citizenship is treated by U.S. law as a nonresident alien and taxed at a flat 30% rate on certain types of passive income derived from U.S. sources, and on net profits from the sale of a U.S. trade or business at regular graduated rates. Expatriates can safely spend only about 122 days a year within the United States. After that, they expose themselves to IRS claims for full U.S. taxation based on alien residency.

Another strict caution: you must be certain to obtain valid foreign citizenship before you surrender your U.S. citizenship – if you fail to do so, you could become a "stateless" person, the proverbial "man without a country." A person without a passport and a nationality is legally lost in this world of national borders and bureaucratic customs officials, and as such is not entitled to the legal protection of any government. *The Wall Street Journal* reported in 1995 that one poor soul had been living on a bench in the international waiting room area of DeGaulle Airport near Paris. He floundered in his "in transit" ambiguity while several governments and the UN Refugee Commission fought over the status of his nationality!

Valid surrender must be an unequivocal act in which a person manifests an unqualified intention to relinquish U.S. citizenship. In order for the surrender to be effective, all of the conditions of the statute must be met; the person must appear in person and sign an oath before a U.S. consular or diplomatic officer, usually at an American Embassy or Consulate. Because of the way in which the law is written and interpreted, Americans cannot effectively renounce their citizenship by mail, through an agent, or while physically within the United States.

Once a surrender is accomplished before an American diplomatic or consular officer abroad, all documents are referred to the U.S. Department of State. The Office of Overseas Citizens Services reviews them to ensure that all criteria under the law are met, but the State Department has no discretion to refuse a proper surrender of citizenship. This personal right is absolute. (If you do surrender your U.S. citizenship, in theory you could get it back, but only through a long and complicated process that any new U.S. immigrant applicant must undergo. And that takes years and involves attorney and other costs.)

Long before such a drastic final step is taken towards ending U.S. citizenship, the new Canadian immigrant should have his or her official Canadian citizenship in order, papers in hand, and an established residence in their new homeland. This will most likely be in the metropolitan areas of Montreal, Toronto, or Vancouver, where the vast majority of immigrants decide to live.

The Canadian Potential

One of the foremost benefits of becoming a Canadian citizen is the ability to take advantage of what is often called an "immigrant offshore trust."

The key to eligibility for this unusual tax-free "window of opportunity" is found in section 94(1) of Canada's Income Tax

Act of 1952. This law ensures that an immigrant who has never been a Canadian resident can move to Canada and earn tax-free foreign source income from a nonresident trust or affiliated corporation for the first five calendar years of his new Canadian residency. But before you surrender U.S. citizenship, you must have already attained citizenship in Canada. As I said, this requires fulfillment of at least the first three of your five-year exemption period. As a U.S. citizen, during that time you are still subject to taxation on your worldwide income, including the trust income.

The Beneficiaries

To qualify for this big tax break, the arrangement must include an immigrant residing in Canada plus either: 1) a foreign corporation or a trust with which the immigrant is "closely tied;" or 2) a foreign affiliate corporation controlled by a person resident in Canada. The essential factor is that the nonresident trust must have one or more beneficiaries who are Canadian residents, or the offshore corporation must be "closely tied" in some manner to one or more Canadian residents. The beneficiaries likely will be your family members, and can include yourself. The foreign trustee will follow your instructions on how the trust assets should be invested and income disbursed.

A "beneficial interest" in a nonresident trust is defined as belonging to a person or partnership that holds any right – immediate or future, absolute or contingent, conditional or otherwise – to receive any of the income or principal capital of the trust, either directly or indirectly. It would be difficult to find a broader definition of "beneficial entitlement" than this – and the implications for tax avoidance are obvious and potentially huge.

Canadian tax officials and court cases have repeatedly stated that such immigration trusts and related businesses, when properly created and managed abroad, are not an abuse of the tax laws. That's because section 94 clearly is designed as a vehicle for exempting new immigrants from taxation for the stated period of five years. In the case of almost every other tax avoidance scheme, Revenue Canada would pounce. Here, the law does more than permit tax avoidance, it approves and encourages it.

Only a change in Canadian law by Parliament could remove this generous tax break, and there is no current talk of removing the provision that has been so successful in attracting much needed capital and business to the nation.

Trust Property Sources

In order for a nonresident trust or a nonresident corporation to qualify as a "controlled foreign affiliate," and to receive section 94 tax-free treatment, it must have acquired its property from a person who meets all of the following requirements: 1) the donor must be the trust or affiliate corporation beneficiary, or related to the beneficiary (spouse, child, parent), or be the uncle, aunt, nephew, or niece of the beneficiary; 2) the donor must have been resident in Canada at any time in an 18-month period before the end of the trust's first taxation year or before his or her death; and 3) if the trust property came from an individual, the individual donor eventually must be a resident in Canada for a period or periods totaling more than 60 months.

As a general rule, a trust donor should transfer only cash and title to intangible assets to an offshore trust. Portable assets, such as gold coins or diamonds, also can be used.

Section 94 applies regardless of the method by which the nonresident trust or corporation acquires its property including purchase, gift, bequest, inheritance or, exercise of a power of appointment by or from an individual. The law treats all such transfers as if you had transferred your property to the trust or corporation.

You must be careful to follow a few rules when donating assets to such a trust or corporation. You cannot retain any reversion right or power to designate beneficiaries after the trust is created. This is what is known in both U.S. and Canadian law as an irrevocable living trust. You cannot retain any control over how the trust property will be disbursed during your lifetime, nor can you retain more than 10% equity ownership in an offshore corporation to which you donate.

As a general rule, a trust donor should transfer only cash and title to intangible assets to an offshore trust. Portable assets, such as gold coins or diamonds, also can be used. Title to real estate or a business located in Canada or the United States definitely should not be made part of the trust property. Transfer of tangible property physically located in either nation does nothing to keep those assets away from Canadian or American creditors or tax authorities. Such action could even subject the trust to the jurisdiction of a Canadian court. By holding title to assets within Canada, the offshore trust could be deemed liable for Canadian taxes.

Foreign Control a Must

In order to determine if an offshore trust is "nonresident" from a tax perspective, Revenue Canada looks at who controls it and its ownership.

The residence of a trust is determined by where the managing trustees or the persons who control the trust assets actually reside. It is therefore important that the offshore trust have a majority of trustees living in the foreign jurisdiction where the trust is registered and where its operation is located. This requirement for majority offshore control does not diminish the ability of a trust beneficiary to serve as a trustee and to live in Canada. Neither status jeopardizes the offshore, and therefore tax-free, status of the trust.

Canadian tax law specifically allows offshore immigration trusts to receive tax-free income from investment business conducted by a resident Canadian citizen during the five-year residency period. Thus, the new Canadian investor-citizen is free to roam the world by e-mail, phone, fax, telex, wire, courier, or letter, using his capital and ability to produce profits for the trust and its beneficiaries. To maximize tax avoidance, the trust should not carry on other active business in Canada or invest in property located in Canada. Income from these sources may subject the trust to certain domestic taxes because of the Canadian source or location.

Creating an Offshore Trust

So where should you establish such an offshore trust? You could conceivably set up shop anywhere in the world.

To do so effectively, you must look abroad for a friendly national jurisdiction in which to locate your assets. The host government must impose little or no taxes on foreign investors. Elsewhere in these pages, I describe several such haven nations, some of them located in the warm waters of the Caribbean, not too far from the U.S. or Canada.

For Example

Let's say you have C$3 million you wish to invest. Like any reasonable person, you want to avoid Canadian taxes on the income produced from your investment. The following strategy can help natural-born Canadian citizens and wealthy new immigrants.

First you need a nonresident of Canada – a friend or relative – to act as manager of your offshore investment corporation. You also need a trust registered in an established asset haven. For this example, let's say you choose to set one up in Panama. You can't do it yourself, since the new Canadian immigrant must live in Canada for five years.

You transfer the C$3 million (US$2.276 million) to the Panama-registered trust, also administered by your friend as trustee, probably in the same Panama office. The trust manager invests that money in Canadian government treasury bills or public company stocks. The interest income this produces can be paid to you, your children, or any other named beneficiaries tax-free. At current interest rates, that means a savings of about C$100,000 (US$75,000) a year in taxes.

While this tax haven structure might be expensive to establish, the arrangement qualifies under section 94 for five years of tax-free income for trust beneficiaries. Even after the five-year period ends, this arrangement can continue to shield the Canadian beneficiary from taxes, so long as it is controlled by non-Canadians.

As I explained in Chapter 2, an offshore asset protection trust (APT) located in a tax haven is proven and effective for offshore financial planning. The APT is the safety vehicle that places personal assets beyond the reach of many irritants: your home country tax authorities, potential litigation plaintiffs, an irate spouse, or unreasonable creditors – wherever such opponents may be located.

Even though an offshore immigration trust can guarantee five tax-free years for new Canadian immigrants, the non-tax benefits are also important. The trust allows Canadians asset protection, a high degree of financial privacy, flexible estate planning and the ability to make internationally diversified investments unrestricted by domestic Canadian law.

Reasonable caution places a premium on pursuing the correct path from the very beginning.

A Need for Caution

The objective of an offshore tax haven is the legal reduction of your tax obligations. Keep in mind that it will do you no good to suffer the bother of restructuring your financial life, only to find yourself embroiled in years of complex and expensive court battles with Revenue Canada. Or worse, facing criminal charges for tax evasion or a variety of other possible tax crimes.

Reasonable caution places a premium on pursuing the correct path from the very beginning. This means the assistance of competent experts from the very start. Cutting corners will only leave you and your financial advisors in deep trouble.

The Mechanics of Offshore Business

The country in which your Canadian immigration trust and the managing trustee are located should be, for obvious reasons, a nation with strong financial privacy laws. As I have said, most tax haven countries do emphasize such statutory privacy rights.

The ideal places for establishing asset preservation or tax

avoidance trusts are tax haven countries such as Panama, Nevis, the Isle of Man, the Channel Islands, or the Cook Islands. These are all countries with statutes tailored to asset protection needs. As I have said repeatedly, all United Kingdom dependent territories are under current pressure from the Labour government to weaken privacy laws and increase reporting requirements for offshore entities. Before you choose a jurisdiction for the location of your trust, check the present state of the laws in the prospect haven.

Tougher Offshore Reporting

Creating an offshore immigration trust will affect your personal tax return, in that a taxpayer must disclose the existence of an offshore trust on his or her annual Canadian federal tax return. Foreign trustees are not required to divulge information about assets held by a trust. They cannot be forced by Canadian courts to turn over trust assets. Revenue Canada and other creditors must first go through the host country's judicial system at great expense.

Reporting laws require that all resident Canadian taxpayers must report the existence of their offshore assets that exceed the aggregate of C$100,000 (US$75,000). This includes offshore bank accounts, securities holdings, and rental properties, and interests in foreign trusts, partnerships, corporations, or any other offshore entities. Prior law required payment of taxes on offshore income by Canadian residents, but did not mandate a listing of assets as does the new law.

Commenting on the reporting law, a leading Canadian financial management company gave this opinion: "Revenue Canada seems to be following the U.S. Internal Revenue Service with respect to offshore entities and transactions. Some of the new reporting is tougher than the IRS, some less, but the intent is the same; the government wants to know everything."

Nevertheless, as I already explained, creditors must get a court to order you to reveal your tax return and the existence of the trust in any civil action. That takes time. If they do discover the trust's offshore location and file a collection suit in the haven country, local laws are hostile to nonresident creditors and the trustee can shift the trust and its assets to another country and another trustee in an emergency. Then, pursuing creditors must begin the process all over again.

The Trust Advantage

This protection in a civil suit gives trusts a distinct privacy advantage over corporations.

In most tax and asset haven countries, at least one person involved in organizing a corporation must be listed on the public record, along with the name and address of the corporation. In many countries, the directors must be listed on the original charter. In a few maximum privacy countries, only the organizing lawyer is listed, but even that reference gives privacy invaders a starting point for nosey investigators.

With a trust, nothing more than its existence is required to be registered in an asset haven nation – and often not even that. The trust agreement and the parties involved do not have to be disclosed, and there is little or nothing on the public record. In privacy-conscious countries, the trustee is allowed to reveal information about the trust only in very limited circumstances.

The country chosen for such a trust must have local trust experts who can assist you in achieving your objectives. The foreign local attorney who creates your trust must be familiar with all applicable laws and tax consequences.

In its simplest form, the offshore immigration trust can be a trust account in a foreign bank. Many well-established multinational Canadian banks can provide trustees for such arrangements and are experienced in such matters. As an extra level of insulation from government pressure, however, use a non-Canadian bank.

With today's instant communications and international banking facilities, it is just as convenient to hold assets and accounts overseas as it is in another Canadian or U.S. city. Most international banks offer Canadian and U.S. dollar-denominated accounts, which often have better interest rates than Canadian institutions.

An International Business Corporation

The offshore corporation is best suited for the needs of Canadian business owners who seriously desire to run a legitimate international business. Establishing your corporation offshore can lower your taxes and increase profits immensely. Under section 94, income from "affiliated" offshore corporations qualifies for the five-year tax exemption. The company can also be for tax avoidance after the five-year moratorium ends, as I explain below.

But foreign corporations, as Revenue Canada demands, must be more than a mere sham. A full-scale company, complete with working offices, staff, international fax and telecommunications facilities, bank accounts, a registered agent, board of directors, a local attorney, and an accountant can cost upwards of C$50,000 annually.

As the Canadian owner, you will want to visit your company offices once or twice a year, a pleasant enough activity if you locate your business in one of the tropical venues specializing in such corporate arrangements.

Members of your board of directors, and associates of the local tax specialists who help you form the company, may be paid about C$2,500 a year. There will be annual taxes to pay and reports to be filed with the local government, and with Canada.

As the Canadian owner, you will want to visit your company offices once or twice a year, a pleasant enough activity if you locate your business in one of the tropical venues specializing in such corporate arrangements. January is an excellent month for Canadians to head south for a visit.

How It Works

Let's say as a new investor-immigrant, you purchase a Canadian manufacturing business that exports products worth C$5 million (US$3.7 million) each year.

Because it is a legitimate business with established foreign transactions, your Canadian company can incorporate an offshore affiliate, in say, Barbados. Like Canada, Barbados is a member of the British Commonwealth. More importantly, it is a place where international companies pay only 2.5% corporate income tax and benefit from credits and inducements for foreign-owned businesses. Compare that to Canada's 45% tax.

You can set up your affiliate with offices in the capital, Bridgetown (population 8,000). It has eight major international banks including branches of the Royal Bank of Canada, the Canadian Imperial Bank of Commerce, Chase Manhattan, and Barclays. Regular air service is offered by Air Canada, British Airways, American, and other major carriers.

Your Bridgetown affiliate will handle all foreign sales and international marketing for your Canadian company. For these services, it will charge a 15% mark-up on the value of the goods it sells. This will amount to about US$750,000 a year at your current export levels.

What you have done is legally transfer the profits from your Canadian company to an offshore affiliate where taxes are much lower – 2.5% vs. 45%! After gladly paying US$18,750 in local corporate income taxes, the rest of the money, US$731,250, can be sent back to Canada as a dividend from exempt surplus income. This is paid to your company – tax-free! During the first five years of your citizenship, you personally can share in that corporate income, again tax-free!

Even after your five-year tax-free period ends, Canadian taxes on the income can be deferred indefinitely. You can do so until the parent company's shareholders need the money for their own use, or until they sell the business. If the shareholders want payment immediately, it can be paid out as dividends. Dividends are taxed at 36%, well below the personal income tax rate of over 50%.

Investment Potential

The Barbados affiliate could also serve as an investment arm for your parent company. In this capacity, it can actively make international investments. All the earned income from such investments – dividends, interest and capital gains – will go to your Bridgetown affiliate. This will be taxed at the 2.5% rate. Investment profits can also be sent to the parent company tax-free. In order to follow this course successfully, all corporate investment decisions must originate with your Bridgetown money manager. He must run your affiliate on a daily basis; i.e., you cannot dictate every move by phone from Montreal or Ottawa. As an added consideration, those with experience say that in order to be successful in using foreign affiliates for investment purposes, a minimum of US$1 million in capital will be needed to start.

In theory, this all sounds grand, but there are practical problems associated with an offshore corporation.

First of all, just as in establishing a domestic corporation, legal formalities must be strictly observed. Revenue Canada will check this carefully. Moreover, the cost of starting up can be considerable. You will need a local legal counsel who knows the law and understands your business and tax objectives. Corporations anywhere are rule-bound creatures requiring separate books and records, meetings, minutes and corporate authorizing resolutions, which make it less flexible than many other arrangements.

But you can pay for a whole lot of recordkeeping with the money you will save in taxes.

If you follow the rules, Revenue Canada will not be able to mount a successful challenge, despite their recent efforts to go after anything they consider to be an "overly aggressive tax strategy."

When the Five Years End

After five tax-free years, it won't be easy to face Revenue Canada. Your offshore trust can either be converted to a domestic Canadian trust (by passing majority control to trustees who reside in Canada), or its affairs can be terminated and the assets distributed to the beneficiaries. In this case, the beneficiaries will owe Canadian capital gains taxes on the fair market value at the time of distribution.

This is especially worrisome when you compare the outrageously high Canadian tax rates with those imposed in foreign tax havens. Luckily, prudent Canadians can take advantage of this wide international tax disparity by establishing an offshore tax shelter that can easily double after-tax disposable income.

This can be accomplished in full compliance with federal law. If you follow the rules, Revenue Canada will not be able to mount a successful challenge, despite their recent efforts to go after anything they consider to be an "overly aggressive tax strategy."

Aggressive Tax Enforcement

The most dangerous attitude one can adopt when dealing with the establishment of offshore business arrangements is the cavalier approach – the stupid idea that "white collar" crimes are somehow less serious than violent crimes, or that the federal government is less concerned about financial offenses than they are about other civil wrongs.

Canadian courts display a stiff attitude towards tax scofflaws, and the long arm reaches across oceans. For example, the Canadian Supreme Court held that the former manager of the Freeport branch of the Canadian Royal Bank could be forced to give testimony at a tax evasion trial in Canada, even though doing so would be a breach of the Bahamian bank secrecy law.

Powerful laws aimed at preventing tax evasion have aided the federal government's vigorous international enforcement efforts. By law, there is no statute of limitations on tax evasion, but a Revenue Canada audit can only cover three prior years. RC has power to obtain "foreign-based information or documents," and elaborate annual corporate reporting requirements were imposed on inter-company transactions between Canadians and any offshore entities. Failure to report, or false statements concerning such transactions, can result in fines of up to C$24,000.

Revenue Canada keeps an eagle eye on the tax shelter industry. Before the adoption of the new offshore reporting requirements, RC officials tracked the offshore business activity of individual Canadians as best they could. Now they have powerful new tools that place personal responsibility to report squarely on taxpayers.

In spite of these tough federal policies, and an array of laws with sharp teeth, there are still many opportunities for profitable offshore financial activities. Offshore tax havens are legal, and in selective circumstances, nonresident owned international investment and business structures can be used to reduce taxes.

Conclusion

There you have it. It may seem a difficult road to travel, but becoming a Canadian citizen investor can save a U.S. citizen millions of dollars that would otherwise go directly to the IRS.

Yes, these savings are predicated on major changes – including surrender of your U.S. citizenship. You must move yourself, your family, and your business to Canada, and possibly to another country later on. Despite these drawbacks, the true bottom line measured in dollar savings can be enormous.

Contacts

Citizenship:

David Melnik, QC, 350 Lonsdale Road, Suite #311, Toronto, Ontario M5P 1R6, Canada; Tel.: 416-488-7918; Fax: 905-877-7751; E-mail: dm1976cp@netcom.ca; Assistant: Carol Bruce, Tel.: 905-877-3156.

Douglas Hendler, Armel Gray Law Firm, Suite 500, 390 Bay Street, Toronto, Ontario M5H 3P5, Canada; Tel.: 416-362-1400; Fax: 416-362-1404.

Joel Guberman, Barrister and Solicitor, 130 Adelaide Street West, Suite 1920, Toronto, Ontario M5H 3P5, Canada; Tel.: 416-363-1234.

Offshore immigration trust:

Derek Sambrook, Trust Services, Ltd., Suite 522, Balboa Plaza, Avenida Balboa, Panama, Republic of Panama; Mailing Address: Apartado 0832-1630, World Trade Centre, Panama, Republic of Panama; Tel.: 507-269-2438; Fax: 507-269-4922; E-mail: sambrook@trustserv.com; Web site: http://www.trustserv.com.

Web sites:

Federal Government of Canada: www.canada.gc.ca/main_e.html.

Revenue Canada: www.rc.gc.ca/.

Chapter 10
The United States as an Offshore Tax Haven

SUMMARY: Unbeknownst to most Americans, the complex tax laws of the United States make the U.S. one of the world's leading offshore tax havens – but almost exclusively for foreign citizens who wish to invest in America. There are ways that U.S. persons can also reap reduced taxes from the U.S. tax laws that benefit foreigners, but those ways are highly complex, requiring costly professional advice and constant management.

In this chapter, I explain the intricacies of the U.S. Internal Revenue Code, so forgive me once again for the legalistic approach. It is much more complex than the chapter on Canada and expatriation. But again I urge you – get competent professional advice and realistic cost estimates before you embark on any plans this chapter may inspire you to attempt.

Tax Haven America

Not many hard-pressed American taxpayers realize it, but the United States is considered a major tax haven for foreign investors.

There are a whole host of laws that provide liberal U.S. tax breaks that apply only to foreigners. While Americans struggle to pay combined taxes that rob them of more than 40% of their total incomes, careful foreign investors can and do make lots of money in the United States – *tax-free*.

On the other hand, foreign corporations operating in the U.S. do pay corporate income taxes on some of their U.S. earnings and often they pay plenty.

---

*While Americans struggle to pay combined taxes that rob them of more than 40% of their total incomes, careful foreign investors can and do make lots of money in the United States – **tax-free.***

A haphazard array of complex provisions in the U.S. IRC, coupled with a host of international tax treaties, provides rich opportunities for the astute foreign investor. Assisting these investors is an elite group of high-priced American tax lawyers and accountants known as "inbound specialists." Their specialty is structuring transactions to minimize taxes and maximize profits.

Foreign investors in America are allowed to get off tax-free because the U.S. government needs and wants foreign investment.

The U.S. Treasury needs the capital to bolster the national economy, to finance huge government current spending, and to refinance constantly the enormous national debt. A large portion of foreign investment goes directly into short and long-term U.S. Treasury securities. This enormous cash inflow keeps the U.S. government afloat from day to day. Billions of dollars of the much talked-about "national debt" is owed directly to European and Asian investors. The communist government of the People's Republic of China is one of America's largest individual creditors by virtue of their investments in U.S. government debt securities. The old saying about government debt that "we owe it to ourselves" doesn't apply any more, if it ever did.

Another scary fact: the annual interest paid on the US$10 trillion government debt now exceeds all other federal budget program costs, except the Defense Department. Some 38% of the entire budget is for interest payments alone, and most of it goes to foreign investors.

We're talking very big money here!

As a consequence, these foreign investors have a lot of power over the U.S.

When the U.S. Congress imposed a 30% withholding tax on all interest payments to foreign residents and corporations doing business in the U.S., foreign investors bluntly let it be known they would take their money elsewhere if the withholding tax remained. Not surprisingly, the IRC is now riddled with exceptions to the 30% tax.

The biggest U.S. tax break for many foreigners comes from a combined impact of domestic IRC provisions and the tax laws of the investor's own country. As Americans are painfully aware, the United States taxes its citizens and residents on their worldwide income. But non-citizens and nonresidents are allowed by their own domestic laws to earn certain types of income from within the U.S. tax-free. As you can guess, droves of smart foreign investors take advantage of this situation.

Where There's a Will

In a qualified, but highly circuitous way, and in the right circumstances, a U.S. citizen or resident alien also can benefit from this tax-free income that makes so many foreign investors wealthy. The qualifying process is complex, but the laws offer clear possibilities.

You can establish an offshore corporation to invest *tax-free* in U.S. securities and other property. But unfortunate things can happen if you don't structure these backdoor, offshore arrangements properly, due to the morass of IRS rules that the U.S. Congress has adopted to keep you from benefiting from this reverse offshore tax avoidance route.

The Offshore Corporation Loophole

Years ago, a U.S. person could pay a pleasant, tax deductible visit to a tax haven nation, say The Bahamas, and form an IBC there.

You could then transfer some cash to the new company and have it put money into selected U.S. investments. If you picked right and this triangle shot paid off, all the corporate income was tax-free. As long as your foreign corporation did not have an office in the U.S., the IRS treated it as a "nonresident foreign corporation" and most of its income was not taxed. As an owner, the company could pay your legitimate business-related expenses, and no income tax was imposed until you decided to pay yourself dividends. Meanwhile, assuming good management, profits could be deferred, ploughed back, and allowed to increase in value.

Part of that happy scenario remains true today.

As long as a foreign corporation does not maintain a U.S. office, or have sufficient contacts with the U.S. that would make it "effectively connected" to this country, the IRS considers it a "nonresident foreign corporation." Under the law, it can avoid taxes on certain U.S. source income as defined by law.

The very big difference today: the U.S. shareholder in an offshore corporation is taxed like a partner in a partnership. This means a controlling U.S. shareholder of a foreign corporation must pay annual income taxes on his or her *pro-rata* share of certain types of the foreign corporation's income when it is earned, even if that income is not paid out in dividends or in any other form, and even if the corporation retains those profits. No longer can the profits sit offshore out of the tax collector's grasp. As you can guess, this has substantially reduced the incentive for Americans to create offshore corporations as a tax avoidance mechanism. If you abide by the law, the tax avoidance is gone.

Except – and there's always an exception when it comes to U.S. tax laws – for two remaining loopholes that still might allow tax-free investment possibilities for Americans using offshore corporations. You need to execute these strategies very carefully to make them both legal and effective.

But first, a little background history and some definitions that hopefully will broaden your understanding of what's going on here.

The Controlled Foreign Corporation

The basic purpose of the complex rules governing *controlled foreign corporations* (CFCs) is to prevent U.S. taxpayers from avoiding or deferring taxes through the use of such offshore companies.

These rules can be found in IRC sections 951 through 964. Essentially, if a foreign corporation is controlled by U.S. taxpayers, those who own 10% or more of the corporation must report their respective share of the CFC income on their annual personal income tax return (IRS Form 1040). The effect is similar to the flow-through tax treatment of a domestic U.S. partnership or subchapter S corporation, but much more complicated.

The basic purpose of the complex rules governing controlled foreign corporations (CFCs) is to prevent U.S. taxpayers from avoiding or deferring taxes through the use of such offshore companies.

The great ingenuity of the American inbound specialist tax advisors has produced numerous loopholes used to circumvent early versions of the CFC tax laws. Over time, the IRS and Congress have repeatedly revised the law, trying to close these loopholes. Undaunted, the tax experts found new loopholes, the IRS reacted, and Congress changed the laws again. The foreign tax area has become an ongoing battle of wits between the international tax experts and the IRS. Much of the Enron scandal came from the too-imaginative use of these offshore tax shelters.

We tell you this because no prudent investor or business person should venture into this offshore tax arena without being fully prepared. You need to be ready to cope with uncertainty and highly complex tax rules that are always in a state of flux. Don't forget the potential cost in accounting and legal fees, just to keep up with constant change.

Just so you understand how complex this area of tax law can

be, I readily admit that most of what I say in this chapter is an over-simplification, a crude condensation of thousands of pages of IRS regulations, rulings and tax court cases. But persevere, for there's a potential for big profits, along with light at the end of the tunnel.

The U.S. Shareholder

First, only a "U.S. shareholder" is affected by CFC rules.

A *U.S. shareholder* is defined as a U.S. person (including any entity), that owns 10% or more of the total voting power of the stock of a foreign corporation. This can mean a citizen or resident of the U.S., a domestic partnership or corporation, or an estate or trust that is not a foreign estate or trust. However, if a foreign trust is a grantor trust, or has U.S. beneficiaries, the U.S. grantor or beneficiary is treated as a shareholder of the foreign corporation.

In the case of a foreign estate, if a U.S. person is a beneficiary, then that beneficiary is considered a shareholder of the foreign corporation. In each instance, the IRS overlooks the legal tangle and only sees U.S. citizens receiving, directly or indirectly, income from a foreign corporation.

But there's another caveat: unless the corporation qualifies as a CFC under the second test described below, the U.S. shareholders are not required to report their share of the corporate income on their personal tax return unless the corporation is also a passive foreign investment company (PFIC).

A Second Test

A *foreign corporation* is considered a CFC only if *more* than 50% of the total voting power, or the total value of the stock is owned by U.S. shareholders having a 10% or greater stock interest on any day of the tax year. (Different rules apply to an insurance company.) If foreign persons (or entities) own 50% or more of the corporation stock, then it is not a CFC.

However, if a U.S. person is related to the foreign person or entity, then the U.S. shareholder is deemed to be a shareholder of the foreign corporation under the *constructive ownership* rules in IRC, section 318, (also called the *attribution of ownership* rules.) These rules apply with respect to U.S. persons and foreign entities, but not to foreign individuals. Section 318(b) refers to section 958(b) with respect to the attribution rules for a CFC. IRC 958(b)(1) provides an exception to the constructive ownership rules in IRC 318. Thus, if a foreign relative (parent, child, grandchild, grandparent, or spouse) owns 50% or more of a foreign corporation, the U.S. owners are not subject to the CFC tax rules.

Third Test

If a corporation qualifies as a CFC for an uninterrupted period of 30 days or more during any tax year, then every U.S. shareholder (as defined above) who owns stock in such corporation on the last day of the tax year in which it was a CFC must report as personal gross income, his or her *pro-rata* share of the CFC income.

Fourth Test

If the corporation is a CFC, its U.S. shareholders are required to report any CFC income that meets the definition of what is called *Subpart F income*. This includes most kinds of foreign source investment income, and foreign income derived from those *related parties* we just mentioned, but not income earned in the U.S.

The *related parties* means anyone who owns or controls (directly or indirectly) more than 50% of the stock of a foreign corporation, or one who is controlled by the foreign corporation, or a person (entity) who is, in fact, in a brother-sister affiliated corporate relationship. The related party can be individuals, corporations, partnerships, trusts, or an estate. These rules apply even though true ownership is masked by a long chain of interrelated controls. The IRS wants to know who controls the income source, and who gets the payoff. All of this legal jargon is laid out in IRC section 954(d)(3).

Subpart F income does not include any income earned in the U.S. because this income is taxable for the foreign corporation, just as it is for a domestic U.S. company. Thus, if a foreign company's domestic income is taxed by the IRS, it's not foreign-source income and is not subject to the CFC rules.

Generally, subpart F income does not include any income derived from doing business in a foreign country, so long as the buyer or supplier is not a related person. In plain language, the CFC rules are aimed at foreign corporations that buy or sell goods or services in a "sweetheart deal" from their related U.S. entities at a presumably favorable price. These underhanded firms then resell their goods or services abroad at a normal market price, thereby shifting the profit into the foreign entity.

Having said all this, we must point out that the specific rules applicable to subpart F income do not require that there be any actual shifting of profits to the foreign corporation in order for the IRS to rule that CFC status exists.

Another point: where the foreign corporation is primarily an investment company that invests in foreign stocks, bonds or other passive income investments (as distinguished from an active trade or business), all of that investment income is treated as subpart F income. Also note that the related party rules are not applicable to investment income.

Tried, But Not True

Now that I've tried to explain what a CFC and a U.S. person are in their tax context, let's look at some related schemes that the IRS has rejected.

Formally assigning title to half the offshore corporation's shares of stock to your offshore attorney, with his or her agreement to vote the shares as you instruct, will not avoid a CFC determination. The IRS looks at the reality of the situation, and easily sees through facades that use a straw man. The use of a foreign corporation with bearer shares that are held by any unrelated party on behalf of the real owner is treated the same as when an attorney holds the shares on behalf of the taxpayer.

Some slick offshore advisors will try to convince potential clients that a chain of legal entities putting lots of paperwork between you and your offshore corporation will fool the IRS into thinking there is no CFC. Of course, the more entities you set up, the more it costs and the more they get paid.

Forget it! An interlocking chain of offshore trusts and corporations, usually with a trust holding the operating corporation's stock, is a dead giveaway to the IRS. It may even provide strong evidence of tax fraud, a criminal act. The IRS is likely to conclude that since you are ultimately responsible for creating the entities in the chain, you are the beneficial owner of the stock. The only remotely attractive feature of this arrangement is that it might be difficult for the IRS to uncover it. Once exposed, however, the sheer complexity would be seen as evidence of deliberate fraud. Don't do it!

What Does Work

Now let's examine some ways to avoid having your investment ruled a controlled foreign corporation. In other words, let's explore a few strategies to help minimize your tax burden. (By the way, you'll often hear a non-CFC called a "decontrolled foreign corporation." It's the same thing).

One way is to make sure that no U.S. citizen or resident alien owns more than 10% of the corporation.

Here's why: for purposes of the CFC rules, if any five or fewer U.S. persons or U.S. residents own 10% or more of an offshore corporation's voting stock, it's a CFC.

Suppose you and at least eleven of your associates (folks unrelated to you - see below) plan to divide ownership interests in an offshore investment company. Divide 100% by 11, and you get a 9.09% share for each U.S. shareholder. Your offshore corporation is not a CFC, because no one U.S. person owns 10% or more of the voting stock. Your group can invest its capital within the United States with little or no tax cost, just as a foreign citizen does. The income can compound tax-free until you decide to pay yourselves dividends.

Caveat: Beware of the *attribution of ownership* rules mentioned above; if related U.S. persons are offshore corporate shareholders, they will be considered as constructive joint owners. Their shares will be added together for purposes of the CFC control test. Don't choose eleven associates who are your family members, and don't use your U.S. entities. If you do, the offshore corporation probably will be ruled to be a CFC.

Your group can invest its capital within the United States
with little or no tax cost, just as a foreign citizen does.
The income can compound tax-free until you decide
to pay yourselves dividends.

If you establish an offshore company with one U.S. person owning more than 50% of the voting stock, and other U.S. persons with less than 10% each, a CFC does exist because of the 50% U.S. shareholder. But here's a twist; only the 50% shareholder is taxed on his pro rata share of the corporation's earned income each year. Because they have less than 10% of the voting shares each, the other U.S. persons are treated as though the company is a decontrolled corporation. They do not have to report their company income share annually, and are liable for taxes only when they actually do receive dividends or other corporate distributions. If a CFC also qualifies as a PFIC, then all U.S. shareholders are liable for their share of taxes on the income of the PFIC.

Real Foreign Partners

Another way to guarantee your offshore company will qualify as decontrolled is to invest along with one or more truly unrelated foreign partners. If the foreign person(s) own 50% or more of the voting power shares, the corporation is decontrolled. It then enjoys tax-free investments in the United States as a nonresident alien. Even though you are an American part owner, you are taxed only as you withdraw money from the corporation, not each year. The foreign person can be a relative of the U.S. owner or owners.

Of course, the foreign persons must be the true owners of the stock. This sort of 50-50 ownership arrangement is particularly popular when foreign investors are from a country with similar tax rules, like Germany. There have been many U.S.-German tax saving joint ventures in real estate that allow both halves to avoid a CFC designation by their respective national tax agencies.

What Kind of Income?

There's another way around the CFC designation, and that depends on the type of income the offshore corporation takes in; only subpart F income is counted as taxable and treated as though it passes through to U.S. shareholders. Non-subpart F income is not reportable annually on a pro rata basis. That income can accumulate and compound tax-free in the corporation until it is taken out as dividends.

Here are the types of income that are counted as subpart F income and are taxable for U.S. shareholders on a pro rata basis annually:

Foreign personal holding company income. All interest, dividends, royalties, and gains on securities, plus rents from related parties, are taxable. In other words, just about every kind of usual investment income is included in subpart F income. One exception: rent derived from the active conduct of a trade or business is not included, unless the rental income is received from a related party.

Example: Suppose your foreign corporation owns an office building in The Bahamas. You occupy 15% for your own business, and your paid staff leases the remainder to unrelated parties and provides maintenance and other services. This would be considered the active conduct of a rental business in a foreign country, and rental income is not subpart F income.

Or suppose your foreign corporation owns an oil drilling company in a foreign nation. When your equipment is idle, it is leased to other oil drilling companies. The rental from the leases is not considered subpart F income and can be accumulated in an offshore corporation. (Because there are special IRS rules for banking, insurance, shipping, or oil services income earned offshore, consult with an experienced international tax advisor who knows these rules.)

The IRS is so generous with the rent income exception because it knows that many tax haven countries prohibit nonresidents from owning land, so not many will be able to qualify for this tax break.

Foreign-based company sales income: This is essentially income from the purchase of property from a related person, or the sale of property to anyone on behalf of a related person. Caveat: to avoid having this kind of income treated as subpart F income, you must purchase your goods or services from unrelated parties, and not sell your goods to a related party.

Foreign-based company service income: This is income from consulting services (legal, accounting, engineering, architectural, or management services) performed for, or on behalf of, a related person, but outside the country in which the foreign corporation is organized. Note: if your offshore corporation performs services for unrelated parties outside the U.S., that service income is not subpart F income.

De Minimis Test Games

Yet another way to avoid offshore company subpart F income is to take advantage of the IRS' so-called *de minimis* rule. Here's the rule: If the sum total of the foreign-based company's service income, plus the gross insurance income, does not exceed 5% of the CFC's total income, or US$1 million (whichever is smaller), none of the income is considered foreign-based company income or insurance income.

For example, suppose that your offshore corporation buys some condominiums in Panama. You rent the condos to tourists who are unrelated to any corporation owners. Since rental income from unrelated persons is not subpart F income, this will not be passed through *pro rata* and taxed to U.S. shareholders. In addition, if the rental income makes up at least 95% of the offshore corporation's total income, it will keep the subpart F income from being passed through to the U.S. shareholders under the *de minimis* rule. (Get it? Five percent is considered as *de minimis*, an amount so small it gets you out from under the CFC taxes).

Yet another way to avoid offshore company subpart F income is to take advantage of the IRS' so-called de minimis rule.

If you have U.S.-based manufacturing or personal consulting services that can be moved offshore, you might be able to use non-subpart F income generated by these operations to shelter investments in the United States. Any importing and exporting of tangible products through a foreign corporation would escape the subpart F rules, so long as the products are not bought from or sold to a related party. In addition, offshore manufacturing and consulting income probably will not be subpart F income, so it is also sheltered from tax in the offshore corporation.

But be careful. There's a flip side, what might be called the reverse *de minimis* rule: if 70% or more of the offshore corporation's income is defined as subpart F income, then all income is treated as such. In that case, you really are stuck tax-wise. You can see how important the character of the income can be.

For clarity's sake (we hope), let's consider another example.

Suppose that your offshore business sells a product with very high production costs and low mark-up. Assume the product costs 90% of its selling price. As we know, investment income is considered subpart F income, but under the rules, if the gross income from the investment measures less than 5% of the gross product sales, then the offshore corporation won't be considered a CFC.

To make it more specific: If the offshore foreign corporation sells US$10 million of widgets, it can make up to US$526,500 of gross investment income without becoming a CFC. (US$10,526,500 x 5% = US$526,325). However, in this example, the profit on the US$10 million of widget sales would be US$1 million, while the profit on the gross investment income might be close to US$500,000 – a third of the total profit.

Now you know why foreign corporations need such good accountants.

Watch Out For . . .

There's a trap that must be avoided when using the *de minimis* rule as a CFC designation avoidance tactic.

The rules say that if 50% or more of the foreign company's total asset value is used to produce passive income, or if 50% of those assets are being held for the production of passive income, the foreign corporation is treated as a *passive foreign investment company* (PFIC), which is discussed further below.

Take it from the experts: as a practical matter, it requires more assets to produce a 5% return in the form of passive investment income than to produce the same amount of net income from a business activity. A business might typically generate a return of 15 to 20% on its net assets, and about 10 to 15% on its total assets. Thus, in the example above, if the foreign corporation needs US$10 million in assets to produce US$1 million in gross profits from widgets sales, it cannot exceed a maximum of US$10 million in passive assets held to produce investment income. If it does, it is considered a PFIC. If the return on those investment assets is 5%, the example given above would work – but just barely

Before venturing into PFIC territory, we'll reiterate the obvious: subpart F income rules offer many possible avenues of tax avoidance. But after reading this, we don't have to tell you the rules are very complicated and riddled with exceptions. Even more discouraging, most of them were not even mentioned here.

As always, consult an experienced U.S. international tax advisor before launching your offshore corporate career.

The PFIC (Pee-fik)

In yet another skirmish between offshore tax specialists and the IRS, Congress attempted to plug even more foreign corporate loopholes with the Tax Reform Act of 1986. This law established the concept of the *passive foreign investment company* (PFIC), and authorized the rules that govern such entities.

First, a definition: *Passive income* is generally considered earnings from interest, dividends, capital gains, royalties, and a few other non-sales or service income types. The PFIC rules that apply to passive income are generally more difficult to avoid than other rules already discussed.

Under the law, a PFIC is any foreign corporation that makes 75% or more of gross income from passive income sources. A corporation will also be considered a PFIC if at least 50% of the value of its assets produce passive income, or are being held for production of passive income. Unlike a CFC, there is no control test for a PFIC. Any offshore corporation which has the minimum amount of passive income, even if its ownership is only 1% American, qualifies as a PFIC.

Owning PFIC shares can be fairly costly. You may face a tax penalty or a loss of your tax deferral. Here are the two possible punishments:

* You pay a penalty tax either when you sell the PFIC shares, or when you receive an excess distribution. The penalty tax assumes that the undistributed PFIC income and gains were actually paid to you annually, but that you didn't report the income and pay taxes owed on it each year. As penalty for your tardiness, you must pay the original tax owed plus interest based on the number of years you held the PFIC shares without paying the taxes. The shares of a PFIC are deemed to be sold at the date of your death, and your estate will be liable for the deferred taxes.

* The other option is to set up your PFIC as a *qualified electing fund corporation* (QEF) from the very beginning. (The IRS has a name for everything). That means you report your *pro-rata* shares of the PFIC's income and gains annually, just as you would with a U.S.-based mutual fund. In other words, you lose any benefit that comes with tax deferral and compounding of profits. In order to make this election, the PFIC must be willing to provide you with annual information on your share of its income. Unless U.S. owners control the PFIC, this is not likely to happen. Another option is to use the mark-to-market election to compute your gain (or loss) each year based on the difference in the market value of the shares at the end of each year. However, this election is limited to widely held foreign fund shares sold through major exchanges.

Your foreign corporation can avoid the PFIC trap by reducing the percentage of the offshore corporation's gross income that is passive. On the other hand, you could increase the amount of the assets used to produce active business income. If the corporation is a PFIC because more than 75% of its gross income is passive income, then it's only necessary to change the percentage by generating more active business income, or less passive investment income. If the corporation is a PFIC because of the 50% asset test, then you can increase assets to produce more active business income, or you can reduce passive investment assets. To qualify, it's necessary to meet both of these tests. Failure to qualify on either ground could subject shareholders to the adverse tax treatment of a PFIC.

Another option is to combine the investment activities of an offshore corporation with an actual operating business. If you have manufacturing or consulting operations overseas, these can be used to avoid the PFIC penalty.

Another potential trap is the *foreign personal holding company* rules. In most cases, if you can avoid the CFC rules, or qualify as a decontrolled offshore corporation, you can also avoid the foreign personal holding company rules.

Offshore Corporations Operating in the U.S.

Once your offshore corporation has done everything necessary to gain a favorable foreign business tax status under IRS rules, it is free to invest in the United States and reap the benefits of tax-free income just as a foreign citizen would.

Once your offshore corporation secures its status as a foreign business, some of the immediate benefits include no obligation to pay U.S. taxes on bank deposit interest, and no tax on capital gains earned on U.S. stocks and bonds.

But what you cannot do as a foreign corporation is "engage in a U.S. trade or business" as defined under U.S. tax law. Lest you be so defined, here are the guidelines to follow:

* No physical office or agent in the United States;

* Books and records must be maintained outside the U.S.;

* Actual management and control must be exercised elsewhere;

* Directors' and shareholders' meetings must be held outside the U.S.; and

* The corporation cannot have a business located within the U.S.

Once your offshore corporation secures its status as a foreign business, some of the immediate benefits include no obligation to pay U.S. taxes on bank deposit interest, and no tax on capital gains earned on U.S. stocks and bonds. Although there could be tax liability for some dividends paid by American stock shares, these taxes often can be reduced or avoided by locating the offshore corporation in a country with a favorable U.S. tax treaty. Some bilateral U.S.-foreign tax treaties provide for a greatly reduced U.S. withholding tax rate on dividends paid to foreign corporations.

A good example of this dividend tax avoidance advantage came to light during the so-called "junk bond" mess and the widespread collapse of insurance companies and savings and loan associations in the 1980s. When these faltering American companies tried to sell assets, many foreign corporations or partnerships submitted the best bids for their portfolios of junk bonds and shares. While potential U.S. bond buyers faced taxes on interest and capital gains, foreign investors, facing no U.S. taxes, could offer bids 10% or more above those of U.S. competitors. If these offshore companies were incorporated in tax-free havens like Panama or Nevis, they escaped dividend and interest taxes on these fire sale stock buys completely.

U.S. Real Estate a Tax Bargain

Investing in U.S. real estate used to be an easy avenue to tax-free income and gains for foreign citizens. But the real estate tax rules were changed in 1980, and profits are no longer tax-free. Still, investment in U.S. real estate through a decontrolled offshore corporation can result in lower taxes on profits if the transaction is structured properly.

In the complicated and rapidly changing area of tax law, an offshore company should be incorporated in a country that has a favorable tax treaty with the United States. The Netherlands is an historic favorite. The offshore company then creates a subsidiary U.S. corporation, which buys the real estate. Sometimes, it makes sense to have one U.S. company hold title to the real estate, while another is created to receive property management fees. Don't forget that foreign investors can also enjoy U.S. stock market trading profits entirely tax-free. This applies whether or not their home country has a double tax treaty with the U.S. The IRS periodically issues revenue rulings attacking current schemes, so obtain up-to-date advice from an experienced U.S. tax advisor.

There is a 10% withholding tax imposed on the gross proceeds from the sale of a U.S. real estate property interest by a foreign person. This term includes an interest in the form of corporate stock, partnerships, trusts, etc. In a case where there is no depreciation taken, a gain on U.S. real estate of 67% of the gross sales price would be subject to a 15% tax, resulting in a tax equal to 10% of the gross sales proceeds. Where the gain is less than 67%, the foreign investor would be paying too much tax with a 10% rate of withholding. Where the property is subject to depreciation, the accelerated depreciation is subject to a 25% rate of tax instead of 15%. This is a VERY complicated subject and one that I have not yet gotten into in any real depth.

Summary

The major points you should remember pertain to the offshore ownership structure (decontrolled corporation vs. CFC), and the type of income to be earned (either subpart F or not).

In evaluating any offshore tax planning proposal, be especially wary of:

1) schemes involving chains of foreign entities, all of which ultimately are controlled by the same person;

2) foreign-based agents who offer to act as accommodation agents to establish proxy control of a foreign entity;

3) any plan that depends on secrecy, non-reporting and hindrance of IRS oversight; and

4) thinly capitalized, low asset corporations. The IRS and the courts often simply ignore such corporations when determining tax liabilities on any specific transaction. They view them as dummy or sham corporations with no continuing business purpose, set up mainly to avoid taxes.

This is not meant to deter you, but to educate you about the risks of haphazard planning. The most disturbing aspect of studying offshore foreign corporations is the number of Americans who are unaware of the possibilities that do exist. If you take the final step and explore these strategies, you won't regret it as long as you are careful to play by the rules.

Also, have an expert on costs "run the numbers" before you create a foreign corporation. It takes a net profit of about US$100,000 in a foreign-based business to justify the added operating expenses with the potential tax savings. Each foreign venture will involve different facts and costs, so that each one will need to be evaluated in terms of whether the potential tax savings is worth the cost and the complexity of operating offshore.

Recommended Attorneys and Accountants

If you want to establish any offshore trust or corporation, your financial future will be determined in large part by attorneys and accountants and their professional abilities. It is vitally important that these professionals be both qualified and experienced in practical offshore business and legal operations.

Below are qualified professionals I know and have worked with over the years and that I recommend.

Vernon K. Jacobs, CPA, P.O. Box 8194, Prairie Village, Kansas 66208; Tel.: 913-362-9667; Fax: 913-432-7174; E-mail: jacobs1@kc.rr.com; Web site: www.vernonjacobs.com.

Michael Chatzky, JD, Chatzky & Associates, 4250 Executive Square, Suite 660, La Jolla, California 92037; Tel.: 858-638-4530; Fax: 858-638-4535; E-mail: chatzky@aol.com.

J. Richard Duke, JD, LLM, Duke Law Firm, 400 Vestavia Parkway, Suite 100, Birmingham, Alabama 35216; Tel.: 205-823-3900; Fax: 205-823-2630; E-mail: richard@assetlaw.com; Web site: www.assetlaw.com.

Gideon Rothschild, JD, CPA, CEP, Moses & Singer LLP, 1301 Avenue of the Americas, New York, New York 10019; Tel.: 212-554-7806; Fax: 212-554-7700; E-mail: grothschild@mosessinger.com; Web site: http://www.mosessinger.com/attorneys/rothschild_g.shtml.

Timothy D. Scrantom, JD, 180 East Bay Street, Charleston, South Carolina 29401; Tel.: 843-937-0110; Fax: 843-937-4310; E-mail: tenstate@aol.com.

Marcell Felipe, JD, 888 Brickell Avenue, 5th Floor, Miami, Florida 33131; Tel.: 305-381-8500; Fax: 305-381-6225; E-mail: mfelipe@marcellfelipe.com; Web site: www.marcellfelipe.com.

Appendices

Glossary

acceptance - Unconditional agreement by one party (the *offeree*) to the terms of an offer made by a second party (the *offeror*). Agreement results in a valid, binding contract.

arbitrage - Buying the securities in one nation, currency, or market and selling in another, to take advantage of the price differential.

asset protection trust (APT) - An offshore trust which holds title to and protects the grantor's property from claims, judgments, and creditors, especially because it is located in a country other than the grantor's home country.

attachment - The post-judicial civil procedure by which personal property is taken from its owner pursuant to a judgment or other court order.

basis - The original cost of an asset, later used to measure increased value for tax purposes at the time of sale or disposition.

bearer share/stocks - A negotiable stock certificate made out only to "Bearer" without designating the shareowner by name. Such shares are unregistered with the issuing company and dividends are claimed by "clipping coupons" attached to the shares and presenting them for payment.

beneficiary - One designated to receive income from a trust or estate; a person named in an insurance policy to receive proceeds or benefits.

bequest - A gift of personal property by will; also called a *legacy*.

capital gain - The amount of profit earned from the sale or exchange of property, measured against the original cost basis.

captive insurance company - A wholly owned subsidiary company established by a non-insurance parent company to spread insured risks among the parent and other associated companies.

civil suit - A non-criminal legal action between parties relating to a dispute or injury seeking remedies for a violation of contractual or other personal rights.

common law - The body of law developed in England from judicial decisions based on customs and precedent, constituting the basis of the present English, British Commonwealth, and U.S. legal systems. See *equity*.

community property - In certain states in the U.S., property acquired during marriage jointly owned by both spouses, each with an undivided one-half interest.

contract - A binding agreement between two or more parties; also, the written or oral evidence of an agreement.

corporation - A business, professional or other entity recognized in law to act as a single legal person, although composed of one or more natural persons, endowed by law with various rights and duties including the right of succession.

corpus - The property owned by a fund, trust or estate; also called the *principal*.

creator - See *grantor*.

creditor - One to whom a debtor owes money or other valuable consideration.

currency - Official, government issued paper and coined money; *hard currency* describes a national currency sufficiently sound so as to be generally acceptable in international dealings.

debtor - One who owes another (the *creditor*) money or other valuable consideration, especially one who has neglected payments due.

decedent - A term used in estate and probate law to describe a deceased person.

declaration - A formal statement in writing of any kind, often signed and notarized, especially a document establishing a trust; also called an *indenture* or *trust agreement*.

deed - A formal written document signed by the owner conveying title to real estate to another party.

domicile - A person's permanent legal home, as compared to a place that may be only a temporary residence. Domicile determines what law applies to the person for purposes of marriage, divorce, succession of estate at death and taxation.

equity - A body of judicial rules developed under the common law used to enlarge and protect legal rights and enforce duties while seeking to avoid unjust constraints and narrowness of statutory law; also, the unrealized property value of a person's investment or ownership, as in a trust beneficiary's *equitable interest*; also, the risk sharing part of a company's capital, referred to as *ordinary shares*.

estate - Any of various kinds or types of ownership a person may have in real or personal property; often used to describe all property of a deceased person, meaning the assets and liabilities remaining after death.

estate tax - Taxes imposed at death by the U.S. and most state governments on assets of a decedent, except on the first US $650,000 in value which is exempt during 1999. The exempt amount by law increases annually until it reaches US$1 million in 2006.

exchange controls - Government restrictions imposed on dealings in a national or foreign currency.

executor - A person who manages the estate of a decedent; also called an *executrix* if a female, *personal representative, administrator* or *administratrix*.

exemption - In tax law, a statutorily defined right to avoid imposition of part or all of certain taxes; also, the statutory right granted to a debtor in bankruptcy to retain a portion of his or her real or personal property free from creditors' claims.

expatriation - The transfer of one's legal residence and citizenship from one's home country to another country, often in anticipation of government financial restrictions or taxes.

family partnership (also, *family limited partnership*) - A legal business relationship created by agreement among two or more family members for a common purpose, often used as a means to transfer and/or equalize income and assets among family members so as to limit individual personal liability and taxes. See *partnership* and *limited partnership*.

fiduciary - A person holding title to property in trust for the benefit of another, as does a trustee, guardian or executor of an estate.

flight capital - Movement of large sums of money across national borders, often in response to investment opportunities or to escape high taxes or pending political or social unrest; also called *hot money*.

future interest - An interest in property, usually real estate, possession and enjoyment of which is delayed until some future time or event; also, futures, securities or goods bought or sold for future delivery, often keyed to price changes before delivery.

gift tax - U.S. tax imposed on any gift made by one person to another person annually in excess of US$10,000.

grantor - A person who conveys real property by deed; a person who creates a trust; also called a trust *donor* or *settlor*.

grantor trust - As used in U.S. tax law, an offshore trust, the income of which is taxed by the IRS as the personal income of the grantor.

gross estate - The total value for estate tax purposes of all a decedent's assets, as compared to net estate, the amount remaining after all permitted exemptions, deductions, taxes and debts owed.

guardianship - A power conferred on a person, the *guardian*, usually by judicial decree, giving them the right and duty to provide personal supervision, care, and control over another person who is unable to care for himself because of some physical or mental disability or because of minority age status.

haven or haven nation - A country where banking, tax, trust, and corporation laws are specially designed to attract foreign persons wishing to avoid taxes or protect assets.

indices of ownership - Factors indicating a person's control over, therefore ownership, especially of trust property, including the power of revocability.

income beneficiary - The life tenant in a trust.

incorporation - The government registration and qualification process by which a corporation is formed under law.

indemnity - An agreement by which one promises to protect another from any loss or damage, usually describing the role of the insurer in insurance law.

inheritance tax - A tax imposed by government on the amount a person receives from a decedent's estate, rather than on the estate itself.

insider dealing - Selling or purchasing corporate shares for personal benefit based on confidential information about a company's status unknown to the general public.

interest - A right, title, or legal property share; also, a charge for borrowed money, usually a percentage of the total amount borrowed.

international business corporation (IBC) - A term used to describe a variety of offshore corporate structures, characterized by having all or most of its business activity outside the nation of incorporation, maximum privacy, flexibility, low or no taxes on operations, broad powers, and minimal filing and reporting requirements.

interbank rate of exchange - The interest rate which banks charge each other in their dealings.

insurance - A contract or *policy* under which a corporation (an *insurer*) undertakes to indemnify or pay a person (the *insured*) for a specified future loss in return for the insured's payment of an established sum of money (the *premium*).

irrevocable trust - A trust which, once established by the grantor, cannot be ended or terminated by the grantor.

joint tenancy - A form of property co-ownership in which parties hold equal title with the right of survivorship; a *tenancy by the entireties* is a similar tenancy reserved to husband and wife in some American states.

judgment - An official and authenticated decision of a court.

jurisdiction - The statutory authority a court exercises; also, the geographic area or subject matter over which a government or court has power.

last will and testament - A written document in which a person directs the post-mortem distribution of his or her property. In the U.S., state law governs the specific requirements for a valid will.

legal capacity - The competency or ability of parties to make a valid contract, including being of majority age (18 years old) and of sound mind.

life insurance trust - An irrevocable living trust that holds title to a policy on the grantor's life, proceeds from which are not part of the grantor's estate.

life estate - The use and enjoyment of property granted by the owner to another during the owner's life, or during the life of another, at the termination of which, title passes to another known as the *remainderman*.

limited partnership - A partnership in which individuals known as *limited partners* have no management role, but receive periodic income and are personally liable for partnership debts only to the extent of their individual investment.

marital deduction - The right of the surviving spouse under U.S. law to inherit, free of estate taxes, all property owned at death by the deceased spouse.

marriage - The legal and religious institution whereby a man and woman join in a binding contract for the purpose of founding and maintaining a family.

money laundering - The process of concealing the criminal origins or uses of cash so that it appears the funds involved are from legitimate sources. A crime in most major nations.

mutual legal assistance treaty (MLAT) - Bilateral treaties between nations governing cooperation in international investigations of alleged criminal conduct.

numbered bank account - Any account in a financial institution that is identified not by the account holder's name, but a number, limiting knowledge of the owner to a few bank officials. Often associated with Swiss banking, the accounts are available in many asset haven nations.

offer - A written or verbal promise by one person (the *offeror*) to another (the *offeree*), to do, or not to do, some future act, usually in exchange for a mutual promise or payment (consideration). See *acceptance* and *contract*.

option - A contract provision allowing one to purchase property at a set price within a certain time period.

partnership - An association of two or more persons formed to conduct business for mutual profit. See *limited partnership*.

policy - In insurance law, the contract between insurer and insured. See *insurance*.

power of attorney - A written instrument allowing one to act as agent on behalf of another, the scope of agency power indicated by the terms, known as *general* or *limited powers*.

preservation trust - Any trust designed to limit a beneficiary's access to income and principal.

primary residence - Especially in tax law, a home place, as compared to a vacation or second home. See *domicile*.

probate - A series of judicial proceedings, usually in a special court, initially determining the validity of a last will and testament, then supervising the administration or execution of the terms of the will and the decedent's estate.

property - Anything of value capable of being owned, including land (real property) and personal property, both tangible and intangible.

protector - In offshore haven nations, an appointed person who has the duty of overseeing the activities of an offshore trust and its trustee.

quit claim deed - A deed transferring any interest a grantor may have in real property without guarantees of title, if in fact any interest does exist.

real estate - Land and anything growing or erected thereon or permanently attached thereto.

real estate investment trust (REIT) - An investment fund in trust form that owns and operates real estate for share holding investors who are the beneficiaries.

remainder - In testamentary law, the balance of an estate after payment of legacies; in property law, an interest in land or a trust estate distributed at the termination of a life estate. The person with a right to such an estate is the *remainderman*.

rescind - Cancellation or annulment of an otherwise binding contract by one of the parties.

revocable trust - A living trust in which the grantor retains the power to revoke or terminate the trust during his or her lifetime, returning the assets to themselves.

right of survivorship - An attribute of a joint tenancy that automatically transfers ownership of the share of a deceased joint tenant to surviving joint tenants without the necessity of probate.

Sparbuch (German) - An anonymous private bank account available only in Austria, identified not by the owner's name, but by a number or password.

spendthrift trust - A restricted trust created to pay income to a beneficiary judged by the trust grantor to be too improvident to handle his or her own personal economic affairs.

subchapter S corporation - Under U.S. tax law, a small business corporation that elects to have the undistributed taxable income of the corporation taxed as personal income for the shareholders, thus avoiding payment of corporate income tax.

trust - A legal device allowing title to and possession of property to be held, used, and/or managed by one person, the *trustee*, for the benefit of others, the *beneficiaries*.

unit trust - In the U.K. and in Commonwealth nations, the equivalent of the investment fund known in the U.S. as a *mutual fund*.

U.S. person - For U.S. tax purposes, any individual who is a U.S. citizen, a U.S. resident alien deemed to be a permanent resident or a U.S. domiciled corporation, partnership, estate, or trust.

Recommended Attorneys Specializing in Offshore Legal Matters

Graeme W. P. Aarons, Solicitor, FM Trust S.A., Rue du Pommier 12, Case Postale 406, 2001 Neuchatel, Switzerland; Tel.: +038-247979; Fax: +038-254664.

Michael Chatzky, JD, Chatzky & Associates, 4250 Executive Square, Suite 660, La Jolla, CA 92037; Tel.: 858-638-4530; Fax: 858-638-4535; E-mail: mgchatzky@aol.com.

J. Richard Duke, JD, LLM, Duke Law Firm, 400 Vestavia Parkway, Suite 100, Birmingham, AL 35216; Tel.: 205-823-3900; Fax: 205-823-2630; E-mail: richard@assetlaw.com; Web site: http://www.assetlaw.com/.

Marcell Felipe, JD, 888 Brickell Avenue, 5th Floor, Miami, FL 33131; Tel.: 305-381-8500; Fax: 305-381-6225; E-mail: mfelipe@marcellfelipe.com.

Gordon Hill, QC, Cox Hallett Wilkinson, P.O. Box 1561, Milner House, 18 Parliament Street, Hamilton HM FX, Bermuda; Tel.: +44-1-294-1530; Fax: +44-1-292-7880; E-mail: tterrell@cw.bm; Web site: www.cw.bm.

Alan Jahde, LLM, Anderson & Jahde, PC, 950 South Cherry Street, Suite 1000, Denver, CO 80222; Tel.: 303-782-0003; Fax: 303-691-9719.

Denis Kleinfeld, JD, CPA, The Kleinfeld Law Firm, Suntrust International Building, One SE 3rd Avenue, Suite 1940, Miami, FL 33131; Tel.: 305-375-9515; Fax: 305-358-6541; E-mail: denis_kleinfeld@kleinfeld.com.

Samuel M. Lohman, JD, LLM, Lohman & Cooper, 11 rue Verdaine, Case Postale 3377 Geneva, Switzerland; Tel.: +41-22-317-8020; Fax +41-22-317-8030; E-mail: lohman@lsfa-law.com.

Robert B. Martin, Jr., JD, 140 South Lake Avenue, Suite 249, Pasadena, CA 91101; Tel.: 626-793-8500; Fax: 626-793-8779; E-mail: petrose @aol.com.

James McNeile, Solicitor, Farrer & Co., 66 Lincoln's Inn Fields, London WC2A 3KG, U.K.; Tel.: +44-171-242-2022; Fax: +44-171-917-7431.

David Melnik, QC, 350 Lonsdale Road, Suite 311, Toronto, Ontario M5P lR6 Canada; Tel.: +416-488-7918; Fax: +905-877-7751; E-mail: dm1976cp@netcom.ca.

Jeffrey J. Radowich, JD, Veneable, Baetjer & Howard, 2 Hopkins Plaza, Suite 800, Baltimore, MD 21202; Tel.: 410-244-7516; Fax: 410-244-7742.

Gideon Rothschild, JD, CPA, CEP, Moses & Singer, LLP, 1301 Avenue of the Americas, New York, NY 10019, Tel.: 212-554-7806; Fax: 212-554-7700; E-mail: grothschild@ mosessinger.com.

Derek Sambrook, Trust Services, Ltd., Suite 522, Balboa Plaza, Avenida Balboa, Panama, Republic of Panama. Mailing Address: Apartado 0832-1630, World Trade Centre, Panama, Republic of Panama; Tel.: +507-269-2438; Fax: +507-269-4922; E-mail: sambrook@trustserv.com; Web site: http://ww.trustserv.com.

Timothy D. Scrantom, JD, 180 East Bay Street, Charleston, SC 29401; Tel.: 843-937-0110; Fax: 843-937-4310; E-mail: tenstate@aol.com.

Recommended Offshore Reading

Books:

Allen, Stuart. *Offshore Finance Handbook*. Asia Law & Practice Pub., Ltd. 1/F Chinachem Hollywood Center. 1-13 Hollywood Rd., Hong Kong, PRC.

American Citizens Abroad. *USA Citizens Abroad Handbook*. USA Today Books, 1988. PO Box 450, Washington, DC 20044. Tel: 703 276 5978.

Azzara, Thomas P. *Tax Havens of the World*. New Providence Press, 1996. PO Box CB 11552, Nassau, The Bahamas. Tel: 242 327 7359

Barber, Hoyt L., *Tax Havens: How To Bank, Invest & Do Business Offshore Tax Free*. McGraw- Hill Book Co.1993. 1221 Ave of Americas, New York, NY 10020 USA.

Bauman, Robert E. & Melnik, David, *The Wealth Protection Series*, The Oxford Club, 2002. 105 W Monument St., Baltimore, MD 21201.

Billon, Christian. *Doing Business in Luxembourg*. Price Waterhouse, 1990. 24-26 Ave de la Liberté, PO Box 1443, L-1930 Luxembourg.

Caribbean Basin Commercial Profile. Caribbean Pub. Co.. Box 688G, 1 Paddington Pl, #306 - N Sound Way, George Town, Gr.Cayman, Cayman Isl., BWI. Tel: 800 227 4835. E-mail: caribbks@pop3.cris.com.

Caribbean Yellow Pages. Caribbean Pub. Co. Box 688G, 1

Paddington Pl, #306 - N Sound Way, George Town, Gr.Cayman, Cayman Is., BWI.

Cayman Islands Yearbook & Business Directory. Cayman Free Press. PO Box 1365, Gr. Cayman, Cayman Is, BWI.

Chambers, Karen, ed., *Australia Investment Guide*. Asiamoney. 20th Fl Trust Tower, 68 Johnston Rd., Wanchai, Hong Kong. Tel: 852 2529 5009; Fax: 852 2866 9046.

Czerlau, Richard. *Tax Haven Road Map*. Uphill Publishing, Ltd.. 190 Attwell Dr., #400, Toronto, ON M9W 6H8 Canada (US$19.95).

Davidson, James D.; Rees-Mogg, Lord Wm. *The Sovereign Individual*, Simon & Schuster, 1997. Rockefeller Center, 1230 Ave of Americas, New York, NY 10020 USA.

Diamond, Walter & Dorothy. *International Trust Laws and Analysis*. Warren, Gorham & Lamont, Boston, Mass. http://www.wgl.com/ Tel: 1-800-431-9025, ext.3.

Diamond, Walter & Dorothy. *Tax Havens of the World*. New York: Matthew Bender Pub. Co, New York, 1997. Web: http://www. bender.com/ E-mail: international@bender.com Tel: 1-800-833-9844

Doggart, Caroline. *Tax Havens & Their Uses*. Economist Intelligence Unit, 2002. 15 Regent St., London, SW1Y 4LR UK. Tel: 44 20 7830 1007.

Dupuch, S.P. *Bahamas Handbook & Businessman's Annual*. Dupuch Pub. Ltd.. PO Box N7513 Oakes Field, Nassau, The Bahamas. Tel: 242 323 5665; Fax: 242 323 5728.

Freeman, Charles. *Freedom Handbook*, The. St. Helier: Freedom Publications. PO Box 115, St. Helier, Jersey, Channel Isl, UK.

Freeman, Charles. *Offshore Secrets*. Douglas: Freedom Publications. PO Box 183, Douglas, Isle of Man, UK.

Fry, William. *Ireland As a Centre for International Investment Funds*. International Financial Services Centre, 1996. Dublin

Investment Funds, Dublin.

Gallo, Roger. *Escape From America*. Manhattan Loft Publishing, 1997. 738 E Burnside, Portland, OR 97214 USA. Tel: 888 314 1592. (US$29.99).

Golding, Jon W. *Tips & Traps of Going Global*. Sterling Westminster Int. Ltd., 1995. Independent Hs, 178 Brompton Rd., London SW3 1HQ UK. Tel: 44 171 5813551; Fax: 44 171 581 3671.

Harris, Richard W. *Doing Business in Cayman Islands*. Price Waterhouse, 1992. First Home Tower - Jennett St., PO Box 258, George Town, Cayman Isl., BWI. Tel: 809 949 7944; Fax: 809 949 7352.

Holland, Ron; Holder, Tami. *The Swiss Franc In the Year 2000*, Offshore Pubs. 1997. PO Box 1201, Skyland, NC 28776 USA.

Holland, Ron; Murdoch, Rachel. *Trading With the Enemy*. Independence Press, 1997. PO Box 1201, Skyland, NC 28776 USA.

Isle of Man Financial & Commercial Handbook. Directory Profiles Ltd. London House, 243-253 Lwr. Mortlake Rd., Richmond, Surrey TW9 2LL, UK. Tel: 44 1481 948 5166; Fax: 44 1481 332 1222.

Jersey Almanac & Trades Directory. St. Saviour: Michael Stephen Pub. PO Box 582, Five Oaks, St. Saviour, Jersey, Channel Isl., UK 611600 611610. (US$35.00).

Johnson, Bryan et al. *Index of Economic Freedom 2003*. Heritage Foundation, 2003. 214 Massachusetts Av. NE, Washington, DC 20002 USA. Tel: 202 546 4400.

Langer, Marshal, J.D. *How To Use Foreign Tax Havens*. Practicing Law Institute, 1977. 810 - 7th Ave., New York, NY 10019 USA.

Langer, Marshall J.; Kleinfeld, Dennis. *Practical International Tax Planning*. Practicing Law Institute, 1996. 810 - 7th Ave., New York, NY 10019 USA.

Milroy, Robert. *MICROPAL Guide To Offshore Investment Funds*. International Offshore Publishing Ltd., Box 549, Les Sablons, St. Peters, Guernsey, Channel Isl, UK. Tel: 44 1481 66759; Fax: 44 1481 66758 (US$100).

Mintz, Robert J.; Rubens, James J. *Lawsuit Proof*. Lawtech Pub. Co. Ltd., 1995. San Juan Capistrano, CA USA.

Mark Nestmann: The Lifeboat Strategy: Legally Protecting Wealth and Privacy in the 21st Century (2003). US$99; Mutual Legal Assistance Treaties (2003).US$25 Big Brother Goes Global: Financial Intelligence Units Exposed (2003). US$25; Critical Analysis of the Cook Islands as an Asset Protection Haven (2001). US$25.; Practical Privacy Strategies for Windows PCs (2003). US$49; 99 Ways to Protect What's Left of Your Privacy and Property Rights (2003). US$25; Available from: The Nestmann Group, Ltd., 2303 N. 44th St. #14-1025, Phoenix, AZ 85008.

Porter, Tom, ed., *Doing Business in Czech & Slovak Republics*. Prague: Price Waterhouse, 1993. 5 patro - Vinohradska 10 121 47 Prague, 2 Czech Republic. Tel: 42 2 235 3571; Fax: 42 2 235 4390.

Sigal, Bill. Switzerland, *Wealth & You*. Librex Ltd/JML SIC, 1995. Baarerstrasse 53 #B, Zug, 06304 Switzerland. Tel: 41 4 223 3165.

Skousen, Mark; Pugsley, John; Browne, Harry. *Why Switzerland?* Offshore Publications. PO Box 1201, Skyland, NC 28776 USA.

Sloma, Diane, ed., *Gibraltar Financial Services Handbook*. Time Off Int. Ltd., 1997. PO Box 555, Gibraltar. Tel/Fax: 79385. (US$25).

Trevellian, Peter. *PTO: Portable Trades & Opportunities*. PT Shamrock Ltd., 1997. Kissack Ct, 29 Parliament St., Ramsey, Isle of Man, UK. Tel: 44 7050 037517.

Weber, Christopher. *An American's Guide to Living Abroad*. Living Abroad Pub. Inc., 1991. 584 Broadway, #606, New York, NY 10012 USA. Tel: 212 941 9602; Fax: 212 941 9690.

Weiss, K.F.B. *PT Offshore Manual & Directory*. Copenhagen: Carlton Press, 1997. Box 1199, Copenhagen K DK 1011, Denmark. Tel: 45 7023 1199, E-mail: weiss@offshore manual.com, Web: www.offshore-manual.com (US$100).

Wessell. Building Your Financial Castle. Presidential Services Inc., 1996. Newhall, CA USA.

Windisch, J.W. Esq. ,*The Swiss Back Door: Campione d'Italia*: Consulting International SAS, 1988. Corso Italia 2, Campione d'Italia CH6911, Switzerland.

Yule, Iain, ed., *Complete Guide To Investment Trusts*, Prof. & Bus. Info. Pub. Ltd. 1997.12-18 Paul St., London, EC2A 4NK UK. Tel: 44 171 377 9977; Fax: 44 171 377 8099. Email: pbi.pub@ ndirect.co.uk.

Yule, Iain, ed., *How To Advise On Investment Trusts*. London: Prof. & Bus. Info. Pub. Ltd., 1997.12-18 Paul St., London, EC2A 4NK UK. Tel: 44 171 377 9977; Fax: 44 171 377 8099. E-mail: pbi.pub@ndirect.co.uk (US$32).

Travel Guides:

South American Handbook, Footprint South American Handbook 2003, by Ben Box Rand McNally Inc., published annually. Best for a visit, or to learn about living anywhere from south of the border in Mexico to the southern tip of Argentina's Tierra del Fuego, or in the Caribbean. This pocket-sized (1,500 page) book is all inclusive, well organized. About US$40, published by Rand McNally in the U.S. At most bookstores or order by mail. In the U.K., write to Mendip Press, Parsonage Lane, Bath BAI IEN, UK. In the U.S. www.randmcnally.com/

Arthur Frommer $25-$35 A Day Travel Guides. Inexpensive paperbacks (US$20) in an efficient, budget-conscious style. Also Frommer Dollarwise Guides. What to see and do and where to stay with an emphasis on good value for the least money. Highly recommended. In all bookstores or order by mail from 1230 Avenue of the Americas, New York City, NY 10020, USA. www.frommers.com/

"Let's Go" Budget Travel Guides, updated regularly, give an honest assessment of exactly what to expect any place you go. 22 guides cover Europe, Canada, the U.S., Mexico, Central America, South East Asia, and the Middle East. In bookstores or by mail: Let's Go, 1 Story Street, Cambridge, MA 02138, USA or in England, Macmillan, Houndmills, Basingstoke, Hampshire, RG21 2XS. www.letsgo.com/

Lonely Planet Shoestring Travel Guides focus on the "Third World" beyond Europe and North America. Published in Australia, they offer the best budget travel advice for all of Asia, Africa, Australia, and New Zealand. In bookstores or order from: Embarcadero West, 112 Linden Street, Oakland, CA 94607, USA or PO Box 617, Hawthorn, Victoria 3122, Australia. www.4travelguides.com/lonelyplanetss.htm

Newspapers, Magazines, & Periodicals:

Aden Forecast. Aden, Pam & Mary Anne, eds., Apartado 754 Centro Colon, San Jose, Costa Rica. Tel: +(506) 225-4674; Fax: +(506) 234-0433. www.adenforecast.com/

Adrian Day's Global Analyst, PO Box 6644, Annapolis, MD 21401, Tel (410) 224-8885 Fax: (410) 224-8229 Email: GlobalAnalyst@AdrianDay.com www.financialnewsletters.com/adcorn/aday.shtml

Asset Protection Newsletter. Jacobs, Vernon K., ed., Research Press Inc., 4500 W. 72nd Tr., PO Box 8135, Prairie Village, KS 66208 USA. Tel: +1 (913) 362-9667; Fax: +1 (913) 383-3505; Web: www.rpifs.com/lawsuits/

Barron's Magazine. 200 Liberty St., New York, NY 10281 USA. Web: http://www.barrons.com/

Business Week International. McGraw Hill Inc., 1221 Ave. of the Americas, New York, NY 10020 USA. Tel: +1 (212) 512-3867; Fax: +1 (212) 512-6556. www.businessweek.com/

Early Warning Report. Maybury, Richard, ed., Box 1616, Rocklin, CA 95677 USA. Tel: +1 (916) 624-2766; Fax: +1 (916) 632-2501. www.webcom.com/beacon/welcome.html

The Economist. 111 W. 57th St., New York, NY 10019 USA. Tel: +1 (212) 541 5730; Fax: +1 (212) 541 9378 or: 25 St. James's St., London SW1A 1HG UK. Tel: +44 (171) 830-7000; Fax: +44 (171) 839-2968. www.economist.com/

Euromoney. Evans, Garry, ed., Euromoney Publications PLC, Nestor House Playhouse Yard, London EC4V 5EX UK. Tel: +44 (171) 779-8888; Fax: +44 (171) 779-8407. www.euromoney.com/

Europe. Guttmann, Robert J., ed., European Union, 2300 M St. NW, Washington, DC 20037 USA. Tel: +1 (202) 862-9555; europa.eu.int/

Expat Investor. Tolley Publishing, 2 Addiscombe Rd., Croydon, Surrey CR9 5AF UK. Tel: +44 (171) 686-9141; Fax: +44 (181) 760-0588. www.expatinvestor.com/

Expat World. Box 1341, Raffles City, Singapore, 09117 Singapore. Tel: +65 446-3680; Fax: +65 339-7048. www.expatworld.net/

Financial Privacy Report. Ketcher, Michael H., ed., PO Box 1277, Burnsville, MN 55337 USA. Tel: +1 (612) 895-8757; Fax: +1 (612) 895-5526; E-mail: ketcher@ix.netcom.com.

Financial Times. FT Publications, 14 E. 60th St. New York, NY 10022 USA. www.ft.com

Financial Times. 149 Tottenham Ct Rd., London W1P 9LI UK. Tel: +44 (171) 873-3000; USA Toll-free: +1 (800) 568 -7625; Fax: +44 (171) 831 9136. www.ft.com

Freebooter. Morgan, Henry, ed., PO Box 191, St. Peter Port, Guernsey GY1 6BZ Channel Island, British Isles. Fax: +44 (171) 223-4295; www.freebooter.com.

Freedom Network News. Miller, Vincent H., ed., International Society for Individual Liberty, 1800 Market St., San Francisco, CA 94102 USA. Tel: +1 (415) 864-0952; Fax: +1 (415) 864-7506. www.free-market.net/

Global Mutual Fund Investor. E.N.R. Asset Management Inc., 2 Westmount Sq, Suite 1802, Westmount, Quebec H3Z 2S4 Canada.

Toll Free (877) 989-8027 Tel: (514) 989-8027 Fax: (514) 989-7060 E-mail: enr@qc.aibn.com. http://www.eas.ca/about_gmfi.html

Hang Seng Economic Monthly. Hang Seng Bank Ltd., Economic Research Dept., GPO Box 2985, Hong Kong. main.hangseng.com/econ/mon/mone.html

Information Line. Checkan, Michael, ed., International Financial Consultants, 1700 Rockville Pike, #400, Rockville, MD 20852 USA. Tel: +1 (800) 831-0007; Fax: +1 (301) 881-6898. www.assetstrategies.com/pages/aboutus.html

International Country Risk Guide. Sealy, Tom, ed., Political Risk Services IBC USA Publications Inc., PO Box 6482, Syracuse, NY 13217-6482 USA. Tel: +1 (315) 472-1224; Fax: +1 (315) 472-1235. http://www.prsgroup.com/icrg/riskdata.html

International Economic Insights. Bergsten, Fred C., ed., Institution for International Economics, 11 Dupont Circle NW, Washington, DC 20036-1207 USA. Tel: +1 (202) 328-9000; Fax: +1 (202) 328-5432.

International Harry Schultz Letter. Schultz, Harry, ed., PO Box 622, CH 1001 Lausanne, Switzerland. www.hsletter.com/

International Herald Tribune. 181 Ave., Charles-de-Gaulle, 92521 Neuilly-sur-Seine, France. Tel: +33 41 43-9300; USA Tel: +1 (212) 752-3890; USA Toll-free: +1 (800) 882-2884; Fax: +33 41 42 9210; E-mail: iht@iht.com. or 850 - 3rd Ave., New York, NY 10022 USA. Tel: +1 (800) 882-2884. www.iht.com

International Living. Peddicord, Kathleen, ed., Agora Ireland Publishing & Services Ltd., 5 Catherine St., Waterford, Ireland. www.internationalliving.com/

International Speculator. Casey, Doug, ed., PO Box 8978, Aspen, CO 81611 USA. Tel: +1 (970) 923-2062; Fax: +1 (970) 923-2064. www.internationalspeculator.com/

Lonely Planet Newsletter. PO Box 617, Hawthorn, Victoria, 3122 AU. www.lonelyplanet.com/comet/index.cfm

Money Laundering Alert, Alert Global Media Inc., 1100 Brickell Ave. #601, PO Box 11390, Miami, FL 33101-1390 USA. Tel: +1 (305) 530-0500; Fax: +1 (305) 530-9434; E-mail: alert@ moneylaundering.com; Web: www.moneylaundering.com.

Offshore Citizen. Addison, Michael E., ed., Promotion Plus (CI), PO Box 337, Guelles Rd., St. Peter Port, Guernsey, Channel Island, UK. Tel: +44 1481-66297; Fax: +44 1481-66398; E-mail: offcit@offcit.com; Web: www.offcit.com.

Offshore Finance USA. Stammer, Brian, ed., 3440 Cote des Neiges, Montreal, QC H3H 1T8 Canada. Tel: +1 (514) 939-2800; Fax: +1 (514) 939-2881; E-mail: island@aei.ca; Web: www. offshorefinanceusa

Offshore Investment. Cain, Charles A., ed., Journal of the Offshore Institute, 62 Brompton Rd., Knightsbridge, London SW3 1BW UK. Tel: +44 (171) 225-0550; Fax: +44 (171) 584-1093; Web: www.offshoreinvestment.com/offshore/.

Offshore Journal, The. Jacobs, Vernon K., ed., Offshore., (E-mail publications) Research Press Inc., 4500 W. 72nd Tr., PO Box 8135, Prairie Village, KS 66208 USA. Tel: +(913) 362-9667; Fax: +1 (913) 383-3505; Web: www.rpifs.com/offshore/

Offshore Red. Grundy, Milton, ed., Campden Publications, Threeway House, 40-44 Clipstone St., London W1P 8LX UK. Tel: +44 (171) 636-1600; Fax: +44 (171) 636-4837; E-mail: red@campden.com; Web: www.campden.com.

Offshore Tax Strategies. Jacobs, Vernon K., ed., (E-mail publications) Research Press Inc., 4500 W. 72nd Tr., PO Box 8135, Prairie Village, KS 66208 USA. Tel: +(913) 362-9667; Fax: +1 (913) 383-3505; Web: www.rpifs.com/taxhelp/

South China Morning Post. GPO Box 47, Hong Kong. Tel: +(852) 2680 8661; U.K. Tel: +44 (171) 587-3683; Fax: (852) 2680 8688. www.scmp.com/

Strategic Investment. Davidson, Jim, ed., 108 N Alfred St., #200, Alexandria, VA 22314 USA. Tel: +1 (703) 836-8250; Fax: +1 (703) 836-4061. www.strategicinvestment.com/

Swiss Perspective. Arguelle, Rosanna, ed., JML Swiss Investment Counsellors, Germaniastrasse 55, Zurich 08033, Switzerland. Tel: +41 1-3601800; Fax: +41 1-361-4074. http://www.cyberhaven. com/fortress/perspective.html

Travel Information Manual (TIM) monthly bulletin on passports, visas, vaccinations, exit permits, currency controls; a joint publication of 14 member airlines of the International Air Transport Association (IATA). Available at major travel agencies. Annual subscription US$37. TIM, PO Box 902, NL-2130EA Hoofddorp, Netherlands. http://www.iata.org/tim/index

Wall Street Journal. Circulation Dept, PO Box 2845, In de Creamer 37, 6401 DH Heerlen, Netherlands. Tel: +31 (45) 576-1222; Fax: +31 (45) 571-4722; U.S. toll-free: +1 (800) 568-7625; http://online.wsj.com/home/us

Book Catalogs:

For catalogues of unusual and difficult-to-find books about personal freedom, individual liberty and survival, send US$5 or equivalent (refundable with first order) to cover postage and handling to any of the following:

Laissez Faire Books, 942 Howard Street, San Francisco, CA 94103, USA. An excellent free catalogue. Web site: http://www.lfb.com/Home.asp.

Loompanics Unlimited, P.O. Box 1197, Port Townsend, WA 98368, USA. Web site: www.loompanics.com/.

Paladin Press, P.O. Box 1307, Boulder, CO 80306, USA. Web site: www.paladin-press.com/.

311

INTERNATIONAL FINANCIAL AND LEGAL NETWORK

Through a winning combination of experience, knowledge and understanding of international financial and legal services, IFLN can provide you with key advantages that few investors will ever have: truly independent advice and introductions to the right professional in the right place from the very start.

In particular, IFLN can assist you with:

- ❖ International Banking and Investment Management
- ❖ Tax and Estate Planning
- ❖ Asset Protection including Family Foundations, Foreign Trusts & Annuity Policies

- ❖ International Corporate Services
- ❖ Residence and Retirement Solutions
- ❖ Real Estate Acquisition and Structuring
- ❖ International Health and Life Insurance

Our online assessment (at www.ifln.com) allows you to have your personal situation reviewed by IFLN specialists on the basis of a comprehensive questionnaire. An initial brief assessment and referral is free of charge.

For more information, visit our web site, or contact us today:

IFLN International Financial and Legal Network
Florastrasse 44 8024 Zurich, Switzerland
Tel: +41 (44) 266 2222 ❖ Fax: +41 (44) 266 2223
Email: info@ifln.com ❖ Internet: www.ifln.com